MONROE'S

Principles
of speech

REVISED BRIEF EDITION

by ALAN H. MONROE

Purdue University

SCOTT, FORESMAN AND COMPANY

Chicago, Atlanta, Dallas, New York

PREFACE

Like the previous abbreviated editions of the author's basic text, *Principles and Types of Speech,* now in its third edition, this *Revised Brief Edition* is designed for use in courses calling for a minimum of textbook work, in short courses, and in courses where training in speech and training in writing are closely related or combined.

The concise development of the previous short editions is retained since its effectiveness has been proved in the classroom. This conciseness was originally achieved, without sacrificing the inclusion of illustrative material so necessary for understanding, by eliminating less essential topics from the larger book and by regrouping the remaining topics. The clarity and brevity so obtained have been preserved in this edition.

Two important chapters have been added, however, in this revision. A thorough treatment of outlining, together with a discussion of the proper arrangement of coordinate and subordinate ideas in a speech, has been included at the request of many who have used the previous brief editions. Likewise, somewhat more thorough discussions of the psychological and rhetorical function of speech, of the speaker's general objectives and choice of specific purpose, and of audience analysis and motivation have been brought together in a new chapter on "The Speaker and His Audience." Without exceeding the limit of a brief edition, these additions should help to strengthen and round out the student's skill and understanding.

The illustrations and references, including the collection of speeches printed in the *Supplement,* have of course been refreshed by including current material wherever possible. On the other hand, what has proved effective in practical classroom use has not been discarded. Brevity, clarity, teachability, usefulness—these were the standards in the preparation of this short edition as they had been for the former ones.

The author is particularly indebted to Professor Milton Dickens of the University of Southern California and to Professor Leland T. Chapin of Stanford University for their detailed criticisms of this revision, and to Mr. James W. McIntyre of Purdue University for his help in assembling new illustrative material. This debt extends, of course, beyond the possibility of specific acknowledgment here, to his other colleagues in the teaching profession, and to the many authors, speakers, and publishers who have assisted in the preparation of this edition and of the previous ones from which it grew.

If the students who use this *Revised Brief Edition* learn more fully to appreciate the value of effective speech and to improve their own intelligence and skill in speaking, its purpose will have been fulfilled.

A. H. M.
West Lafayette, Indiana
May 1951

TABLE OF CONTENTS

v

List of illustrations

Chapter 1 BASIC

REQUIREMENTS

On the front page of a recent newspaper appeared the headline, PRESIDENT SPEAKS TO NATION 8:30 TONIGHT. Of course, everyone wanted to know how the government planned to meet the developing crisis; but why did the President *speak* instead of merely issuing a statement? Obviously he felt that by speaking he could make a more personal appeal for unified national support. Because of the circumstances, the President's speech was front-page news. That same day, however, a hundred forty million other citizens of this country also spoke. They ordered groceries, discussed the neighbor's new car, sold life insurance, taught school, held conferences, argued on street corners, paid compliments to their sweethearts. Their speech was not headline news, but to each of them it was a necessary part of daily life.

Consider the telephone industry. It represents millions of dollars of invested capital and employs thousands of operators, repairmen, and clerks, to say nothing of the highly trained business, legal, and engineering staffs. It maintains expensive laboratories for research and large factories for the manufacture of equipment. In the city of Chicago alone over a million instruments are in daily use. For what? So that people can talk to one another even at a distance. Most of us talk so much and have been talking for so long that we are likely to forget how important speech is to us; yet here is a vast industry built entirely upon our desire to talk. Over thirty billion times a year someone in the United States wants to say something so urgently that he cannot wait to see his listener face to face and is willing to pay to talk with him by telephone.

But talking is not enough for most of us; we need to talk *well*. Consider the ten or fifteen most influential men or women in your home community. Is it not true that most of them are good speakers? Imagine a mute Jefferson or Lincoln, or a Wilson or Roosevelt with clumsy speech. The simple truth is that in a democratic society such as ours the ability to express ideas is just as essential as the capacity to have ideas. Even in your own intimate circle you will find that the impressions you make will depend largely upon the manner in which you talk, the clearness with which you develop your ideas, and the pleasantness of your voice.

This does not mean, of course, that training in speech will make you overnight a "leader of men." Such hasty miracles seldom occur outside the covers of "success" books. But if you have intelligence and character, careful training in speech will help you express your ideas with clearness and force; it will help you become a more useful and influential citizen. Let us begin, then, by examining the basic requirements of effective speaking and the procedures useful in developing our abilities to meet these requirements.

Characteristics of the successful speaker

What are the characteristics of the successful speaker? In most important human activities success depends upon *knowledge, self-confidence,* and *skill.* These same characteristics form the basis for effective speech. Without knowledge speech becomes empty; without self-confidence the speaker stumbles and lacks power; without skill expression is often crude and monotonous.

In each of these respects you have already developed considerably. You have been talking for the past sixteen to twenty years. You are, of course, better able to express yourself now than you were at the age of six. You have had more experience, and more information is at your command; your vocabulary is larger, and your ability to put words together is better. But you may have developed bad habits of speech as well as good. You may have unconsciously acquired peculiarities of thought and expression that are irritating or clumsy. The job before you, therefore, is not a new one which you will start at the beginning, but one which is already in progress. You can build on the foundation you have already laid, and you will need to correct any mistakes in yesterday's building.

DEVELOPING A BACKGROUND OF KNOWLEDGE

There is no substitute for knowledge that is thorough and varied, and acquiring this knowledge is a lifelong and cumulative task. If you are wise, you will begin your formal study and practice of speech by talking about things within your personal experience, and will gradually expand your range of subject matter as you develop. Start with "talking shop." Talk about the things you are doing and studying in the other courses you are taking and about your experiences at home, in the shop, or on the farm. Do not be afraid of choosing too simple a subject at the start, but as you go further, choose subjects which will draw you out and develop your store of knowledge.

INCREASING SELF-CONFIDENCE

What are the qualities which characterize a self-confident speaker? Among other things, an erect but comfortable posture free from dependence on chairs, tables, or other artificial support; easy movement free from fidgeting or jerkiness; direct, straightforward, eye-to-eye contact with the listener; earnestness and energy in the voice; and an alertness of mind enabling the speaker to think on his feet.

A great many things go to determine the amount of nervousness or confidence a speaker may feel—including the amount of sleep he had the night before and the quantity of mince pie he ate for dinner. But the experience of many generations of speakers has provided us with a few simple rules which, if followed, are bound to increase our poise and self-control:

Pick an interesting subject. Have you ever noticed how, in speaking, the more one thinks about the subject and the less he thinks about himself, the less self-conscious and the more confident he becomes? Avoid dry and dusty topics; choose something that will make you want to talk.

Know your subject thoroughly. Compare the way you feel when called on in class after you have thoroughly studied your assignment with the way you feel when you are unprepared. The speaker who is well informed is always more confident than the one who is not; he is not afraid of having his ignorance exposed.

Learn thoroughly the sequence of the ideas you intend to present. Photograph upon your mind the four or five main points in the order in which you intend to make them. You will feel more confident if the sequence of your main points is firmly fixed in your memory. Do not, however, memorize your speech word for word. To do so often defeats its own purpose because attention is fixed on the words rather than on ideas, and the failure to remember one phrase is likely to destroy the entire sequence. Confidence will come from the feeling that at all times you know what you are going to say next.

Practice aloud as often as you can. Say aloud and on your feet what you expect later to tell your audience; begin by following a written outline and gradually discard this outline as the sequence of points becomes fixed in your mind. With each repetition you will become more and more sure of yourself.

4

Focus your attention on your audience. Forget yourself as much as possible; think only about getting your audience to understand and to agree with you.

Be physically active while you speak. Walk from one part of the platform to another as you begin presenting a new idea; go to the blackboard and draw a diagram or write down the points you want the audience to remember; show your listeners the article you are talking about and demonstrate how it is used; imagine you are on the scene you are describing and use your arms and hands to point out where each thing is as you tell about it. By doing so you will increase your confidence and the vitality of what you say. Of course you must not overdo this—don't appear to be merely pacing the platform.

Remember that some nervous tension is both natural and good for you. Even in the deepest sleep our muscles are never completely relaxed; there is a certain amount of tension in them which physiologists have called "muscle tonus." If, then, you feel keyed up just before you start to speak, regard this fact as a good sign; it means that there is small chance of your making a dull and listless speech.

Welcome every opportunity to speak. Each time you meet a situation and master it, the more confident you will become. Therefore, welcome each assignment in your speech class as an opportunity, a step along the road to confidence. Your classmates will be a friendly audience. Your assignments will be planned in a natural and helpful sequence. Attend every class and take part enthusiastically in all of its activities. Seek other opportunities to speak: at your fraternity, in campus organizations, or before your church groups. Confidence grows with each successive well-prepared and effective speech you make.

DEVELOPING SKILL

Fluency, poise, control of voice, and coordinated movement of the body mark a skillful speaker. Combined with self-confidence and a background of knowledge, such skill heightens the speaker's effective-

5

ness. Special drill on gesture, intonation, distinctness, and the like may be needed to improve your technique (these will be taken up in Chapter 3), but, after all, skill in speaking is developed mainly by practice in speaking. However, in practicing to develop skill you must take care not to develop artificiality. Good speaking is distinct and lively, but it does not strive for artificial effect; it is forceful but often informal; it commands attention, but does so only because of the speaker's desire to communicate. The following list may suggest some types of speakers who do not maintain this strong sense of sincere communication:

The *Elocutionist*—one who permits himself to be carried away by the sound of his own voice and the graceful manipulation of his body, at the expense of the thought behind them. He talks for display rather than for communication.

The *Verbal Gymnast*—one who makes a display of the language he uses. He never uses a short word if he can find a long one; he delights in complex sentences and in mouth-filling phrases. Disraeli referred to one of them as a man who "is intoxicated with the exuberance of his own verbosity."

The *Oracle*—one who "knows it all." He is ponderous in making the simplest statement; his attitude suggests, "When I speak, let no dog bark!"

The *Hermit*—one who mumbles to himself. He may have a wealth of good ideas, well organized and developed, but he looks off at the ceiling or floor, talks in a weak, monotonous voice, and in general makes no effort to be heard or understood. He shrinks from his audience and refuses to raise his voice, on the apparent assumption that the fewer who hear him, the fewer enemies he will have.

The *Gibberer*—one who emits a continuous stream of words with little or no thought behind them. He jumps around from one point to another until both he and his audience are thoroughly confused. He usually stops by saying, "Well, I guess that's all I have to say on the subject."

How, then, can you avoid speaking like one of the types of speaker just described? How can you develop an energetic, conversational manner of speaking? Your instructor will help you overcome any genuine difficulties that face you. The course of training you are beginning is designed to develop your power of expression steadily and naturally; and Chapter 3 will suggest specific ways of improving your voice and your platform behavior. For the present, however, to make sure that you are talking in a lively conversational way, remember just three things:

1. Have something you want to say.
2. Want someone else to understand it.
3. Say it as simply and directly as you can.

problems

1. Evaluate and compare as to knowledge, self-confidence, and skill as many of the following as you have heard speak (or any other speakers you have heard recently):
   a. The mayor of your home town or city.
   b. The principal of your high school.
   c. Your high-school class orator.
   d. The president of your college or university.
   e. The governor of the state.
   f. A United States congressman from your state.
   g. The football (or basketball, etc.) coach.
   h. A member of the debating team.
   i. A convocation speaker at your college or university.
2. Take a simple topic from the list on the next page (or a similar topic which interests you) and prepare to give a two- or three-minute speech on it. Follow the suggestions for increasing self-confidence presented on pages 3 and 4; make a rough outline of the points you expect to make, and practice aloud often enough to be sure of the sequence. When you step before the class, do so firmly; move about occasionally as you talk; and make what you say interesting to the audience.

a. What I expect from college.
b. In defense of popular music.
c. High altitude flying.
d. Radio advertisement I dislike.
e. Initiation into a chemistry (physics, biology, home economics, etc.) lab.
f. Military training.
g. Hunches.
h. Deep sea fishing.
i. Candid camera techniques.

Classroom discussion

In nearly every class you will be called on to do one of three kinds of speaking: simple recitation, informal discussion, or short oral reports. A few suggestions here may help make your classwork more effective and help develop your speaking skill for later use.

Discussion procedure will vary from answering rapid-fire questions to giving fairly long explanations, comments, or demonstrations. In some classes you will speak sitting down; in others, standing at the blackboard or before the class. (If you stand at a blackboard in use for the class, be sure you stand to one side so that the class can see what is written on it; and guard against talking to the blackboard instead of to the audience.) At some schools the student is required to stand up for class discussion in order to develop his confidence in being on his own before a group. In every instance, however, these rules apply:

Be prepared. There is no substitute for knowledge, and much of your acquisition of knowledge depends on the effort you spend on investigation and preparation. If you study your assignments daily, you will have little trouble.

Act alert. Sit or stand erect; even when not speaking, avoid a slouched position. Keep awake mentally as well as physically; listen to what is said and keep track of the discussion.

Talk loudly enough to be heard. Do not mumble or swallow your words; remember that everyone has a right to hear you. If what you say is not worth being heard, don't say it at all. But if you are asked a question, at least answer, "Yes," "No," or even "I don't know," with alertness and vigor.

Do not remain silent when you have something worth while to say. Avoid giving the impression that the discussion is beneath your dignity or that the subject is uninteresting. At least show your interest by facial expression, and if possible express that interest by participation. This comment does not imply that you must talk when you have nothing to say. Ask sensible questions and add useful comments.

Speak to the point; do not ramble. In most discussions time is valuable. Don't waste it by saying things that are unimportant or by using five minutes to express an idea that could be stated in one. Be definite in statement. Avoid vague statements, uncertain opinions, and equivocal answers. Do not stretch the facts, but be as conclusive as possible with your information.

Do not try to show off. Sarcasm, flamboyant statement, the continuous suggestion that "I know it all"—any of these will irritate your listeners. It is not desirable to efface yourself completely; self-assurance is to be desired, but avoid the appearance of arrogance.

Accept criticism with dignity. Avoid irritating replies to criticism. If you think the criticism justified, accept it graciously; if not, refute it politely or ignore it.

Above all remember that you are in a discussion group and that every member has as much right to consideration as you.

When to take part in discussion

Sometimes, instead of conducting a formal recitation period, your instructor may present a topic for general discussion by the class, or he may outline a problem and ask you to discuss its solution. When this occurs, you may wonder particularly about the question "When should I talk and when should I keep quiet?" There can be no dogmatic answer. The situation becomes much like any group discussion, and the rules just given should be observed. But note the following expansion of these suggestions:

Speak, of course, when you are asked a direct question. A direct question naturally requires a direct answer. Do not let your answer become long-winded. Unless you can contribute a new point of view or additional information, cut your answer short. If the question itself is not clear, ask to have it explained.

Speak when you have an intelligent comment or suggestion to make. Frequently some aspect of the subject has been neglected, or some important point has slipped by without notice. Even when you have no tangible information upon this particular point, a brief comment may stimulate others to contribute the information needed.

Speak when you can make clear an idea another has badly muddled. Quite often someone else may make a point which is very important, but he may express it so vaguely that no one else appreciates its significance. If you can tactfully make the point clear, you will have performed a valuable service.

Speak when you can correct an error. In doing this you must exercise a great deal of tact, else you may start a bad argument. If the point is important, however, and you know the other man is wrong, develop your correction courteously.

Speak when you can offer added information upon the question. No one person knows everything. Only by the combined information of the entire group can a sound judgment be made. If, therefore, you can illuminate the problem by an apt illustration, if you can cite accurate figures bearing upon it, or if you can relay the testimony of someone outside the group, by all means do so. Be sure of one thing: that what you say has a direct bearing upon the point at issue. Remember that nothing is so disconcerting as to have someone inject irrelevancies into a discussion.

10

Speak when you can ask an intelligent question. If you are in doubt about something and are fairly sure that others are also in doubt, find out about the matter at once; do not allow the decision to be made without being informed. Obviously, to be continually asking questions is unwise, but a question asked at the proper moment will often save a great deal of muddled thinking and discussion. Moreover, a question may frequently be used to bring the discussion back to the main issue when it has begun to wander off the point.

Speak when you can inject humor into an otherwise dry discussion. This suggestion needs to be followed with extreme caution. Once in a while, however, a little humor temperately injected may serve to liven up a lagging discussion.

Do not speak beside the point. This rule is by all means a cardinal one. If you have nothing to say directly bearing on the point at issue, keep quiet. Too often someone wanders far off the point to discuss another far removed, and by doing so drags out the settlement of the main point interminably. No matter how important what you have to say is, wait until the point under discussion is settled before you turn to a different subject. One point must be settled at a time.

PRESENTING SHORT ORAL REPORTS

Often in class meetings—and for that matter eventually in board or committee meetings—you may be called on to give short oral reports. For instance, you may be asked to discuss "The sources of raw material for synthetic rubber" or "Additional office equipment needed to handle a 15% increase in next year's business." Such reports have for their purpose one of two things: to present information, or to make suggestions for action by the group. In either case they should be brief. (Directions for longer reports will be given in Chapter 6.)

Reports should always be clear, accurate, and well-pointed. Your report will be stronger if you develop an outline of the main points to be covered. Begin by stating in one short sentence just what your report is on. Then develop the substance of the report in some coherent order. Arrange the main points in time sequence if the report is to tell about a series of events; arrange them in space sequence (north to south, left to right, front to back, ground level on up, etc.) if the report is to describe a piece of machinery, the location of buildings, etc. Sometimes there is a standardized sequence natural to a given subject, as in financial reports; if so, follow that sequence. In any case, emphasize at the end, in summary fashion, facts or conclusions which are of particular importance, together with any suggested action you recommend. In short:

1. State the subject of the report.
2. Present the substance of it in—
    a. time sequence,
    b. space sequence, or
    c. standardized sequence.

3. Summarize the important points or recommended action. The following outline will serve as an example:

Subject: THE DUTIES OF A SCHOOL THEATER STAFF
    I. The Staff Backstage.
        A. The stage manager is responsible for:
            1. Building the set.
            2. Painting the set.
            3. Setting up the scenes on stage.
            4. Shifting scenes between acts.
            5. Storing the set after performances.
        B. The chief electrician has charge of:
            1. Arranging the lights.
            2. . . . etc.
        C. The property manager . . .
        D. The costume mistress . . .
        E. The make-up chairman . . .
    II. The Auditorium Staff.
        A. The ticket manager . . .
        B. The chief usher . . .
Summary: (of important points)

Notice that the *space* sequence was used in the two main points of the outline, that a *special* sequence natural to this subject was used in A, B, C, etc., and that the *time* sequence was used in the minor points—1, 2, 3, etc.—listing the duties of the stage manager.

When you present the report orally, stand up and speak up. Refer to your notes when accuracy demands your doing so, but not otherwise; train your memory to grasp and retain the essential points so that you can look at your listeners when you talk.

problems

1. Take critical notes of any class discussion in which you participate during the next few days. As objectively as possible, rate yourself on your performance and contribution.
2. Go to the blackboard and explain a problem in mathematics or in chemistry or in one of your other courses. Speak distinctly and loudly enough to be heard. Make your comments as brief as clarity will permit.
3. Conduct a discussion in class of some problem suggested by your instructor, such as:
   a. The most efficient methods of study.
   b. How to develop photographs.
   c. The reasons for the defeat of Japan in 1945.
   d. Choosing clothes to fit climatic conditions.
   e. How to plan a well-balanced menu.
   f. Use of the atom bomb.
   g. Special characteristics of famous contemporary speakers.
   h. The use of electricity on the farm.
4. Using the formula discussed on pages 11, 12, and 13, make an outline for a short report on each of the following:
   a. Some recent event you have observed.
   b. Your inspection of some workshop, office, gymnasium, dormitory, etc.
   c. The solution to some problem such as those implied in Problem 3 above.
5. Prepare and present a short oral report on some phase of any one of the topics listed in Problem 3.

Preparing to speak
in public The term "public speaking" too often brings to mind the picture of a large auditorium and a very formal address. Of course there are many such occasions. Far more frequently speeches are "public" only in the sense that there is but one speaker and an audience which may be made up of two or twenty to two hundred listeners. In this sense the "short oral report" discussed in the preceding section is a public speech. But not all the speaking you do before a group will be so simple. You will need to give longer reports on more complex subject matter; you may give instruction in the form of lectures; you may even be called upon to talk before large audiences.

Leaving until later more detailed directions for the particular types of public speaking you may be required to do, you should consider now the *process* of preparing to speak. How should you go about getting ready? What preliminary steps are involved? How should you limit the scope and purpose of your speech?

There are three principal methods of speaking, which differ primarily in the degree of preparation which they involve. These are the *impromptu* method, the *extemporaneous* method, and the method of *memorizing*.

By the impromptu method is meant speaking "on the spur of the moment." No specific preparation is made for the particular occasion; the speaker relies entirely on his general knowledge and skill. The ability to speak impromptu is useful in an emergency, but its use should be limited to emergencies. Too often the moment arrives without the "spur." Whenever possible it is better to plan ahead than to risk the rambling, incoherent speech which the impromptu method so often produces. The method of memorizing goes to the other extreme. The speech is not only planned but written out and committed to memory word for word. Some speakers can use this method effectively, but too often it results in a stilted, inflexible presentation. There is a tendency to hurry through, saying words without thinking of their meaning; besides, with this method there is difficulty in making the changes so often needed to adapt a speech to the reactions of the audience. (Many speakers, delivering a radio talk or a speech on some special occasion where precise wording is required, often read the speech from a written manuscript. When this method is used, the speaker should practice to make the delivery sound flexible and spontaneous.)

The extemporaneous method is the one usually advised and employed. This method takes a middle course. The speech is very carefully planned and outlined in detail; sometimes a complete draft of it is written out; but the wording is never specifically committed to memory. Instead, having prepared an outline or manuscript, the speaker lays it aside and practices saying his speech aloud, choosing his words each time as he goes. He uses the outline to fix firmly in mind the sequence of ideas, and by practicing a variety of wordings he develops flexibility of expression. If the extemporaneous method is used too sketchily, it will be no more effective than the impromptu method, a fact which sometimes leads to a confusion of these two terms; but a thorough and careful use of it will result in a speech nearly as polished as a memorized one and certainly more vigorous, flexible, and spontaneous.

Although the extemporaneous method is usually advised and employed, it is well to remember that the best method for a given speaker often depends on the way his mind works before an audience. The best method for a given occasion depends on such factors as the importance of the occasion, the amount of time available for preparation, and what the audience expects. It is unlikely that a president would attempt an extemporaneous report to the nation.

The essential steps involved in the thorough preparation for a speech, whether memorized or extemporaneous, are as follows:

Selecting and narrowing the subject

Sometimes you will be asked to talk on an assigned subject. But whether you are given a subject or choose it yourself, you must narrow it down to fit the time limits of your speech and the interest and capacity of your audience. A subject may be interesting to the audience for any of these reasons:

1. Because it vitally concerns their affairs.
2. Because it concerns the solution to a definite problem.
3. Because it is new or timely.
4. Because there is a conflict of opinion on it.

Moreover, your own interest and knowledge must be considered. Whenever possible, talk about something with which you have had personal experience and about which you can find out more than your audience already knows. Try to speak on a subject in which you are vitally interested and to which you can make a real contribution.

Determining the purpose of the speech

Too often a speaker arises to "say a few words" with no idea what he is speaking for. When this happens, the net result is merely the consumption of a certain amount of time. It is not enough just to center the speech about a definite subject; the speech should be thought of always in terms of the response desired from the audience. You may want the audience to be informed, or to understand a difficult point, or to believe a proposition, or to become emotionally aroused, or to take some definite action. In any event you must think of your speech as an instrument of utility—a means of getting a reaction. If you determine your purpose for speaking and keep in mind the response you seek, you can save much time that might otherwise be consumed with nonessentials. But once you have determined the specific purpose, you should continually refer to it throughout the entire preparation of your speech. To insure doing this, you will find value in writing down your specific purpose in a simple sentence and fixing that sentence in mind.

16

If your speech is to have its maximum effect, you must get in mind early in the process of preparation (indeed this will often be the first step) a clear picture of the conditions under which you are to speak. Will the speech be given out of doors or inside? Is it likely to be hot, cold, or comfortable? Will the audience be sitting or standing; and if sitting, will they be crowded, comfortable, or scattered around in a big room? How large a place will the speech be given in? Will there be echoes? Can the speaker be seen and heard easily? Are there likely to be disturbances in the form of noise or interruptions from the outside? All these things and many other physical factors have their effect on the temper of the audience, their span of attention, and the style of speaking you will find necessary. Many an audience has been lulled to sleep by the fact that the speaker seemed to be addressing an imaginary audience. People like to feel that they are being talked to directly—that they are at least silent partners in the conversation. Further, they do not like to have too heavy a diet of thought forced upon them at a jovial gathering, nor are they pleased by facetious comments in the face of tragedy. Whenever possible, therefore, find out ahead of time what sort of gathering you are to address. Find out what kind of people will make up the audience, what brings them together, what their ages and interests are, who else is going to speak to them, and what will be their probable attitude toward you and your purpose. Figure out what the people in your audience want most and what they are chiefly interested in. How are their wants and desires related to the subject and purpose of your speech? How can you best appeal to these basic desires?

Sometimes, of course, you will not be able to learn all these things in advance, and you will have to adapt yourself to conditions as you find them; sometimes you will have a very small audience and will be able to size up the situation quickly and exactly; but always the more accurately you can picture the audience and occasion beforehand, the easier this adaptation will be.

Gathering the material

Having completed your survey of the problem by considering the subject, purpose, and audience, you are now ready to begin building the talk. Ordinarily you will start by drawing together what you already know about the subject and deciding roughly what points you want to include in your speech. Frequently, however, you will find that what you already know is not enough. You will want to gather additional information—facts, illustrations, stories, and examples—with which you can develop your speech. It is very often necessary to inquire from those who know more about the subject than you do and to investigate the written sources. Newspapers, magazines, books, reports—these form a valuable storehouse of information which is readily available in the library. Gradually, what you already know and the new material you find can be brought together, sifted, and made ready for the detailed building of the speech.

Making an outline of the speech

As implied in the last paragraph, you will make a rough sketch of the points in your speech even before you make a search for material to develop it; but the detailed outline cannot be drawn up until you have most of the information at your disposal. With the material at hand, you will first set down the main points you expect to make in the order you expect to make them. Then under each main point you will fill in the detailed items, being careful that these details are related to the point under which they are included. This outline should be worked out in detail at first to insure unity and coherence in your speech; later a skeleton outline can be made to fix the points in your memory.

Wording the speech

With the detailed outline before you, there are two ways in which you may develop the wording of your speech. You may write it out word for word and memorize it, or you may use the extemporaneous method recommended on page 15, whichever is easier for you to do effectively. All that you know—or can learn—about English composition, usage, and style will apply at this stage. *Of course in developing your speech on paper you must remember that your material must eventually seem natural and appropriate as you deliver it orally.*

PRACTICING ALOUD

You are now ready for the final step in your preparation: the actual practice for oral presentation. The best method for most speakers is to take the outline or manuscript and, in the privacy of a room, to talk aloud, following the sequence of ideas as written. Do this until the sequence of ideas is clearly in mind. Then think through the outline, point by point, to make sure that the ideas have really become fixed in mind. Next go through the speech aloud without looking at the written speech at all. The first time through you may leave out a good deal, but do not let this worry you. Practice until the ideas have become fixed in an orderly fashion and the words flow easily. Finally, decide whether the situation which will confront you can best be handled by a vigorous, lively presentation or by a quiet, dignified one; whether the situation will call for straight talk or a tactful approach. Above all, remember that you will be speaking *to* people, not *at* them. Throughout your practice, preserve a mental image of the audience you expect to face and project your speech as if they were actually before you.

To summarize, then, thorough preparation to speak in public will require you to take these seven steps:

1. Select and narrow your subject.	⎫	Survey
2. Determine the purpose of your speech.	⎬	the
3. Analyze the audience and the occasion.	⎭	Problem
4. Gather your material.	⎫	Build the
5. Make an outline of your speech.	⎬	Speech
6. Develop the wording of it.	⎭	
7. Practice the speech aloud.	⎰	Practice

It will not always be possible, or perhaps even advisable, to arrange your work in just this order. For instance, your analysis of the audience may actually determine your selection of a subject, and step 3 may therefore precede step 1. Ordinarily, of course, you will want to survey the problem before you start building the speech, and you will have to build a speech before you can practice it; otherwise the sequence should remain flexible.

These essential steps in preparing to speak, so briefly mentioned here, will be treated in more detail in succeeding chapters. When you study these later chapters, however, remember that the problems discussed in them should not be considered in isolation but rather in relation to the integrated process of preparation.

problems

1. List instances of each of the three types of preparation (memorized, extemporaneous, impromptu) as exemplified in speeches you have heard, and comment on their effectiveness.

2. Assuming that you were asked to speak before your class for five minutes one week from today, indicate *(a)* how much time you would reasonably expect to spend in the process of preparation and *(b)* how you would divide that amount of time among the seven essential steps in this process.

3. Make a short report to the class on one of the following:
   a. The hardest step in speech preparation for me is———.
   b. How an effective speaker whom I know prepares his speeches.
   c. How Abraham Lincoln prepared the Gettysburg Address (or one of his other speeches).
   d. In the past the extemporaneous (or the impromptu, or the memorized) method of preparation has proved most satisfactory for me. (Give examples from your experience.)

4. Narrow the following general topics into subjects suitable for a five-minute talk. Give at least five specific topics for each general one.
   a. Photography.
   b. Extra-curricular activities.

c. Life in a dormitory.

   d. Movies.

   e. Winter sports.

   f. Modern literature.

5. Analyze some audience of which you were recently a member and, in a brief oral report to the class, *(a)* bring out the essential nature of the audience, and *(b)* indicate how the speaker did or did not adapt his remarks to his listeners and to the occasion.

6. Make a list of sources from which you could get additional material on one of the topics listed in Problem 4. List the names of several persons you could ask about this subject and visit the library to compile a list of written sources.

7. In a composition handbook, such as Perrin's *Writer's Guide and Index to English* (Scott, Foresman), find a discussion of oral and written English. Prepare a digest of the material for presentation to the class.

Chapter 2 THE SPEAKER

AND HIS AUDIENCE

In order to apply intelligently the detailed suggestions about speech composition and delivery contained in later chapters, the student will first want to gain some insight into the rhetorical and psychological foundations of the principles later to be studied. What is the nature and function of speech? For what purpose do speakers talk? Since audiences differ, how does one analyze and motivate them? A brief survey of some of these matters should prove useful here. Let us begin with the development of language as an illustration of the social function of speech.

The social function of speech Many interesting theories have been suggested about the origin of language in the human race. Some scholars believe that the automatic cries of alarm, the screams of pain, the snarls of rage, and other emotional expressions formed the basis of language. A different suggestion is that as men found it necessary to work or fight together in groups for their common good, they discovered the utility of audible signals to coordinate their effort. Another theory suggests that language began with man's attempt to imitate the sounds of nature. None of these theories can be proved because we have no records of those primitive ages.

We can observe directly, however, the development of speech in children. Beginning with simple emotional cries of hunger, pain, and pleasure, the child soon reaches the "babble" stage; that is, he plays with sounds, making all sorts of noises apparently just "for the fun of it." He gradually finds that certain of these noises produce reactions: his mother responds to some of his "speech" but not to other sounds he makes. Then he associates the sound and the response it secures, and begins to use the sound consciously for this purpose; he has discovered a "word." His parents meanwhile talk to him, and he notices similarities between their sounds and his own; through imitation, and encouraged by his parents, he thus learns additional words and their meanings. Later, words are put together into simple sentences ("Bobby go," etc.), and gradually this process is extended to more complex phraseology and more accurate pronunciation as it keeps pace with the growing complexity of his own thoughts and actions.

Note that speech develops in the child in order to meet a social need. It serves a communicative function. The child at first cries and gurgles merely to express his own emotions, but his speech develops only as he discovers how to use these sounds *to get responses from other people.* As he grows older, he finds that speech is used on the playground and in the schoolroom, at home and at the store, in the club and at work—but he always speaks to a listener, always to someone else.

This communication of ideas to impart knowledge and to secure cooperative action is what we mean by the social function of speech. By means of this tool we cease to be isolated individuals, relatively weak in face of the forces of nature. We join forces to control our environment, developing the great strength of our industrial and political organizations. We hold these joint enterprises together and direct their course of action through language, written and oral.

24

By learning to think and to speak in language symbols, the human race has speeded greatly the rate of its own development. In his interesting book *Human Destiny,* Lecomte du Noüy, the biologist, points out, "The incomparable gift of the brain, with its truly amazing powers of abstraction, has rendered obsolete the slow and sometimes clumsy mechanisms utilized by evolution so far. Thanks to the brain alone, man, in the course of three generations only, has conquered the realm of air, while it took hundreds of thousands of years for animals to achieve the same result through the processes of evolution. . . . Articulated speech alone has already considerably shortened the time necessary for certain adaptations. What we call the education of young children can be considered as an extraordinarily quick short-cut, replacing the biological process of adaptation, and obtaining in one generation results better than those which required ages amongst the animals at the cost of innumerable deaths."[1]

Thus, in the evolution of man, social processes involving speech have replaced the slower biological processes of adaptation. This social function, the communication of knowledge from one individual to another, is the most important role of speech. As we study speech, therefore, we must be careful not to think of it as an isolated thing; we must think of speech in its functional setting, as a means of communication, as something going on *between a speaker and a listener.* We shall then be less concerned by what speech *is* than by what it *does;* its form and beauty will be important only in terms of the response it secures from those who hear it.

The nature of the speech act

What is the chain of events involved in this process of communication that we have just considered? What happens when one person speaks to another?

1 From *Human Destiny* by Pierre Lecomte du Noüy (Longmans, Green and Company, Inc., N. Y., 1947), pp. 120-22.

Speech as a circular response

We must realize first that the act of speaking is not a one-way process; it involves a series of interacting elements. Thus, the sound of my voice reaches my own ears as well as my listener's and causes me to talk louder, perhaps, or more slowly. Likewise, my listener, if he cannot hear, may cup his hand behind his ear; seeing him do so will cause me to raise my voice. A frown of perplexity on a listener's face may impel me to clarify my explanation, or a look of doubt may cause me to offer added proof. This interaction is, of course, most obvious in the give and take of conversation and group discussion, but, although less obvious, it is present and important even when only one is speaking and the rest are listening. This continuous interaction is often called a *circular response* and is a fundamental characteristic of the act of speaking.

For the sake of simplicity, however, let us break this chain of interaction at some point, and describe the process of speaking as if its various elements occurred in a direct sequence. (1) We shall begin with an

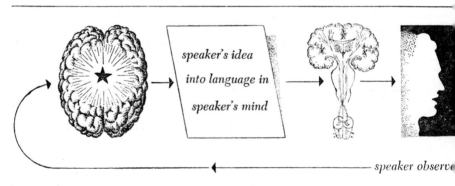

Here is a diagram of the circular response. Notice that each step is required to make the process complete. An idea forms in the speaker's mind, where it is translated into language symbols; reacting to impulses from the nervous system, the muscles used in speech convert these language symbols into audible speech; the sounds are carried as wave patterns in the air until they strike the eardrums of the listener; as nerve impulses, they travel to the brain, where they again be-

idea in the speaker's mind which he wants to communicate to a listener's mind. How he got the idea—through observation, reading, or listening to others—is of no concern to us at the moment, nor is the reason why he feels impelled to transmit that idea to another. We begin at the point where he has the idea and wants to tell it. (2) He must translate the idea into language symbols of some kind: words, phrases, sentences—in English or some other language. As yet, however, these language symbols are mental concepts only; they have not emerged from the speaker's mind. To make these symbols audible, (3) nerve impulses from the central nervous system must actuate and control the complex systems of muscles used in speech—the breathing muscles, the muscles of the larynx and jaw, the tongue, the lips, etc.—and (4) these muscles must react in a coordinated movement to produce the proper sounds.

But these sounds are now no longer words and sentences; they are merely disturbances in the molecules of air surrounding the speaker, a wave pattern of compressed and rarefied particles of gas. (5) The out-

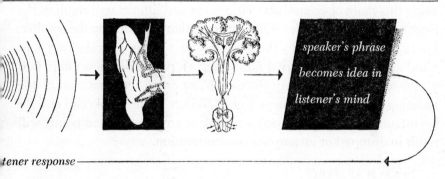

speaker's phrase becomes idea in listener's mind

listener response

come language symbols which convey meaning to the listener's mind; the listener reacts to what he has heard; the speaker observes this reaction and responds to it.

Thus we see that the process of communication depends not only on the speaker's saying something to a listener, but also on his constant awareness of the listener's reaction to what he says.

ward movement of these wave patterns through the air transmits the sounds the speaker made until they strike the eardrums of a listener. (The use of telephone or radio, of course, introduces additional steps by changing sound waves to electronic waves and back again to sound waves.) (6) In the ear of the listener, the waves of compressed and rarefied air are again translated into nerve impulses and (7) are carried to the brain by the auditory nerve. When this happens, the listener has "heard" the sounds but he has not yet understood the speaker. He must (8) recognize these nerve impulses as language symbols—words and sentences—and he must (9) attach a meaning to this series of symbols. Thus, what the listener hears arouses thought and feeling in him. (10) Finally, the listener reacts at this point, and the speaker, observing his reaction, responds to it, thus continuing the circular response. The process of communication is complete only when these ten steps have occurred. (See diagram on pp. 26 and 27.)

From this description, it is easy to see why speakers are so often misunderstood by those who hear them. A break or distortion *anywhere* along this chain of events between speaker and listener will result in the listener's receiving an idea different from that intended by the speaker. Poor choice of language by the speaker (step 2), poor articulation (steps 3 and 4), interfering external noise (step 5), partial deafness (steps 6 or 7), possession of an inadequate vocabulary or misinterpretation of the meaning by the listener (steps 8 or 9), failure of the speaker to observe his listener's reaction (step 10)—a break at any one of these points will result in distorted or incomplete communication.

SPEECH AS HABIT

If each step in this process of oral communication required the conscious effort of the speaker and listener, talking to one another would be slow and painfully laborious. Yet we know that, in spite of the complexity of the process described above, speech is, for most of us, easy, natural, and spontaneous. This is because so much of the act of speaking and of listening to the speech of others is automatic. By practice, we have reduced much of the total process to the level of habit. Thus, when we see a certain animal, the word "cat" automatically occurs to us, and if we wish to talk about that animal, habit has established appropriate neuromuscular patterns so that our speech mechanism produces the sounds of the word "cat" without much conscious effort. Even the sentence structure we use and to some extent the arrangement of the larger units of thought we express are profoundly influenced by our habits of thinking and speaking. To the extent that the various steps in the act of speaking become habitual through practice, therefore, the easier speaking becomes for us. By the same token, however, the more our speech becomes a habit process, the less conscious we are of it *regardless of whether our habits are good or bad*. Practice makes permanent—but not necessarily "perfect." As students of speech, we may profit by examining our habits of speech at each stage of the communicative process described above to see whether our habits contribute to the clarity with which our ideas are transmitted or whether they distort or prevent easy communication.

Thinking and emotion in speech

Behind the actual process of communication we have just examined lie the thinking processes of the speaker and the listener and the patterns of emotional reaction which they possess. Leaving the details of their practical application in speech composition for later study, let us here consider a few aspects of their fundamental nature.

THE THINKING PROCESS

Thinking consists essentially of *identification, classification, determining relationships,* and *solving problems*. We begin by observing the environment around us. A certain object catches our eye and we note its shape, color, and size; we feel its texture, and perhaps lift it to note its weight; we may smell or taste it as well. This combination of impressions is remembered, and serves to *identify* that object for us if we are confronted by it again. Suppose later in the day we come across another object similar in every respect except size; the second object is a little larger. In spite of this difference, we note how similar our impressions of this new object are to our memory of the first one and we say to ourselves, "This is the same sort of thing." Later, we repeat this process as we encounter more and more similar objects, until we become aware that all of them may be thought of together as a *class of things* having similar characteristics. At this point we are likely to coin a name for our classification—we say to ourselves, let us call these things "rocks."

From this point on as we observe new objects we say, "This is a rock," or "This is *not* a rock," depending on whether they have similar characteristics. Similarly, we classify other objects, events (falling—not falling), and qualities (hot-cold, black-white). As our thinking proceeds, we subdivide our classes into smaller units (limestone, gravel, etc.) and combine them into larger classes (rocks + dirt + humus, etc. = land), and give each of them a name. We even note intangible similarities in qualities and behavior and group them together in such categories as "beautiful" and "friendly." This form of thinking enables us to arrange our impressions in an orderly way; we are able to deal with relatively few *classes* of things instead of an infinite number of slightly different *individual* things. On the other hand, we run the risk of forgetting the differences which always exist between individuals in a class, and at times of mistaking the *name* we have given a class of things for the things themselves. (Just what, for example, is "New York State"?) The study of logic and of semantics is concerned with these problems.

Another type of thinking deals with relationships other than mere classification. We note, in the objects around us and in the events which occur, certain connections and sequences that are regular. One type of event *follows* another; one type of object is *larger* than another; qualities A and B always occur together, but never when quality C is present. We note these relationships, and use our knowledge of them to analyze our experiences and predict the results of our actions. Thus we think *back* and think *ahead* in terms of related phenomena.

Much thinking of the types described above would be purely academic were it not for its application to another form of thinking which we do, namely, problem solving. Suppose a man is separated from his dinner by a high board fence which he cannot scale. If he does not *think about it,* he may waste his energy in aimless running back and forth and fruitless efforts to jump high enough to climb over; failing in his effort, he sinks down exhausted and hungry. But if he thinks about the problem, he does his running and jumping *in his mind;* employing the processes of classification and relationship applied to his previous experience, he concludes that such action would be fruitless. By analyzing the nature of his problem and reviewing his experiences in solving similar problems, he concludes that he must build a platform or ladder of some sort and goes about doing so. This type of thinking, then, is creative and imaginative. By manipulating and combining mental concepts, one *puts together a pattern of action* in his mind before expending energy to apply it.

In all these thinking processes, you will note the important part played by language, for it is the names of things we manipulate in our thinking to save the effort of manipulating the things themselves. Thus the speaker uses language in his own thinking and in leading the thinking of his audience. In general, it may be said that clear thinking and sloppy language do not occur together.

EMOTION AND ITS EFFECTS

From our discussion of the thinking process it might be inferred that human beings are ruled by reason. This, however, is not the case. A very large part of human behavior is emotional in nature or at least colored by emotion. Ages ago, in the struggle for survival, the human race developed certain patterns of reaction to the dangers that beset it. The basis of these patterns still persists in what we now call anger, fear, excitement, and the like. These reactions have a strong physiological foundation: when we become angry or afraid, adrenalin is secreted, blood sugar pours into the bloodstream, the heart beats faster, and our breathing rate is changed. Our bodies prepare, as bodies did in past ages, to meet the emergency—to run or to fight. Civilized man, of course, has largely substituted words for deeds, the language symbol for the act. Thus we become angry when we are struck by a word just as much as if by a fist, and we strike back in the same symbolic way. *But the physiological processes go on just as they did in the past*—and we feel angry! The thinking processes described above may serve to modify and direct our behavior, but the basic emotional patterns are automatic to a large extent and beyond our conscious control.

Emotion, of course, varies in intensity. Most psychologists agree that a *mild degree of emotion* is nearly always present and serves a beneficial purpose. Such emotion exhibits itself in a feeling of pleasantness and controlled enthusiasm or in mild irritation which stirs us to improve our lot. (A speaker, for example, who does not feel somewhat stimulated when confronted by an audience is likely to speak poorly as a result of his very apathy.) A second level of emotion, which we may label *strong emotion,* tends to differ in type as well as degree. Usually, strong emotion has a focal point: we are angry *about* something or *at* somebody; we are afraid *of* something. Moreover, strong emotion usually (though not always) is of a definite type—fear, rage, love, etc.—rather than being a vague and general feeling. The physiological changes are greater than in mild emotion, and we are prepared to exert strong effort, but we are still capable of coordinated action. We can consciously control to some extent what we do though it is difficult to keep from doing something. Our energies demand release, but we can direct them in an organized fashion. The extreme degree of emotion, however, is a *disrupting emotion.* When emotion is very strong we may lose control of ourselves entirely. We may "freeze" as some animals do when startled, unable to move or speak, or we may break out in random and unintegrated movements having no value whatsoever. The level of emotion at which disruption sets in varies from person to person, but it is rarely reached in situations where previous experience has established appropriate action to solve the problem. Thus the trained soldier is deathly afraid, but he does not easily go to pieces under fire *because he has practiced what to do about it.*

The speaker may use his knowledge of emotion both to manage his own emotional reactions and to stir the feelings of his listeners. He may increase the vigor of his own speaking, and minimize his fear of criticism, by talking about subjects which arouse his own enthusiasm or strong feeling. He may arouse his listeners to action by describing emotion-provoking situations to them. To put it simply, he may use his own and his listeners' thinking processes to give sensible direction to his proposals, and he may use his knowledge of emotion to give power and exhilaration to his own speaking and to the active response required of his audience.

problems

1. Prepare to take part in a class discussion of "The social function of speech" as used in the following:

   a. Buying or selling merchandise in a retail store.

   b. A long-distance telephone conversation with your parents on the occasion of some family anniversary.

   c. A political speech by a candidate for public office.

   d. A classroom lecture or discussion in a course in mathematics, science, language, or history.

   e. The play-by-play broadcast of an athletic contest.

   f. Conversation with a "date" at some social event.

   g. A doctor asking questions of his patient while making his diagnosis.

2. In your own past experiences or in those of people you know, find examples where the "circular response" has been broken or distorted at each of the ten stages involved in the speech act as described in this chapter.

3. Pick out ten things you do when you speak which can be identified as "habits of speech." In one or two sentences each, explain why you think they are good or poor habits.
4. Report to the class on the speech habits exhibited by someone you have recently heard speaking from the platform or on the radio.
5. In speeches you have heard or in articles or editorials you have read, find examples of each kind of thinking described in this chapter. Be prepared to discuss in class the relationship between *thinking* and *language* as employed in these examples.
6. From your own experience, select occasions when you have experienced each of the three degrees of emotion (mild, strong, disrupting) described in this chapter. As accurately as you can remember them, write out a brief description of your feelings and outward reactions.
7. Describe to the class an instance you have observed in which a speaker aroused the emotions of his listener (or listeners). Did this emotional response help or hinder him in achieving the purpose for which he spoke?

The speaker's prestige

How completely your listeners will believe what you say and do what you request—even how closely they will listen to your explanation or argument—will depend in large measure on their opinion of you yourself. Whenever you speak before a group you become, temporarily at least, the leader of the group, a position in which you must have prestige to be successful.

Some elements involved in a speaker's prestige were discussed in Chapter 1. Obviously a leader must have confidence in himself if he expects others to follow with confidence. For this confidence to be genuine, it must be based on knowledge both theoretical and practical; and to impress one's hearers, skill in speaking developed through practice is required. All these things help to establish the speaker's prestige as soon as he stands up and affect his prestige throughout his speech. The chairman's introduction, of course, is important in creating respect for the speaker before he starts; his remarks about the character, past experience, and present position of the speaker may help to qualify him as an expert in the opinion of his audience. But a timid, poorly informed, or mumbling speaker is likely to lose all the respect created for him by the chairman. When he stands up to speak, the speaker must be *prepared to lead* and, without overstepping the bounds of modesty and propriety, he must *assume leadership* with confidence and authority. Your ability to do this will develop as you grow in maturity both as a person and as a speaker.

Importance of the speaker's integrity

What has just been said does not mean, of course, that confident speaking will in itself make you a leader. Nearly nineteen hundred years ago, Quintilian said that a good speaker must first of all be a good man: he must be intelligent and observant, but above all he must have integrity of character. People do not listen merely to a speech, but to a *person speaking;* and they are influenced quite as much by their confidence in the speaker as by what he says. The man who is honest and sincere, who has a reputation for knowing the facts and speaking the truth, is respected when he speaks. He influences his listeners by his own character—by what classical writers used to call "ethical persuasion."

If, however, a young man or woman has little character or intelligence to begin with, speech training can do little more than make him a glib rascal or a slightly more efficient parrot. His actions will contradict his words; he cannot long urge honesty in government if he cheats in school or business; his request for an open mind in others will fall on deaf ears if he is stubborn and bigoted himself. Even his own speaking will betray his character, for he will find it easier to dodge the issue than to face it—to say the popular thing than to support justice in the face of prejudice. Such a speaker may win easy applause at first; but the man who lacks the courage of his convictions, who seeks unfair personal

There are two ways of democracy functioning and ruling men. One is by force and the other is by law. . . . Our government, democracy, is a government by law.

What makes it possible for men to govern themselves by law?

A law is just a piece of paper with some words on it. Some laws, some of our most important laws, are not even written down.

Nevertheless, laws are the most powerful instrument that society has ever invented. In the history of mankind they have proved themselves to be more powerful than armies or navies or any kind of war machinery.

Laws derive this great, strange power from one source, from the faith that one man or one woman has in other people. I have a great faith that you will obey the laws and you have a great faith that I will obey the laws. That faith makes our democracy strong. That faith binds us together.

If that faith should weaken, if I should lose faith in you, or you in me, our system of laws would be weakened. Our democracy would begin to break down.

What gives us this faith in each other?

Essentially it is that each of us knows that the other has a conscience. The conscience of a democratic people is a great and a very noble achievement. We have groped for it through centuries of darkness, through generations of oppression.

The sincerity of a speaker is extremely important. Wendell Willkie's sincerity was so dynamic that even these pictures of him seem audible. From the portion of his speech reprinted here it is plain that he realized the importance of the factors of interest in gaining an audience's attention.

36

advantage, who suppresses the facts or warps the evidence to prove his point, eventually loses his prestige. As soon as the currency of his speech is recognized as counterfeit, his influence is lost.

When Winston Churchill took over the British government during the Second World War, he offered his countrymen only "blood, sweat, and tears" in the struggle with Nazi Germany. Yet this very rugged honesty captured their support far quicker than rosy promises could have. To the British people during the war, Winston Churchill became the symbol of their courage and their faith. His mastery of the art of speech made people listen, but it was confidence in his integrity that made them follow him.

The speaker's purpose

Assuming that a speaker has all the elements of prestige, including known integrity of character, knowledge, confidence, and skill in speaking, he may yet fail in his effort if he does not keep clearly in mind his purpose in speaking. Many a speech has been ruined by aimless wandering or needless padding with extraneous material. A leader must first of all know where he is trying to lead! Earlier in this chapter, while considering the social function of speech, we saw that *the aim of every speech is to get a reaction from the audience.* As a speaker, then, you must decide very early *what kind of reaction* you desire and, specifically, *what particular reaction* you propose to secure.

THE GENERAL TYPES OF SPEECH PURPOSE

Writers on practical speaking, from classical times to the present, have grouped the purposes of speech into a few fairly definite types and pointed out valuable differences in the methods of accomplishing them. Many such classifications have been used, varying in size and detail. The following one, listing the "general ends" of speech, will be found quite workable:

THE GENERAL ENDS OF SPEECH

General Purpose	Method	Audience Reaction Sought
To Entertain	Interest and Amuse	Enjoyment
To Inform	Explain and Amplify	Clear Understanding
To Persuade	Motivate and—	
	a. Convince with Proof	Belief
	b. Stimulate by Vivid Appeal	Emotional Arousal
	c. Use Strong Suggestion	Action

A general end, as the term is used above, denotes a general class of speech purpose in terms of the reaction which the speaker wants from his audience. Merely because your purpose falls within one of the general ends it does not follow that you will have no concern with any of the others. You will sometimes need to entertain during your speech in order to inform; you must usually inform in order to secure belief; to get action you will need to convince or stimulate. But one of these will be the end, and the others means to that end; one will be your objective and the others only contributory. For this reason you must take care that the secondary purposes do not run away with the speech—that they are included only when they advance the principal aim of the speech, and only for as long as they do so. The following discussion treats each general end in its capacity as a *primary* aim of this sort.

To ENTERTAIN

When your primary concern is to have your audience enjoy themselves, the general end of your speech will be to entertain. This is a frequent purpose of after-dinner speakers, but this type of purpose is by no means limited to speakers at such occasions. Humor is, of course, the primary means of entertainment, but curious bits of information serve the same purpose if they are striking or unusual ones; vividness and originality of statement will play an important part. You will then need to avoid heavy discussion and controversial issues; above all you must avoid the attempt to "grind an ax" in a speech of this sort.

To inform

When the object of your speech is to inform, your main purpose will be to make the audience understand something, or to widen the range of their knowledge. This is the purpose of the foreman who is showing a workman how to operate a new machine. The teacher lectures to his class primarily to inform, and the county farm agent desires chiefly that his audience understand when he explains the results of tests carried on at the agricultural experiment station. To do this, he must relate his ideas to the existing knowledge of his audience; he must watch that the structure of his speech is clear; and he must present enough concrete examples and specific data to avoid becoming abstract and dry.

To persuade (*To convince, stimulate emotion, or evoke action*)

The object of your speech will be to persuade when you desire to strengthen or change the beliefs or emotional attitudes of your listeners or to arouse them to action. Many times all three aspects of persuasion will combine in the objective of a single speech; at other times your purpose may be more limited, merely to establish logical conviction or primarily to arouse emotion.

If the main purpose of a persuasive speech is to influence the beliefs or intellectual attitudes of the audience, the objective will be primarily *to convince* the listener. A very large share of present-day speeches have this as their general end. Political speakers urge their constituents to believe in the principles and performances of their respective parties; attempts are made to create belief in the superiority of certain products, principles, or forms of government; the truth of scientific and philosophical hypotheses is debated pro and con. The essential characteristic of a speech made to convince is the fact that it attempts to prove something; hence, it is usually filled with argument supported with fact, figure, and example. New situations are referred to old beliefs, and evidence is brought to substantiate the speaker's assertions. Very often, emotional appeal is added in order to lend a dynamic force to the argument but not to replace the basic logic which underlies it. In this way the attempt is made to establish or change the convictions of the audience.

Sometimes, however, the main purpose of a persuasive speech is *to stimulate emotion*; this is true when the speaker tries to inspire, to arouse enthusiasm, or to deepen a feeling of awe, respect, or devotion on the part of his audience. Speeches commemorating great events, such as Memorial Day or Armistice Day, and those given at rallies, pep sessions, and as keynotes to conventions usually have stimulation as their general end. Sometimes a speaker attempts to change the attitude of the audience in this way, but usually he attempts merely to strengthen an existing attitude. Rarely does he try to prove anything; but such a speech is full of striking statements, vivid descriptions, and strong emotional appeal. Very often, no specific performance is demanded of the audience.

There are times, however, when the speaker desires *to evoke action*—to obtain some definite observable performance from the audience. This performance may be to vote "yes" or "no"; it may be to contribute money, to sign a petition, to form a parade and engage in a demonstration; or it may be any one of a hundred types of observable public acts. The basis of this action may be the creation of a strong belief, or it may be the arousal of emotion, or it may be both. For this reason the development of the speech which aims at action will follow closely the methods suggested for speeches which aim to convince or to stimulate. The only distinguishing feature of the actuating speech is that it goes further than the other two; in it you definitely ask your audience to do something active and observable, at a specified time.

The speech to evoke action differs from other persuasive speeches, therefore, only in the *degree* of reaction sought from the audience. The content and method of development will parallel closely that used in any other persuasive speech.

40

These, then, are the general types of purpose which a speech may have. To attempt speaking with no more precise objective in mind, however, would be dangerous. The general purpose must be narrowed to a more specific one before you proceed with the building of your speech.

The specific purpose—
limiting factors

We may define the specific purpose of a speech as the *specific response* desired from the audience by the time the speaker has finished. It is the exact thing that he wants the audience to do, feel, believe, understand, or enjoy. The following example will illustrate the relationship between the subject, general end, and specific purpose:

Subject: Fire Insurance for Students.

General end: To persuade—evoke action.

Specific purpose: To get members of the student council to approve the group policy offered by the ABC Fire Insurance Company.

Or again—

Subject: High Altitude Flying.

General end: To inform.

Specific purpose: To make the audience understand the difference between the problems of flying above and below an altitude of twenty thousand feet.

Before going very far with the preparation of a speech, you must determine not only the type of reaction you want from your audience, but the exact response wanted with reference to the subject of your speech. While making this decision, you will need to keep in mind certain factors which should limit or modify your choice.

THE AUTHORITY OR CAPACITY OF THE AUDIENCE

To demand of a group of college students that they "abolish all required courses" is foolish; they do not have the authority to do so since curricular requirements are in the hands of the faculty. But students do have the right and ability to bring pressure on the faculty toward this end. Limit your request to something that is within your listeners' power and ability. Do not ask the audience to do something which they couldn't do even if they wished.

THE EXISTING ATTITUDE OF THE AUDIENCE

A group of striking workmen who believe that they were badly underpaid and unfairly treated by their employer would probably be hostile to the suggestion that they return to work under the same conditions as before; but they might approve submitting the dispute to arbitration by some disinterested person whose fairness and judgment they respect. Your purpose, then, must be reasonable in the light of your listeners' existing beliefs.

THE OCCASION

To ask people to contribute money to a political campaign fund might be appropriate at a pre-election rally, but to do so at a church dinner would be decidedly out of place. The celebration of a football victory is hardly the place to secure an understanding of Einstein's theory. Be sure that your purpose fits the spirit of the occasion at which you are to speak.

THE TIME LIMIT OF THE SPEECH

A hostile majority may be induced by what you can say in a few sentences to postpone action until a later time; but to change the attitude of your audience completely so that they will favor your proposal may take an elaborate discussion. Moreover, if the subject you are to discuss is a complex one, you may be able *to inform* your audience, to get them to understand your proposal, but the time may not be adequate for you *to convince* them of its desirability. Given an hour to speak, you may be able to get an audience to understand the working of the Federal Reserve System in expanding and contracting credit; but if you have only five minutes, you had better limit your efforts to an emphasis of the importance of this function and to suggestions for finding out more about it. Do not attempt to get a reaction which would take more time to secure than you have for your speech.

If these limiting factors are kept in mind when you determine the specific purpose of your speech, the success of your effort will be more probable. Write down your specific purpose in a simple sentence; check it against the limitations listed above; then fix it firmly in mind. Rarely will the audience be told this purpose in so many words in the speech itself; certainly no such didactic statement will be made at the beginning of the speech. But whether the purpose is obviously revealed to the audience or not, it should remain in the focus of your own thoughts both during the preparation of the speech and during its presentation.

problems

1. Make a list of five speeches that have become historically important. Explain why these are considered great speeches. Keep in mind the following questions.
   a. What had the speaker done to establish confidence in his personal integrity?
   b. How did the speaker make use of his knowledge and background?
2. Supposing the class to be your audience, select a subject, and phrase three sentences, each one stating a specific purpose appropriate for a different general end but all concerned with the chosen subject.
3. Go to hear some speaker; write down the subject and title of his speech; determine the general end and specific purpose of it; and note to what extent he accomplished his specific purpose.
   a. Write a brief report of your observations covering these points.
   b. Be prepared to discuss your observations orally before the class.
4. Visit the library and find a book or magazine containing a number of printed speeches. (For example, such books as *Models of Speech Composition,* edited by J. M. O'Neill; *Representative American Speeches,* edited by A. C. Baird; or any issue of the magazine *Vital Speeches of the Day.*) Determine the general end and specific purpose of at least five speeches and state to what extent you believe each speech moved toward accomplishing its purpose.

5. List three subjects upon which you could talk, and, for each one, phrase a title that would command attention.
6. Select some simple physical response which the members of the class can make (such as laughing, looking at some object in the room, adjusting their hair or neckties) and in a one-minute speech evoke this action from them.
7. For each of the three general ends, list one occasion which has occurred in your experience during the past year at which a speech for that general purpose would have been appropriate.

Analyzing the audience

Unless there were someone to listen, speech would be a mere verbal exercise. Talking to hear one's own voice may help to bolster up courage on a dark night, but it is hardly communicative speech. Yet it is a curious fact that, without meaning to, many a speaker has done this very thing. Too often we become so engrossed in our own interests, so impressed by the facts that seem important to us, that we forget we are talking to other people whose knowledge and interests may differ widely from our own. It is a fairly safe assertion that more speeches fail of their purpose for this one reason than for any other. The most important lesson a speaker can learn is to see things from the viewpoint of his audience. He must continually ask himself, "How would I feel about this if I were in their places?" To do this effectively means a thorough analysis of the audience since it is obvious that an argument which would convince some people would leave others unmoved, and that what would be highly interesting to one audience would be dull to another.

But how are you to find out these things? The best way, of course, is to ask some of those who you know will be members of your audience; or if you do not know any such persons, a great deal can be learned from others who have had dealings with them. Even this method is sometimes impossible, and you will then be forced to infer the attitudes and beliefs of your audience from what general knowledge you can gather about their education, occupation, age, and the like.

44

Some general facts about the audience should be determined early in the analysis. They include:

The size of the audience.

The age of those making up the audience. It is important to note whether they are of the same age level, or of widely divergent ages. Age will affect their ability to understand you and will determine how far back their experience runs.

The sex of members of the audience. Is it a mixed audience or not? Men and women differ in their interests though these interests overlap. Some subjects suitable for discussion before one sex are unsuitable for the other or for a mixed audience.

The occupation of the members of the audience. Occupation tends to suggest interests which people will have and the type of knowledge which they will show. A talk to the University Club members will doubtless differ from one before the local labor union. A fair index of income level can also be gained from this information.

The education of those in the audience. Both formal education in the public schools and colleges, and that education which has come through training, are important. A Chicago cab driver may not have a broad formal education, but his knowledge of the ways of human nature and of the conditions in that city may be profound. Remember to consider both schooling and experience.

Membership in social, professional, and religious groups. Memberships in special groups often indicate both interests and prejudices. Rotary Club, Knights of Columbus, Sigma Chi, Country Club, Young Republican League, Business and Professional Women's Club, Elks, United World Federalists—what do these organizations mean to you? They should represent types of people, points of view, interests, and special abilities. Whenever you find out that a sizable part of your audience is affiliated with some special group, you will have gained a valuable clue for your analysis.

45

THE AUDIENCE'S KNOWLEDGE OF THE SUBJECT

Through either the general data about the audience or some special information which you have secured, you should be able to infer what the members of your audience know about the subject of your speech. Will they understand technical terms without explanation? Will too elementary a discussion of it seem boring and trivial to them? What facts will be new to them, and what material will be old stuff? For a speaker to imply by his remarks that he thinks his listeners ignorant, or for him to assume toward them a condescending manner is decidedly tactless; but it is equally bad policy to talk over their heads. A plan which has been found fairly successful generally is to aim the speech at a level of knowledge characteristic of the average member of the group.

THE PRIMARY INTERESTS AND DESIRES OF THE AUDIENCE

A cardinal rule laid down by Webb and Morgan in their stimulating book *Strategy in Handling People,* based on the experience of successful men, is this: "From a practical standpoint, the first precaution in managing people is to discover what they really want, especially the exact nature of the most active wants which touch upon us and our plans."[2] The most carefully built speech of all time is likely to fall flat unless it contains an appeal to the people who hear it. Before going further, then, we will consider briefly the universal motives which control human behavior. If the speech is to influence the audience, the main points of that speech must appeal to these motives, and nothing must be said that will contain a counterappeal.

Nearly everything we do or think or feel is based upon some fundamental motive or urge or drive within us that has been set in motion by some event or condition in our immediate experience. Someone calls me a liar, and I order him out of my room; he pressed the fighting button, and I became angry. Someone shows me that the only way I can get a job is to join the union; so I pay my union dues and join. I am told that

2 From *Strategy in Handling People* by E. T. Webb and J. J. B. Morgan (Boulton, Pierce, and Company, Chicago, 1931), p. 73.

46

membership in a fraternity will insure my social prestige on the campus and help me get into activities—I become interested. My bed is so warm and the room so cold that I decide to stay in bed and miss my eight o'clock class, but recalling that I must pass that quiz at nine o'clock or flunk the course, I brave the cold and shiver into my clothes at eight-thirty. In each of these instances some latent force within me has been stirred to action.

Psychologists have called these powerful tendencies by different names depending upon the point of view of the particular psychologist represented. They have been called instincts, emotions, prepotent reflexes, purposive or wish-fulfilling drives, habitual action tendencies, and many other names. Many have been the arguments about the number of basic drives which exist and the degree in which they are inborn or acquired through experience and habit. With the technical details of these arguments we are not here concerned. It is more important for us to note the facts agreed upon by all: (*a*) that in all human beings there are certain universal action tendencies—the organism has within it the capacity and the tendency to move in different directions; and (*b*) that these tendencies are set in motion and modified in their direction by pressure put on the individual by his environment.

In terms of the speaker this means that *the normal condition of the people in an audience is one of physical relaxation, mental inertia, and emotional equilibrium unless something has happened already to stir these people into motion or unless the speaker does so through the appeal which he makes.* If, then, you are to accomplish the purpose of your speech, you must overcome the inertia of the audience or counteract an opposite tendency by setting in motion some fundamental reaction which will move them in the direction of your purpose. You must puncture a hole in their apathy or opposition which will make them feel unsatisfied until they have reacted as you wish. But before you can do this, you must understand what these basic urges or reaction tendencies are, and you must know how to arouse them.

The primary motives. Fundamentally, there are four primary motives which influence human beings. Behind every act, belief, or emotion will be found one or more of these basic desires:

1. Self-preservation and the desire for physical well-being.
2. Freedom from external restraint.
3. Preservation and increase of self-esteem (ego expansion).
4. Preservation of the human race.

Thus, we build a fire to keep from freezing or even from feeling cold (1); we abhor imprisonment and dislike laws which infringe upon what we call our personal liberty (2); we wear fine clothes, try to excel others in our accomplishments, enjoy praise, and dislike appearing in unfavorable circumstances (3); we marry, have children, organize governments, impose legal penalties for anti-social conduct (4). The only limit to such an enumeration is, of course, the infinite variety of human conduct itself.

These four basic motives vary in their power with different individuals. One man may care more for his comfort than his freedom; another, more for his family than himself. Experience modifies the influence which these motives have upon us. Moreover, there are certain periods in our lives when one or another motive matures and becomes most powerful. Furthermore, the immediate situation confronting us may call one of them into play more than any of the others. Regardless of these variations, however, all four of them are powerful factors in the life of every human being.

But the complexity of human life prevents the simple and direct fulfillment of these desires. Experience produces a large variety of composite desires, combinations of the four primary motives as they relate to the concrete objects of our environment. *To these more specific and familiar patterns the speaker must make his motive appeals.*

Types of motive appeal. A motive appeal, then, is an appeal to some sentiment, emotion, or desire by which the speaker may set the *primary motives* into action. There are, of course, an infinite number of these specific human wants, and any list of them must of necessity be incomplete and overlapping to some extent. The list which is to follow has both of these faults, but it will nevertheless be found quite practical. In it you will find the specific desires and sentiments to which appeals are almost universally effective. It will be extremely worth your while to study this list, and to begin basing your analysis of people and the main points of your speeches upon them.

1. Acquisition and Saving.
2. Adventure.
3. Companionship.
4. Creating.
   a—Organizing.
   b—Building.
5. Curiosity.
6. Destruction.
7. Fear.
8. Fighting.
   a—Anger.
   b—Competition.
9. Imitation.
10. Independence.
11. Loyalty.
    a—To friends.
    b—To family (parental or filial love).
    c—To social groups (school spirit, civic pride).
    d—To nation (patriotism).
12. Personal Enjoyment.
    a—Of comfort and luxury.
    b—Of beauty and order.
    c—Of pleasant sensations (tastes, smells, etc.).
    d—Of recreation.
    e—Of relief from restraint (sprees, etc.).
13. Power and Authority.
14. Pride.
    a—Reputation.
    b—Self-respect.
15. Reverence or Worship.
    a—Of leaders (hero worship).
    b—Of institutions or traditions.
    c—Of the Deity.
16. Revulsion.
17. Sex Attraction.
18. Sympathy.

These, then, are some of the sentiments or desires to which motive appeals may be made. Observe, however, that these appeals are not always made singly but that they are often combined. For example, most students attend college in order to improve their chances to get ahead when they are through; they seek training that will improve their chances of self-advancement. But what is involved in this desire for self-advancement? A desire for greater income, the power of higher position, and the pride of a higher station in life—all these, acquisition, power, pride, are combined into the one pattern called "getting ahead." Or let us take another common experience: suppose you were going to buy a suit of clothes or a dress. What would influence your decision? One thing would be its price—*saving;* another would be its comfort and appearance—the *pleasure* to be derived from beauty or luxury; another consideration would be its style—*imitation*—or its individuality of appearance—*independence;* and finally, a combination of these items would make an appeal to *pride:* Would other people think the clothes in good taste, would they envy your selection? Some of these desires might be stronger than others in your choice, some might conflict with each other, but all of them would be present; whichever suit or dress made the strongest appeal to them would be the one chosen.

Yet, while a variety of appeal is valuable in a speech, this appeal should not be dissipated by too diffuse scattering. Usually, the better method is to select two or three motives which you think will have the strongest appeal to your audience on the subject of your speech, and to concentrate your appeal on these few motives, allowing other appeals to be incidental. You can accomplish this result by selecting as the main points of your speech arguments that contain these basic appeals. For example, a student who was urging his classmates to participate in interclass athletic contests chose the following as the main points of his speech:

1. Concentrated study without exercise will make your mind stale and ruin your grades. *(Fear)*

2. By playing with others you will make new friends. *(Companionship)*

3. Interclass competition may lead to a place for you on the varsity teams. *(Power* and *pride)*

4. You will have a great deal of fun playing. *(Enjoyment of recreation)*

In the complete development of his speech, this student incidentally made appeals to imitation through examples of those who had previously engaged in interclass sports; he stimulated the desire for competition; he suggested that participation would indicate loyalty to the class; but the principal appeal was made to those few motives which were incorporated in his main points.

Quite clearly, you cannot in most cases express your appeal to motives directly or in too obvious a manner. To do so would make the technique too prominent and would develop resistance in the audience. You would not go before an audience and say, "I want you to *imitate* Jones, the successful banker," nor would you say, "If you give to this cause, we will print your name so that your *reputation* as a generous man will be known to everybody." Rather you must make the appeal effective through the suggestion of these things carried in the descriptions and illustrations that you use. Furthermore, some motive appeals which are privately powerful, such as the appeal to fear, imitation, personal comfort, or pride, we hesitate to acknowledge publicly. Therefore, when these appeals are used in a public speech, they must be worded tactfully and supplemented by other appeals which we can publicly admit as the cause for our action.

AUDIENCE'S FIXED ATTITUDES AND BELIEFS

From the time a child first begins to receive impressions of his environment he starts to form opinions or to establish attitudes toward things in that environment. These opinions and attitudes are modified by his later experience, but most of us by the time we grow up have by habit and repetition established some of them as the fixed bases for our conduct. Some people, for example, believe firmly in the value of science; others (though they may not admit it openly) believe in hunches, jinxes, and the like. A man may be fixed in his belief in a high tariff, or in the law of supply and demand, or the superiority of a certain race. Such proverbs as "Honesty is the best policy," and "Spare the rod and spoil the child," are but traditional ways of stating rather common fixed beliefs.

The speaker who knows beforehand what beliefs and attitudes have become the fixed bases of his hearers' thinking can avoid arousing needless hostility and can often make use of these stereotypes as pegs upon which to hang his proposal. If you can show how your idea fits in with one already fixed in the minds of your audience, or how your proposal merely applies some of their existing principles of conduct, your battle is won.

ATTITUDE OF THE AUDIENCE TOWARD THE SPEAKER

Ask yourself what will be your listeners' attitude toward you personally and toward your qualifications to address them on the chosen subject. Two things must be considered: (*a*) the degree of their *friendliness* toward you, and (*b*) the degree of their *respect* for you or your knowledge of the subject. These two phases of their attitude may vary extremely and sometimes in opposite directions. A father's friendship for his small son, for instance, amounts to a very strong affection, but he may not respect the son's judgment very much. On the other hand, this son may have the greatest respect for a neighborhood policeman but hate the ground that man walks on. Respect and friendliness are two different things, but they must both be taken into account.

Adaptation to personal hostility. When your analysis predicts personal hostility on the part of your audience, your first job as a speaker is to wean them away from it. You can hardly accomplish your purpose without doing so. The method will vary, of course, with the cause of that hostility and will be less of an obstacle if their respect for you is high. Nevertheless, try in some way to *establish common ground* with your audience. This can often be done by one of the following methods:

1. By showing a friendly attitude toward your audience.
2. By an attitude of fairness, modesty, and good humor.
3. By pointing out your own agreement with some of their cherished attitudes or beliefs.
4. By referring to experiences held in common with them.

52

5. By tactful compliments to their abilities, accomplishments, or friends.
6. By humor that is in good taste, especially that which is at your own expense.

Adaptation to an attitude of condescension. The thing *not* to do when an audience has a condescending attitude toward you is to assume a conceited or antagonistic attitude yourself. Of course, you must appear self-confident, but this confidence must be tempered with a large measure of modesty. Gain the respect of your audience by the soundness of your thinking and the grasp you show of the facts about the subject rather than by parading yourself. Avoid saying "I think —"; present rather the evidence which makes that conclusion evident. If you have occasion to call attention to your own accomplishments in a pertinent connection, do so in a matter-of-fact, unassuming way.

ATTITUDE OF THE AUDIENCE TOWARD THE SUBJECT

Roughly speaking, people are either *interested* in a subject or they are *apathetic* toward it. The latter attitude is usually present if they see no connection between the subject and their own affairs. When your diagnosis indicates that this will be their attitude, you will need to show the audience some connection with their affairs which they had not realized, or you will need to arouse their curiosity in some novel aspect of the subject. Utilize all the methods for holding attention that you can. Of course, you cannot neglect doing these things even if the audience is already interested—you must be careful not to lose that interest; but when an audience is apathetic, you will find that more effort is required to this end.

ATTITUDE OF THE AUDIENCE TOWARD THE PURPOSE

If, with no preliminaries at all, you told the audience the specific purpose of your speech, what would be their attitude toward it? The answer indicates the meaning of "attitude toward purpose." It is not the attitude you hope for at the end of your speech, but what it is before you begin. Of course, only rarely will you actually state your purpose at the start. Yet, to build a speech that will get the proper response when it is asked for, you must try to determine the audience's attitude toward your purpose, assuming you had stated it baldly to them. Since an audience is never uniform throughout, it will represent many differing shades of attitude. It is usually best, therefore, to determine what attitude is predominant and to adapt your speech to that predominant viewpoint while making allowances for any marked variations you expect.

When the general end of a speech is *to entertain* or *to inform,* the attitude toward the purpose will be governed largely by the attitude toward the subject as explained above; hence, it will be either (*a*) an interested attitude or (*b*) an apathetic attitude. When the general purpose is *to persuade,* however, the attitude toward the purpose will be governed largely by the attitude toward the specific feeling, belief, or action to be urged; hence, it will be one of the following: (*a*) favorable but not aroused, (*b*) apathetic to the situation, (*c*) interested in the situation but undecided what to do or think about it, (*d*) interested in the situation but hostile to the *proposed* belief, attitude, or action, or (*e*) hostile to any change from the present situation.

Let us assume property taxes in your college community are high and that fraternity property is tax-exempt. Under these conditions, suppose your purpose were to start a movement for the removal of this exemption so that fraternity houses would be placed on the assessment sheet. An audience of local property owners (provided they were not fraternity alumni) would most likely be favorable, but they would need to be aroused before they would take any concerted action. Nonfraternity students would ordinarily form an apathetic audience since they would not see what connection the proposal had with them. The university administration and faculty on the whole would be interested in the situation because of its connection with both students and community but would be undecided whether to support the plan or not (excepting those who were influenced by owning property themselves or were fraternity alumni). Property owners who were also fraternity alumni or sympathizers would be interested in the situation and desirous of some way to relieve themselves of the heavy property tax, but they would probably be opposed to this particular way of doing it because of their fraternity connections. Student fraternity men, on the other hand, would be frankly hostile to any change from the present situation under which they were obtaining a distinct advantage. Thus, a knowledge of the proportion of each of these groups in the specific audience you were to address would give you a good estimate of the complexion of their attitude toward your purpose.

Having determined the attitude of your audience toward your purpose, you will need to adjust the method of approaching your audience, and the structure and content of your speech, to that attitude. If your listeners are apathetic, you must begin your talk on a point of compelling interest or startling vividness; show them how your subject affects them. If they are hostile to a proposal, you must approach it more cautiously; emphasize some basic principle with which they do agree and relate your proposal to it. If they are interested already but undecided, pile on the proof. If they are favorable but not aroused, use strong motivation embodied in vivid descriptive detail.

No analysis made beforehand is proof against mistaken judgment. Moreover, the attitude may change even while you are speaking. Hence, it is highly important to watch the reactions of the audience closely when your subject is announced and throughout your entire speech. The way your hearers sit in their seats, the expressions on their faces, their audible reactions such as laughter, applause, sharp breathing, shifting about, whispering—all these are vivid symptoms of their attitude toward you, your subject, or your purpose. If you are wise, you will develop a keen sensitivity to these signs and adapt your remarks to them as you go on.

"I am convinced by my own experience, and by that of others," said Henry Ford, "that if there is any secret of success, it lies in the ability to get the other person's point of view and to see things from his angle as well as your own."[3] A systematic method for finding out the other fellow's point of view has been presented. Your task is to apply this method in the specific situations that arise.

problems

1. Covering the points discussed on pages 44 to 56, make an audience analysis of:
   a. Some speech situation in which you were a member of the audience—or better, go to hear some speaker and make this analysis on the spot.
   b. Your own speech class as an audience for your next class speech.
   c. Some student group (such as a particular fraternity, club, young people's society, student council) which you might address on some subject which you specify.
   d. A group in your home community (such as a luncheon club, political club, religious organization, high-school assembly, city council) before which you might speak on a selected subject.
2. Given the facts stated in the audience analysis of your speech class (**1b** above), what would be the difference in attitude toward speaker, subject, and purpose in the following situations:

SPEAKER	SUBJECT	PURPOSE
a. The instructor.	Preparation of class work.	To get students to spend more time in preparing speeches.
b. A visiting student from England.	Life at Oxford.	To secure appreciation of the difference between English and American customs.
c. A senior.	Athletic rally.	To urge attendance at a rally to be held that evening.

3. Clip ten advertisements from some current popular magazine and for each one list the motive appeals made in it. Select the strongest motive appeal made in each advertisement and explain how the appeal was made.
4. Pick out the motive appeals made in one of the speeches printed at the end of this book.

3 From *Strategy in Handling People* by E. T. Webb and J. J. B. Morgan (Boulton, Pierce, and Company, Chicago, 1931), p. 73.

5. In one or two sentences each, phrase ten different motive appeals calculated to stimulate reaction in the members of your class.
6. Prepare a short speech concentrating upon one type of motive appeal. Employ as many different methods as possible to make that appeal strong.
7. Make an analysis of some audience of which you were recently a member and, in a brief oral report to the class, (a) bring out the essential points of your analysis, and (b) indicate how the speaker did or did not adapt his remarks to the audience.

Chapter 3 HOW TO STAND UP

AND BE HEARD

The first chapter offered some brief suggestions for meeting the basic requirements of effective speaking. We turn now to study in more detail the development of speaking skill.

Just as the pitcher who throws the ball controls it, giving it direction and power, so the speaker may give to his speech strength and vitality by the manner of his delivery. Physical bearing and tone of voice are of particular importance. As we noted in Chapter 2, one must not only know enough to assume leadership; he must look and sound the part if he is to obtain respect and cooperation. In this chapter we shall consider first the *physical behavior* of the speaker and second, his *use of the voice.*

PHYSICAL BEHAVIOR

Through visual impressions the audience makes its first estimate of the speaker—of his sincerity, his friendliness, and his energy. An audience reads these things from his facial expression, from the way he stands and walks, and from what he does with his arms and hands.

Eye-contact with the audience

The first thing a speaker must do when he addresses his listeners is to make them feel that he is talking to them personally. Nothing is quite so important as the simple device of looking them in the eye. Reading a speech or even too close a use of notes invariably reduces the effectiveness of the speaker so far as contact with the audience is concerned. Of course, it is impossible to look in the eyes of each member of the audience at the same time. Pick out one person and talk to him personally for a short while, looking him in the eye as you do so; then shift your attention to someone else in a different part of the audience.

Posture

Posture, or the speaker's stance, is of prime importance. How do you stand when you talk to people? Are you erect? comfortable? alert? There is no one way to stand that is best for a speaker, but there are several things which all speakers should avoid. In general your posture should be comfortable without being slouchy, erect without being stiff. It should be such that it gives the impression that you are alert and "on your toes." Avoid too much hiding behind the speaker's table or stand. Let the weight of your body fall on the balls of your feet rather than on the heels but do not jiggle up and down on them. Be alert, self-possessed, and at ease. Stand with the assurance of one in command of himself and the situation.

Movement

The eye instinctively follows moving objects and focuses upon them. You can often awaken a sleepy audience by the simple expedient of moving from one part of the platform to the other, but continuous or aimless pacing back and forth should be avoided.

On the other hand, transitions from one main point in the speech to another can often be indicated by merely shifting the weight from one foot to the other, or by a lateral movement of a step or two. Such a movement is a signal that "I am done with that point; now let us turn our attention to another." Forward or backward movements usually serve to imply the degree of importance attached to an idea. A step forward implies that you are coming to a more important point which you do not wish your audience to miss. Backward movement suggests that you are willing for them to relax a bit to let the last idea take root before you present another important one.

The way you walk to the platform and the way you leave it are also important; the audience's first and last impressions of the speaker are gained from these movements. Instead of walking up in a slovenly, meandering fashion, walk briskly and purposefully. Let your manner breathe confidence; do not tiptoe forward timidly, as though you were afraid the audience would see or hear you. On reaching the platform, don't rush into your speech. Take time to get a comfortable stance and to look out over the audience; *then* begin to talk. And when you are through speaking, don't rush off too abruptly. Pause at the end long enough to let your final words take effect; then step down and walk firmly back to your seat.

But, you may ask, how much movement is desirable? How often should one move around while speaking? The basic principle to remember here is moderation: Don't remain glued to one spot and don't keep on the move all the time. If you avoid these two extremes, your natural impulses will be apt to provide enough movement. In the beginning you will be better off with too much activity than with too little. Even random movement is better than none, for it serves to release pent-up energy and to reduce muscular tension in the nervous speaker. To the lethargic speaker, on the other hand, vigorous movement is stimulating, quickening his pulse and making him more lively and animated.

Gesture

In addition to moving around on the platform, you can use gestures to increase the force and clarity of your speech. By gestures we mean the movement of some *part* of the body, such as the head, shoulders, or arms, to emphasize or demonstrate what you say. Fidgeting with coat buttons and aimless arranging of books or papers on the speaker's table are not gestures—they do not relate to what you say.

That gestures do aid in the communication of ideas is the unwritten testimony of nearly all great speakers. A simple experiment will make the importance of gestures convincing: try to direct a stranger to a place several blocks away and notice how necessary it is for you to point the way and show him every turn he must take. Observe two persons in a heated argument and notice how often their hands come into play to emphasize the points they are making.

The attention value of gesturing is apparent. Just as we watch the moving ballplayer rather than the stationary one, so will we give our attention to the active speaker rather than to the quiet one. Unless he compensates for the lack in some other way, the speaker who uses no gestures will seem sluggish and apathetic, and his audience will respond with sluggishness and apathy. But a physically active speaker will be apt to stimulate among his listeners a lively, attentive attitude.

Types of gesture

Roughly speaking, there are two types of gestures: *conventional* and *descriptive*. Let us consider these two types as they are made with the hands and arms, the principal agents used in gesturing, and then give brief attention to the uses made of other parts of the body.

Conventional gestures. There are six basic movements of the hands and arms which have been used so universally that people recognize the meanings which they have always been used to convey. These gestures have become a sort of generalized sign language.

62

1. *Pointing.* The index finger has been used universally to indicate direction and to call attention to objects at which it is pointed. You might, for example, point at a map hanging on the wall as you say, "That map you see is already out of date; the boundaries have been changed since it was made." Or if you were to say, "The whole argument rests upon this one principle: . . . ," you might use the index finger to point in front of you as if that "principle" were there in tangible form before you. An accusation or challenge can be made doubly effective by pointing your finger directly at the audience or at some imaginary person assumed to be on the platform beside you.

2. *Giving or receiving.* If you were to hand someone a sheet of paper or were to hold out your hand to accept one given to you, you would find that the palm of your hand would be facing upward. This same movement is used to suggest the giving of an idea to the listeners or the request that they give you their support. This gesture indicates, "This is the information I have discovered," or "The ideas I am holding before you are worth your attention," or "I appeal to you to give me your help in this matter." No other conventional gesture is used quite so much as this one, because of the variety of uses to which it can be put. Sometimes it is even combined with the pointing gesture described above—the idea is, as it were, held out in one hand while the other hand is used to point at it.

3. *Rejecting.* If a dog with dirty paws were to jump up on your clothes, you would push him down and to one side with your hand. In the same way you can express your disapproval, or rejection, of an idea. This movement with the palm of the hand turned down can be used to reinforce such statements as "That proposal is absolutely worthless," "We must put that idea out of our heads."

4. *Clenching the fist.* This gesture is reserved for use with expressions of strong feeling such as anger or determination. The clenched fist may be used to emphasize such statements as "We must fight this thing to a finish!" or "He is the worst scoundrel in the world!"

5. *Cautioning.* If you wished to calm a friend who had become suddenly angry, you might do so by putting your hand lightly on his shoulder. A similar movement of the hand as if on an imaginary shoulder before you will serve to caution an audience against arriving at too hasty a judgment or against making too much noise. This gesture is often used with such statements as, "Don't take this thing too seriously," "If you'll just keep quiet a moment, I think I can make the point clear." By using this gesture you check your hearer's thoughts and get him ready to listen to another idea.

6. *Dividing.* By moving the hand from side to side with the palm held vertical, you can indicate the separation of facts or ideas into different parts. You might, for instance, appropriately use this gesture while saying, "We must be neither radical in our ideas nor ultra-conservative"—moving your hand to one side on the word "radical" and to the other on the word "conservative."

These are the basic movements of conventional gesturing. From what has been said about them, you must not infer that they are set and invariable. No two persons will make these movements exactly alike or on exactly the same occasions. Moreover, these movements do not always start from the same position. Frequently one gesture begins at the point where another stopped, so that the effect is one of continuity rather than jerkiness. And usually it is the movement of the hand rather than the fixation that effectively emphasizes the speaker's ideas. Practice alone will make your use of these gestures smooth and effective; this practice is most valuable when supervised by your instructor.

Descriptive gestures. The movements discussed above are rather traditional, but there are many other movements of a more descriptive nature which are quite as effective. Descriptive gestures are imitative. The speaker describes the size, shape, or movement of an object by imitation. You may show how vigorous the punch was by striking the air with your fist; the height of a younger brother may be indicated by holding the hand high enough to rest on his head; the speed of an auto-

64

mobile may be suggested by a quick sweep of the arm; you may show the details of a complicated movement by performing it as you describe it. Because of their spontaneous and imitative nature, descriptive gestures cannot be cataloged as were the more conventional ones. Some suggestions can be obtained by watching other speakers, but the best source is your own originality. Ask yourself, "How can I *show* my audience this?"

GESTURES OF THE HEAD AND SHOULDERS

Shrugging the shoulders and shaking the head have the same implication in public speech as they do in conversation, and vigorous nods of the head are frequently used for the purpose of emphasis.

Whether you are speaking or listening, your posture, gesture, and facial expression will reflect your attitude. Here, Alfred P. Sloan, Jr., Chairman of the Board of the General Motors Corporation, shows clearly his feelings about what has been said at the Congressional Monopoly Committee he is attending. Notice how different he looks when he is intent on proving a point himself. Superficial skill in platform manner is not enough: you must feel and believe what you say.

Such movements of the head and shoulders are useful, but they should not be used to the exclusion of the hands and arms.

FACIAL EXPRESSION, PANTOMIME, AND IMPERSONATION

Whether we like the fact or not, the expressions on our faces carry our thoughts to the audience. Of course, to attempt mechanically to put on an effective expression is not wise. Too often such an attempt results only in an artificial grimace or a fixed smile. A better way is to work on your facial expression from the inside. If you have a cordial feeling for your audience, are interested in the subject of your talk, and are enthusiastic about speaking, your face will reflect your attitude and emphasize the oral expression of your ideas. Sometimes a speaker may want to make his story more vivid by acting and talking as if he were the person described. In this imitative process the speaker's posture, movement, gesture, and facial expression all combine. The shoulders are perhaps allowed to droop and the walk develops a slight limp; the hand trembles as it knocks on the door and the face shows surprise at what is seen when the door opens—all together, these few vivid details present a character and tell what he is doing. In moderation, pantomime and impersonation are useful devices for a speaker to use.

CHARACTERISTICS OF GOOD GESTURES

Gestures, like most other things, can be made well or poorly. The only way to perfect your use of them is through practice, but that practice will be more effective if you keep in mind the qualities which are characteristic of good gestures:

Relaxation. When the muscles which move the human skeleton are held in tension, jerky, awkward movements result. Paradoxical as the advice may seem, the best way to relax is to move. Warm up as the athlete does by taking a few easy steps and making a few easy gestures with your arms. Avoid stiffness; before you start to speak, let all the muscles of the body slacken. Avoid awkwardness by relaxation.

Vigor. Gestures should not go to the extreme of being insipid and lifeless. Put enough force and life into them to make them convincing. A languid shaking of the clenched fist is unconvincing to support a threat or challenge. On the other hand, sledge-hammer pounding of the table or continuous violent sawing of the air on minor points is monotonous and often ludicrous. Vary the vigor of your gestures, but in the main be vigorous enough to suggest reality.

Definiteness. If you point out the window, make the movement so distinct that there will be no doubt where you are pointing. This is especially important when several gestures follow each other rapidly. Too often the effect is a blur. While being careful to avoid jerkiness, be sure that each movement is definite and clean-cut.

Timing. The comedian gets many a laugh from his audience merely by making his gestures a little late. The effect of making a gesture after the word or phrase it was intended to reinforce has already been spoken can be nothing but ridiculous. The stroke of the gesture should fall exactly on, or slightly precede, the point it is used to emphasize. If you practice using gestures until they have become habitual with you and then use them spontaneously as the impulse arises, you will have no trouble with this matter. Poor timing usually comes from the attempt to use "canned" gestures—gestures planned out and memorized ahead of time for a particular word. The impulse to gesture should come from within rather than from without. Gestures should never be "laid on." It is fatal to decide ahead of time that at a certain sentence in your speech you are going to point at your audience and a moment later point dramatically at the heavens above. Gestures naturally arise from enthusiasm, excitement, or emotion. Practice gesturing all you please—the more the better—until you can feel the easy swing, the abandon, the power in it; but when you stand before an audience to speak, do not force your arms to move. If you have practiced the movements, if you feel enthusiastic about your subject and let yourself go, the gestures will come naturally and with effect.

ADAPTING GESTURES TO THE AUDIENCE

Just because one type of gesturing is effective with one audience you cannot assume that it will suit all occasions. You will need to adapt your gestures to both the size and the nature of your audience.

The size of the audience will govern the sweep of the gesture. Roughly, the larger the audience, the wider should be the arc through which your arm should travel. Remember the effect of perspective: what would seem a wild swing of the arm to a person with whom you were conversing close at hand will appear quite moderate before an audience of two hundred. Conversely, small gestures of the hand hinged at the wrist, while effective in conversation, would seem weak and indefinite to the larger audience.

The nature of the audience and the occasion will govern the number and degree of vigor of the gestures. People who are young or who are engaged in vigorous physical activities are attracted to a speaker who uses many gestures vigorously made. Older, more conservative persons are likely to be irritated by too strong or too frequent gestures and to lose respect for the speaker. Moreover, some occasions such as formal dedication exercises call for dignity of movement as well as expression, while others such as rallies require more violent and enthusiastic activity.

All these elements must be considered to make the most effective use of gesture. Begin by using as many gestures as you can. Get your arms out from your body and let the swing be complete. If some friend tells you that you are using too many gestures, make sure that the criticism is not really that you are using too many of the *same kind* of gesture. Instead of cutting down the number, increase the variety.

And remember: to have a good posture, adequate movement, contact with the audience, and effective gesture is just as natural as to comb your hair or to handle a knife and fork with ease. You were not born doing either, but practice made them habitual until now they seem a part of you—they seem natural. Practice until good posture, movement, and gesture also become habitual and natural. Then you can forget them

68

as most good speakers do. They will be automatic in their obedience to your impulse and effective in reinforcing your ideas.

problems

1. Imagine yourself in the following situations—picture in detail all that has led up to them—and react spontaneously with whatever physical behavior your impulse suggests. Speak out also if you feel the urge to do so.

   a. Someone has fired a gun just behind you.

   b. A child just in front of you is in the path of a fast-moving automobile.

   c. Someone has just slapped your face.

   d. You catch a grounder and throw to first base; there are two outs with a runner on second.

   e. Someone shouts to warn you of a heavy object about to fall on the spot where you are standing.

   f. You are marooned on an island and are trying to catch the attention of men on a passing ship.

2. Think of something which arouses your fighting spirit—injustices, favoritism, cruelty, unnecessary red tape, thoughtless, unsympathetic officials or teachers, unfair requirements or restrictions, dangerous demagogues—something which makes you genuinely angry, excited, indignant. Deliver a short "tirade" on this subject. Let yourself go vocally and physically.

3. In your own room, before a mirror, stretch and manipulate your facial muscles in the following ways:

   a. Raise your eyebrows.

   b. Wink one eye while raising the other eyebrow.

   c. Pucker your nose.

   d. Wiggle your ears—if you can!

   e. Draw down the corners of your mouth.

   f. Stretch your lips in a wide grin.

   g. Pucker your lips.

   h. Move your lips as far as you can to one side of your face and then as far as you can to the other side.

   i. Drop your jaw as far as it will go.

   j. Wrinkle your forehead in a frown.

   k. Combine the movements listed above two, three, four at a time.

69

Remember that these exercises are for the sole purpose of developing facial flexibility; you cannot prepare facial expressions in advance to be assumed at given points in a speech; genuine facial expression must reflect genuine feeling.

4. Try to communicate the following ideas silently by means of physical action alone. Of course you will need to use descriptive as well as conventional gestures.

   a. "Get out of here!"

   b. "Why Tom (or Mary)! I haven't seen you for ages!"

   c. "You men on that side, sing the first line, and we'll sing the second."

   d. "Right in front of me was a big field with a brook running straight through the middle of it."

   e. "If we're going to get what we want, we'll have to fight for it, and fight hard!"

   f. "Quiet down a little, won't you? Give him a chance to explain."

   g. "Come here a minute, Jim, will you?"

   h. "Every penny I had is gone."

   i. "Now the first thing to remember is this: . . ."

   j. "If you think it was easy, you're all wrong."

5. Listen to a speaker and write a brief report of your observations regarding his platform behavior. Note both good and bad qualities in his audience contact, posture, movement, and gesture. A good way to proceed is to make, before you go, a brief outline of the suggestions and warnings contained in this chapter and then to check the speaker on these points while he is speaking.

6. Attend a motion picture or a play and report on the physical behavior of the actors. Comment on such points as these:

   a. What special meanings were conveyed by facial expression and by movements of the head or shoulders?

   b. What conventional gestures and what descriptive ones were especially effective?

7. Make a short speech describing some exciting event you have witnessed; use movement and gesture to make the details clear and emphatic. Try to make your description so vivid and your action so dynamic that your listeners will tend to project themselves into the situation. Remember that to succeed in doing this you will need to imagine yourself back in the situation while you describe it; you must feel the excitement in order to communicate that feeling.

70

USE OF THE VOICE

The statement has often been made that the first duty of the speaker is to be heard and understood. You may speak with a voice of pleasing quality and with all the gestures that could be desired, but if the utterance of your words is so indistinct that your listeners have to strain to understand you, they will soon tire of the effort. Strong, distinct speech is obviously one of the first requirements you must meet if you are to be heard correctly and are to be respected.

The mechanics of speaking

Logically, the study of vocal delivery begins by gaining an elementary knowledge of the mechanics of it. Accurately speaking, of course, there is no such thing as a speech mechanism or vocal mechanism. We shall use these terms, however, to include those parts of the body which are used in the speaking process. All those muscles, bones, cartilages, and organs have, as you know, many other functions which are biologically far more important than producing the voice. The tongue, for example, even though so vital a part of the speaking mechanism, is far more important in eating. Even the vocal cords have as their chief function the protection of our lungs from cold air, smoke, and other forms of dangerous irritation. Indeed, the very fact that speaking is a secondary function of these organs makes doubly important a program of vocal training, for although we were born instinctively prepared to eat and to breathe, we had to learn how to talk. This fact explains why so many of us use our voices badly. We have established bad habits of speaking. We have developed improper methods of coordination. But even though we may have inadequate speech habits, or bad ones, we have all learned in childhood how to use these organs together in some form of speaking. Let us therefore forget for the present their primary biological functions and consider them together as a single

71

The voice is a wind instrument

This diagram shows how the speaking mechanism functions as a wind instrument. The motor compresses the air in the lungs as shown by the arrows; this compressed air is sent through the vibrator, which first produces the speech sound; the speech tone next enters the resonators of the throat, mouth, and head to be amplified and modified in quality; finally, the tone is affected by the modifiers, which alter the quality further and serve also to produce the consonant sounds.

mechanism—the instrument of speech. We may divide this mechanism conveniently, for discussion, into four parts: the motor, the vibrator, the resonators, and the modifiers. Refer to the diagrams on pages 72 and 73.

THE MOTOR

For the purposes of speech the motor is essentially a pump for compressing air. It consists of (*a*) the *lungs,* which contain space for the air, (*b*) the *bronchial tubes,* which converge into the windpipe, or *trachea,* thus forming a nozzle out of which the compressed air is released, (*c*) the *ribs,* and other bones, cartilages, and tissues, which serve to hold the motor in place and give leverage for the application of power, and (*d*) the *muscles,* which alternately expand and contract the space occupied by the lungs, thus serving alternately to draw air into the lungs and to compress it for expulsion afterward. A large number of muscles are used in this process, but to detail them would be beyond the scope of this book. One thing should be noted, however. This air pump works in two ways: Certain muscles draw the ribs down and in when we exhale so as to squeeze the lungs after the fashion of a bellows, while others—the strong abdominal muscles—squeeze in below to exert pressure up against the bottom of the lungs after the manner of a piston. Likewise, air is drawn into the lungs by double action: One set of muscles pulls the ribs up and out to expand the horizontal space, while the diaphragm—a layer of muscles and flat tendon tissue—expands the vertical space by lowering the floor of the chest cavity; this two-way expansion creates a suction, drawing air into the lungs. Thus, both inhaling and exhaling can be done in two ways: by movement of the ribbed walls of the chest and by raising and lowering its floor.

THE VIBRATOR

The air compressed in the lungs is directed through the trachea into the *larynx*, which contains the vibrating unit. The larynx is situated at the upper end of the trachea and is movably attached above and below by muscles which shift it up and down. The larynx itself consists of a group of small cartilages joined together so that they move as if on joints like the bones of the arm. The position of these cartilages is changed by a number of small muscles which are delicately intertwined. Within the larynx, stretched between the cartilages, are the *vocal cords*—the vibrators proper. These are not really cords, but a pair of membranes very much like thin lips. When a tone is to be produced, they come together until there is but a very small slit between them. The compressed air from the lungs, pushing against and between the vocal cords, causes a vibration which forms the original speech tone. This tone may be changed in pitch up and down the scale by the muscles which control the tension and length of the cords. The position of the larynx as a whole is adjusted to a proper relation with the air cavities above by the action of the larger outside muscles which hold it in place. The action of these two sets of muscles, particularly the small internal ones, is largely automatic; that is, they cannot be controlled individually. The muscles of the larynx can, however, be operated as a group to make the pitch of the voice higher or lower, as we wish.

73

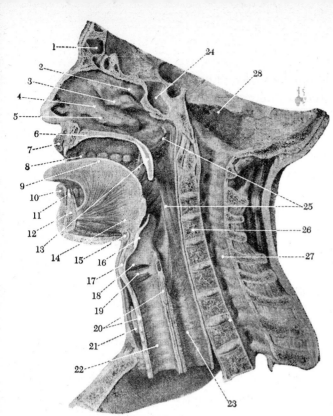

1. Frontal sinus
2. Upper nasal bone
3. Middle nasal bone
4. Nasal cavity
5. Lower nasal bone
6. Hard palate
7. Upper lip
8. Upper teeth
9. Tongue
10. Lower lip
11. Lower teeth
12. Lower jaw (mandibula)
13. Soft palate
14. Base of the tongue
15. Hyoid (tongue) bone
16. Epiglottis
17. Thyroid cartilage
18. False vocal cord
19. True vocal cord
20. Cricoid cartilage
21. Thyroid gland
22. Windpipe (trachea)
23. Gullet (esophagus)

Speech sounds are formed here

(sagittal section of the head and neck— tongue drawn out for clearer view)

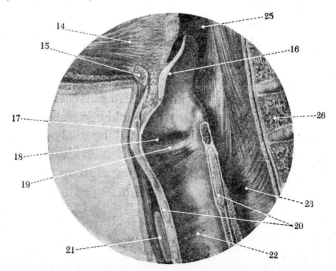

Detail showing structure of the larynx

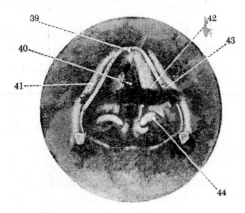

The vocal cords
(laryngoscopic view of the
vocal cords in relaxed posi-
tion at normal breathing)

24. Sphenoidal sinus
25. Region of the pharynx
26. Vertebrae of the neck
27. Spinal cord channel
    (cord removed)
28. Cranial cavity (brain
    removed)
29. Larynx
30. Windpipe (trachea)
31. Rib bones (numbers 6, 7,
    and 9 cut away)
32. Abdominal muscles
33. Chest muscles
34. Lungs
35. Diaphragm
36. Peritoneum
37. Abdominal muscles
38. Rectal sheath
39. Base of epiglottis
40. Rima glottids
41. Thyroid cartilage
42. False vocal cord
43. True vocal cord
44. Arytenoid cartilage

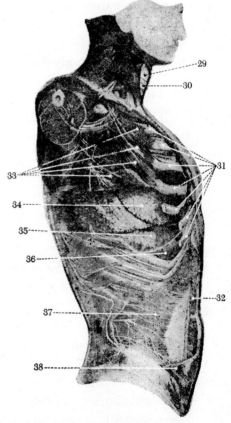

The vocal mechanism
(anatomy involved in speech)

75

The sound originating in the larynx would be thin and weak were it not for some means of building it up. This function is performed by a group of air chambers in the head and throat. Of these, the principal ones are the upper part (or *vestibule*) of the *larynx,* the throat (*pharynx*), the *nasal cavities,* and the *mouth.* These cavities act much as the resonating parts of musical instruments do: they amplify the sound, making it louder; and they modify its quality, making it rich and mellow, or harsh, or whining. Moreover, by a proper manipulation of the size and shape of some of these cavities, various tone qualities recognized as the different vowel sounds are formed.

THE MODIFIERS

The *tongue, lips, teeth, jaw,* and *palate* act as modifying agents in the production of speech sounds. These agents form the movable boundaries of the resonators mentioned above, and by moving them we modify the shape of these resonators and affect the quality of the tone. Another function of the modifiers, quite as important as this, is the formation of consonantal sounds; the stops, hisses, and other interruptions to the steady flow of vowel tone make an important part of our spoken language. It is the "p," "m," "k," "s" sounds and their companions that serve to make words out of what would otherwise be mere vocal tones. Precision and sharpness of articulation come from active use of these modifiers.

Physical requirements for a good speaking voice

To what has been said about the mechanics of speaking we may add a few simple requirements for the effective use of that mechanism. These suggestions must be general; for more specific suggestions to fit your individual problems, you must seek the advice of your instructor. Three things, though, are always important:

CONTROL OF BREATHING

Singing tones are often sustained, but most speech sounds are not. They are usually short and precise. Therefore, you do not need a big lung capacity; what you need is control over what you have. By controlling the pressure exerted on the vocal cords by the air in your lungs, you may vary the strength of your voice and give your utterance power or delicacy as you will. Lack of control, on the other hand, results in lack of power, jerkiness, or a breathy, wheezing tone. Exercises such as panting, expelling the breath slowly with a long slow whistle or hum, counting from one to ten with increasing force, reading aloud passages which require varying numbers of words to be spoken between inhalations to prevent breaking continuity or sense—these and similar ones help to increase breath control.

RELAXATION OF THE THROAT AND NECK

Tension in the throat and neck results in strain and soreness. In addition, it results in harshness and a loss of tone flexibility. Good voice quality comes from a relaxed condition of the throat coupled with the breath control mentioned above. Letting the head hang limp, yawning, soft singing of vowel tones—these are good ways to practice relaxation. Of course, none of these can be done when you are actually speaking, but the habit of relaxing the throat and neck can be developed through them.

FLEXIBLE AND ENERGETIC USE OF THE JAW, LIPS, AND TONGUE

If the jaw remains frozen tight or the tongue and lips fail to move in a lively fashion, the result is a jumble of unintelligible sound. Mumbling speakers can seldom be heard clearly and, even when heard, are not given full credit for what they say. Sharp and precise utterance comes only when you keep your jaw, lips, and tongue moving, and moving with precision. For practice, exaggerate these movements, watching yourself in a mirror to make sure the movements are as vigorous as they feel.

77

Practice saying words difficult to pronounce, and develop ability in saying tongue-twisters (such as "She sells sea shells") rapidly without mistake.

Vocal quality

When you describe someone's voice as being harsh or mellow or guttural or nasal, you are describing its quality. Quality is often referred to as "timbre" or "tone color." It is determined by the combination of resonances in the voice. Just as the quality of tone produced by one violin differs from that produced by another even though the same strings are used on both, so does the quality of one person's voice differ from that of another. In the human voice the quality is determined in part by the initial tone produced in the larynx and in part by the influence of the resonating air chambers above. In general, pleasant quality results from a relaxed throat coupled with a full use of the resonating cavities; unpleasant quality arises from lack of breath control, tension in the throat, or inadequate use of the resonating cavities.

Unpleasant vocal qualities

Let us consider a few of the more common types of voices having poor quality and see what causes them.

Thin, weak voices lack carrying power. A number of causes may combine to result in such a voice: the muscles of the tongue and palate may be so inactive that inadequate use is made of the resonating cavities; the pitch level may be too high—even a falsetto—so that the lower resonances are not used (similar to what happens when you tune out the lower partials on your radio with the tone control); or the power given to the voice originally by the breathing muscles may be inadequate. Of these causes, the last two are the most common. If your voice is thin, try lowering the pitch of your voice (come down the musical scale a bit) and at the same time talk a little louder. Open your mouth wider,

78

especially on vowels like "ah," "oh," or "aw," in order to increase the size of the oral cavity and improve its resonating effect.

Huskiness and harshness result either from tension in the throat or from forcing too much air through the vocal cords. An irritated or diseased condition of the throat may have the same effect. If a throat examination fails to disclose any pathological condition, you can be sure that harshness can be reduced by proper breathing and relaxation. Let the neck muscles become slack; then say such words as "one," "bun," "run," very quietly, prolonging them almost to a singing tone. Huskiness can often be diminished by adjustment of the pitch level, usually in an upward direction. Work at this until you are sure the tone is clear and free of all breathiness; if you have trouble, use less breath. When you are sure the tone is clear, increase the volume gradually until you can produce a strong tone without tension or huskiness and harshness.

Nasality, contrary to popular notion, is just as often the result of too little nasal resonance as of too much. Nasality of this type results from failure to open up the nasal passages enough. Say the word "button" or "mutton." Notice what happens to your soft palate—did you feel it tighten up just before the explosion of the "t," and then relax to allow the explosion to carry the "n" sound out through the nose? For all the explosive consonants like the "t," "p," etc., the palate has to close tight; but if this tension is continued during the production of the vowel sounds, a flat, nasal (or really, "de-nasal") sound is likely to result. On the other hand, if the nasal passage is always left open (as in severe cases of cleft palate) or is not closed sufficiently, an excess of nasal resonance occurs which is equally unpleasant. The correction of serious nasality requires special individual training which you should seek if you have this difficulty; and if you have a nasal obstruction or palatal cleft, you should seek medical advice about it. These are by no means the only types of unpleasant quality, nor have all the causes that produce poor quality been mentioned. Only the most common have been discussed.

th ese

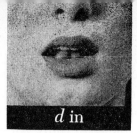

d in

th

Clear speech depends on distinct consonant sounds and requires a vigorous use of both tongue and lips. Notice the positions of these organs in pronouncing th, v, w, *and* d, *as shown in these pictures.*

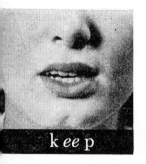

k *ee* p

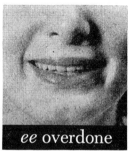

ee overdone

ee

While the position of the lips is important in producing the right vowel sound, that of the tongue is even more important. Say "keep" and "car," noticing the difference in your tongue and jaw positions.

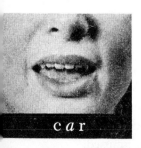

c *a* r

h *a* t

a

New Englanders say "car" with an a *vowel very seldom heard in the midwest. Compare the pictures above with those on the next page,*

EFFECT OF EMOTION ON VOCAL QUALITY

Changes in quality of tone are closely related to emotion. Our voices automatically register any strong feeling that comes over us. To tell an angry man by the tone of his voice is not difficult. Ordinarily, if you really feel what you are saying, your voice will change of its own accord to suit the feeling. Only in mimicry and impersonation can a change of quality be purposely made by most people without suggesting insincerity; when the speaker is obviously impersonating someone else, an effective imitation of that person's voice quality even to the point of suggesting its emotional tone is perfectly in order.

PRECISION

For the effective speaker, precision—that is, speech so distinct it cannot be misunderstood—is of great importance. You will do well, therefore, to take very seriously the suggestions made on pages 77 and 78, for precision is primarily a job for the jaw, tongue, and lips. Only by developing skill and energy in the muscles which manipulate these members can clean-cut speech be had. Do not be satisfied with sloppy articulation. Bite off your words even in an exaggerated fashion for a time until you find the habit of precision growing on you.

There are four faults that are responsible for most of the indistinctness in speech. By avoiding or eliminating them you will have done a great deal to improve the understandability and precision of your utterance. These faults are *(a)* the "immovable jaw," *(b)* the "idle tongue," *(c)* "lazy lips," and *(d)* too much speed.

Some oriental peoples move their jaws very little in speaking; so much of the meaning in their language is conveyed by variation in the tone of voice that scarcely any jaw movement is required. In the English language failure to open the jaws adequately is a serious fault because so much meaning is conveyed by consonant sounds, which cannot be made effectively unless the tongue is given enough room for vigorous movement. Even the vowel sounds are likely to be muffled if the

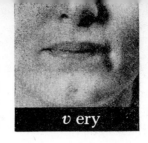 

v ery   *w* ool

Many small children—and even adults who are not careful—have difficulty with the v *sound; failure to bring the lower lip back near the upper teeth makes their pronunciation of "very" sound like "wery."*

v

y *ou*   l *et*

Certain vowels require a rounding of the lips while others require a wider opening produced by lowering the jaw. Compare the two pictures above with those below and with those on the opposite page.

ou

 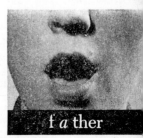

j *aw*   f *a* ther

The positions of the lips in the two pictures above are those normally taken in saying the vowels in words like "jaw" and "father."

a

jaws are kept nearly closed. As you talk, therefore, strive for free and active movement of your jaws. The tongue has more to do with the distinct formation of speech sounds than any other organ; even when the jaw moves, if the tongue lies idle or moves sluggishly, the sounds produced cannot be sharp. The lips, too, are made of muscle; if they are allowed to become lazy, they will hang like soft flaps, and a mumbled articulation will be the result. This is especially true of sounds like "p," "b," "m," and "f," which require vigorous action of the lips. But there is a limit to the speed with which the jaw, tongue, and lips can move. A great deal of indistinctness could be avoided if speakers took time enough to get the sounds out instead of being in such a hurry to be through. Take time to be distinct; as your jaw, tongue, and lips develop more flexibility and precision, you can speed up more, but for the present avoid rushing.

Briefly, then, loosen your jaw until a lively movement of it can be noticed when you are talking, practice moving your lips with energy, whip your tongue into vigorous activity, and don't talk too fast. Practice repeatedly the exercises for distinctness at the end of this section and watch to see that the effect of this practice is carried over into your daily conversation. There is nothing which will create so much unconscious respect for you as a crisp and decisive utterance.

Using the telephone and microphone

Talking over the radio or telephone is influenced by two major factors inherent in the situation. The first is that your listener cannot see you (unless television is also employed) and he is therefore robbed of all the visual cues so meaningful to the ordinary listener. Gestures, for example, may help you to emphasize points, but your radio listener won't see them, and the visual emphasis will be lost on him. A great deal of meaning is conveyed by facial expression; again, your listener can't see it, and you must make up for this loss in some other way. Charts and maps help a speaker convey his explanations, but, except through television, you can't broadcast them; all you can do is to refer to them. All of your meaning must be conveyed by sound alone a large share of the time.

The second factor is that your voice must pass through the telephone or microphone, the transmitting set, and the receiver before reaching your listeners. Regardless of the perfection of the equipment, some distortion will occur. Frequently this distortion is beneficial, making one's voice sound better than it naturally is, but many little faults otherwise unnoticed may be exaggerated with ruinous effect. Moreover, failure to use the proper technique may result in indistinctness or even in disagreeable noises.

Both because the instrument is sensitive and because your listeners, undiverted by facial expression or gesture, have focused their attention entirely upon your voice, the distinctness of your speech and accuracy of pronunciation are especially important.

Microphone technique

There are many different types of microphones in use. Some pick up sound equally well from all directions; others transmit sound made directly in front of them with much greater volume than that made at the side or above or behind. Always ask your instructor, the announcer, or the technician in charge about the particular microphone you are to use.

With most microphones the loudness of the sound picked up varies in geometric ratio to its distance from the sound source. That is, if you speak with the same degree of force, the sound picked up by the microphone at a distance of one foot will be four times as loud as at a distance of two feet. It is important to remain at approximately the same distance from the microphone all the time in order to avoid fading or undesired increase in volume.

Most radio equipment is very sensitive, and sudden increases in volume are apt to produce "blasting." Something very similar occurs to what would happen if you hit the keyboard of a piano with a sledge hammer. For this reason avoid shouting, or for that matter any sudden increase of volume.

In aviation and in communication at sea a great many numbers are used in connection with distances, direction, and weather data, to say nothing of code numbers. You must be especially distinct in pronouncing them. One good method is to repeat the number, first giving each digit separately, and then giving the whole number. Thus: "ceiling, one-two-five-zero feet; repeating, ceiling twelve hundred fifty feet; one-two-five-zero feet." Be particularly careful with "three"; exaggerate the *r* sound because over a poor circuit "three" may sound like "two." Likewise, "nine" can be distinguished from "five" by pronouncing the former as if there were two syllables—"ni'-yun" (or say "fi'-yuv" and "niner" as recommended by the Navy). Say "zero" instead of "oh" to avoid confusion with "four," which is pronounced "fōh" in some sections of the country. In noisy surroundings, as in airplanes, you must hold the microphone close to your lips and talk in a very loud voice, prolonging each syllable.

Special comment should be made here about the sibilants—sounds such as "s," "z," "th," "sh," and the like. The high frequencies characteristic of these sounds tend to produce a whistling or hissing sound on some circuits if they are given too much emphasis. Some persons are worse than others in this respect; if you are one who "whistles when he speaks," use sparingly words in which these sounds occur in stressed positions—or better, learn to subdue your production of them. The only way to check the effect of transmission on your own voice is to have an audition or to have a phonograph recording made to which you yourself can listen.

Public address systems and television

The same instructions apply to using a microphone attached to a public address system as to one used with radio equipment, except that here you will ordinarily have an actual audience before you. Likewise, in television your listeners can see as well as hear you. Because of this you can employ gestures to emphasize your points, but you must be careful not to move away from the microphone or the focal area of the television camera. Even turning your head away will sometimes make your voice fade. Look at the audience but talk to the "mike."

Telephone technique

In general, the same cautions and suggestions which apply to the use of microphones apply also to the use of telephones. Usually, however, the telephone mouthpiece is not as sensitive as a microphone, and you must therefore keep your mouth close to it when you talk. There is not nearly as much likelihood of "blasting"; in fact, a fairly loud voice is often necessary. With some very poor circuits, you will have to exaggerate the distinctness of your consonant sounds.

Pronunciation standards

Spoken words are the sound symbols of meaning. If they are not given the conventional pronunciation, they may not be recognized as symbols for the meaning you intend.

To find an acceptable standard of pronunciation is sometimes difficult, because standards differ. Certain pronunciations which would be acceptable in Chicago would not be in Boston. The native of Louisiana pronounces his words in a way different from that of the man from Montana. That this is true is perhaps unfortunate, but the fact remains; and for you to insist on a pronunciation foreign to the locality in which you are living is extremely unwise. On the other hand, to attempt by main force to vary your pronunciation to suit every group which you address is equally foolish. The best criterion to follow is the usage of the educated people of your community. For most words a dictionary provides a very helpful guide. But with respect to certain words which are constantly changing, dictionaries are likely to be out of date and should not be followed too slavishly. Moreover, most dictionaries do not take sufficient notice of regional differences in dialect. Nevertheless, since most words do not vary greatly from the recorded pronunciation, a dictionary will usually be reliable.

Be particularly careful about misplacing the accent in words; no fault is quite so noticeable as this one. For example, if you say "genu-*ine*," "*de*-vice," "the-*ay*-ter," "pre-*fer*-able," instead of the more accepted forms, "*gen*-uine," "de-*vice*," "*the*-ater," "*pref*-erable," your error will be obviously crude. Other errors arise from the omission of sounds (such as "pro'ly" for "probably"), from the addition of sounds (such as "ath*a*lete" for "athlete"), and from the substitution of sounds (such as "set" for "sit"). The way words are spelled is not always a safe guide, for English words contain many silent letters, and many words containing the same combinations of letters require a different pronunciation. (For example: of*t*en, b*ough*, r*ough*, thr*ough*, call*ed*, shout*ed*, gasp*ed*.) In addition, the formality of the occasion exerts considerable influence; many omissions acceptable in conversation become objectionable in a formal address. In radio broadcasting, careful pronunciation is particularly important since listeners are more likely to be critical of it. In general, however, what is good pronunciation elsewhere is also good "over the air." Do not be so labored and precise as to call attention to your pronunciation rather than to the idea, but do not take this warning as an excuse for careless speech.

In brief, gain control of the mechanics of your speech. Learn to control your breathing, to relax your throat, and to develop energy and flexibility in your jaw, tongue, and lips. Develop a pleasing quality in your voice; bite your words so that they will be distinct and clean-cut; establish habits of acceptable pronunciation. Learn to adjust your speech to radio and telephone transmission. Finally, remember that only by using your voice can you improve it; all this book can do is point the way. First, last, and always—practice.

problems

1. Practice expelling the air from your lungs in short, sharp gasps. Place your hand on your abdomen to see that there is a sharp inward contraction of the muscle wall synchronous with the chest contraction on each outgoing puff.

   a. Then vocalize the puffs, saying "Hep!—Hep!—Hep!" with considerable vigor.

   b. In the same way, say "one, two, three, four," with staccato accents.

2. Fill your lungs; then exhale *as slowly as possible* until the lungs are empty. Time yourself to see how long you can keep exhaling without a break. (Note that the object here is not to see how much air you can get into the lungs, but how slowly you can let it out.)

   a. Then, filling your lungs each time, vocalize the outgoing breath stream first with a long continuous hum, second with an "oo" sound, and then with other vowel sounds. Be careful not to let the sound become "breathy"; keep the tone clear.

   b. Place a lighted candle just in front of your mouth and repeat the series outlined above. The flame should barely flicker; don't blow it out.

3. Intone the following words quietly at first, then louder, and louder; try to give them a ringing quality; put your fingertips on the nose and cheek bones to see if you can feel a vibration there. Avoid breathiness due to the use of too much air.

one	home	tone	alone	moan
rain	plain	mine	lean	soon
ring	nine	dong	moon	fine

4. Read aloud the following passages in as clear and resonant tones as you can. Be sure you open your mouth wide enough and that you make the tones vibrate.

   from THE TWENTY-FOURTH PSALM

   Lift up your heads, O ye gates;
   And be ye lift up, ye everlasting doors;
   And the King of glory shall come in.
       Who is this King of glory?
       The Lord strong and mighty,
       The Lord mighty in battle.

Lift up your heads, O ye gates;
Even lift them up, ye everlasting doors;
And the King of glory shall come in.
   Who is the King of glory?
   The Lord of Hosts,
   He is the King of glory.

from Childe Harold's Pilgrimage, *Byron*

Roll on, thou deep and dark blue Ocean, roll!
 Ten thousand fleets sweep over thee in vain;
Man marks the earth with ruin—his control
 Stops with the shore;—upon the watery plain
 The wrecks are all thy deed, nor doth remain
A shadow of man's ravage, save his own,
 When for a moment, like a drop of rain,
He sinks into thy depths with bubbling groan,
Without a grave, unknelled, uncoffined, and unknown.

from The Chambered Nautilus, *Oliver Wendell Holmes*

Build thee more stately mansions, O my soul,
 As the swift seasons roll!
 Leave thy low-vaulted past!
Let each new temple, nobler than the last,
Shut thee from heaven with a dome more vast,
 Till thou at length art free,
 Leaving thine outgrown shell by life's unresting sea!

5. Make a list of words which you have heard pronounced in more than one way. Look them up in the dictionary and come to class prepared to defend your agreement or disagreement with the dictionary pronunciation. Here are a few words on which to start:

abdomen	deficit	gladiola	recess	route
creek	evidently	humble	research	theater
data	forehead	idea	roof	vaudeville

6. Check the pronunciation in your locality of the following words:

bath	water	I	down
roof	dictionary	hot	girl
tomato	either	necessary	barn

88

7. Stretch the muscles of articulation:

   a. Stretch the mouth in as wide a grin as possible; open the mouth as wide as possible; pucker the lips and protrude them as far as possible.

   b. Stretch out the tongue as far as possible; try to touch the tip of the nose and the chin with the tongue tip; beginning at the front teeth, run the tip of the tongue back, touching the palate as far as it will go.

8. With vigorous accent on the consonant sounds, repeat several times over the series *pah, tah, kah*. Then vary the order, emphasizing first *pah,* then *tah,* then *kah.* In the same way practice the series *ap, at, ak* and *apa, ata, aka.* Work out additional combinations of this sort, using different combinations of consonants and vowels.

9. The words grouped in fours below have been found experimentally to be easily mistaken for one another under conditions of noise interference.[1] Practice articulating them distinctly and with precision. Then with your back to the class, and with three or four other students creating a noise by reading aloud from the textbook at the same time, read down one column or across one row, choosing one word at random out of each four. Announce before you start which column or row you are going to read from, pause briefly after each word, and have other members of the class check the word they understood you to say. (Used in this way, the following list is not an accurate *test* of intelligibility, but it should provide interesting material for practice.)

	A	*B*	*C*	*D*	*E*	*F*
	system	firm	banner	puddle	carve	offer
1	pistol	foam	manner	muddle	car	author
	distant	burn	mother	muzzle	tarred	often
	piston	term	batter	puzzle	tired	office
	heave	detain	scream	porch	fable	cross
2	heed	obtain	screen	torch	stable	cough
	ease	attain	green	scorch	table	cloth
	eve	maintain	stream	court	able	claw
	roger	pure	petal	vision	bubble	thrown
3	rupture	poor	battle	bishop	tumble	drone
	rapture	tour	meadow	vicious	stumble	prone
	obscure	two	medal	season	fumble	groan

1 Taken from answer sheets for standardized tests developed by C. Hess Hagen, printed in *Intelligibility Measurement: Twenty Four-Word Multiple Choice Tests,* OSRD Report No. 5567 (P.B. 12050), issued by the Office of Technical Services, Department of Commerce, p. 21.

art	sponsor	game	cape	texture	eye
4 heart	spotter	gain	hate	lecture	high
arch	ponder	gage	take	mixture	tie
ark	plunder	gang	tape	rupture	hide

comment	exact	made	process	glow	single
5 comic	retract	fade	protest	blow	jingle
cannon	detract	vague	profess	below	cycle
carbon	attack	may	possess	low	sprinkle

bumper	cave	pier	divide	kitchen	baker
6 number	cake	pierce	devise	mission	major
lumber	cage	fierce	define	friction	maker
lover	case	spear	divine	fiction	banker

gale	glamour	ward	leap	second	rich
7 jail	slimmer	wart	leaf	suction	ridge
dale	swimmer	wash	lease	section	bridge
bail	glimmer	war	leave	sexton	grip

danger	enact	hold	crater	seaport	joy
8 feature	impact	old	traitor	keyboard	going
nature	relax	ode	trainer	piecework	join
major	intact	hoed	treasure	eastward	dawn

10. Gather as many tongue-twisters as you can and practice saying them rapidly and precisely. Here are a few to start on:
    a. She sells sea shells on the sea shore.
    b. National Shropshire Sheep Association.
    c. "Are you copper-bottoming them, my man?" "No, I'm aluminuming 'em, mum."
    d. He sawed six long, slim, sleek, slender saplings.
    e. Dick twirled the stick athwart the path.
    f. Rubber baby-buggy bumpers.

g. "B—A, Ba; B—E Be:
B—I, Bi; Ba Be Bi;
B—O, Bo; Ba Be Bi Bo;
B—U, Bu; Ba Be Bi Bo Bu!"

11. Read aloud the following passages in a distinct and lively or forceful fashion; move the tongue, jaw, lips with energy:

from THE PIRATES OF PENZANCE, *Gilbert and Sullivan*

I am the very model of a modern Major-General,
I've information vegetable, animal, and mineral,
I know the kings of England, and I quote the fights historical,
From Marathon to Waterloo, in order categorical;
I'm very well acquainted too with matters mathematical,
I understand equations, both the simple and quadratical,
About binomial theorem I'm teeming with a lot o' news—
With many cheerful facts about the square of the hypotenuse.

I'm very good at integral and differential calculus,
I know the scientific names of beings animalculous;
In short, in matters vegetable, animal, and mineral,
I am the very model of a modern Major-General.

I know our mythic history, King Arthur's and Sir Caradoc's,
I answer hard acrostics, I've a pretty taste for paradox,
I quote in elegiacs all the crimes of Heliogabalus,
In conics I can floor peculiarities parabolous.
I can tell undoubted Raphaels from Gerard Dows and Zoffanies,
I know the croaking chorus from the *Frogs* of Aristophanes,
Then I can hum a fugue of which I've heard the music's din afore,
And whistle all the airs from that infernal nonsense *Pinafore*.

Then I can write a washing bill in Babylonic cuneiform,
And tell you every detail of Caractacus's uniform;
In short, in matters vegetable, animal, and mineral,
I am the very model of a modern Major-General.

from ALICE IN WONDERLAND, *Lewis Carroll*

"You are old," said the youth, "and your jaws are too weak
   For anything tougher than suet;
Yet you finished the goose, with the bones and the beak—
   Pray, how did you manage to do it?"
"In my youth," said his father, "I took to the law,
   And argued each case with my wife;
And the muscular strength which it gave to my jaw
   Has lasted the rest of my life."

from THE CATARACT OF LODORE, *Robert Southey*

Dividing and gliding and sliding,
And falling and brawling and sprawling,
And driving and riving and striving,
And sprinkling and twinkling and wrinkling,
And sounding and bounding and rounding,
And bubbling and troubling and doubling,
And grumbling and rumbling and tumbling,
And clattering and battering and shattering;

Retreating and beating and meeting and sheeting,
Delaying and straying and playing and spraying,
Advancing and prancing and glancing and dancing,
Recoiling, turmoiling and toiling and boiling,
And gleaming and steaming and streaming and beaming,
And rushing and flushing and brushing and gushing,
And flapping and rapping and clapping and slapping,
And curling and whirling and purling and twirling,
And thumping and plumping and bumping and jumping;
And dashing and flashing and splashing and clashing;
And so never ending, but always descending,
Sounds and motion forever are blending,
All at once and all o'er, with a mighty uproar,
And this way the water comes down at Lodore.

92

from FIRST INAUGURAL ADDRESS, *Thomas Jefferson*

Friends and Fellow-Citizens:

Called upon to undertake the duties of the first executive office of our country, I avail myself of the presence of that portion of my fellow-citizens which is here assembled, to express my grateful thanks for the favor with which they have been pleased to look towards me, to declare a sincere consciousness that the task is above my talents, and that I approach it with those anxious and awful presentiments which the greatness of the charge and the weakness of my powers so justly inspire. A rising nation spread over a wide and fruitful land, traversing all the seas with the rich productions of their industry, engaged in commerce with nations who feel power and forget right, advancing rapidly to destinies beyond the reach of mortal eye; when I contemplate these transcendent objects, and see the honor, the happiness, and the hopes of this beloved country committed to the issue and the auspices of this day, I shrink from the contemplation, and humble myself before the magnitude of the undertaking.

Utterly, indeed, should I despair, did not the presence of many whom I here see remind me that in the other high authorities provided by our constitution I shall find resources of wisdom, of virtue, and of zeal on which to rely under all difficulties.

SEA-FEVER,[2] *John Masefield*

I must go down to the seas again, to the lonely sea and the sky,
And all I ask is a tall ship and a star to steer her by,
And the wheel's kick and the wind's song and the white sail's shaking,
And a gray mist on the sea's face and a gray dawn breaking.

I must go down to the seas again, for the call of the running tide
Is a wild call and a clear call that may not be denied;
And all I ask is a windy day with the white clouds flying,
And the flung spray and the blown spume, and the sea-gulls crying.

I must go down to the seas again to the vagrant gypsy life,
To the gull's way and the whale's way where the wind's like a whetted knife;
And all I ask is a merry yarn from a laughing fellow-rover,
And quiet sleep and a sweet dream when the long trick's over.

2 From John Masefield's *Collected Poems*. By permission of the Macmillan Company, and Society of Authors.

from THE SANTA FE TRAIL—A HUMORESQUE,[3] *Vachel Lindsay*

I want live things in their pride to remain
I will not kill one grasshopper vain
Though he eats a hole in my shirt like a door.
I let him out, give him one chance more.
Perhaps, while he gnaws my hat in his whim,
Grasshopper lyrics occur to him.
I am a tramp by the long trail's border,
Given to squalor, rags and disorder.
I nap and amble and yawn and look,
Write fool-thoughts in my grubby book,
Recite to the children, explore at my ease,
Work when I work, beg when I please,
Give crank drawings, that make folks stare,
To the half-grown boys in the sunset-glare;
And get me a place to sleep in the hay
At the end of a live-and-let-live day.

In an even, deliberate narrative manner

I find in the stubble of the new-cut weeds
A whisper and a feasting, all one needs:
The whisper of the strawberries, white and red,
Here where the new-cut weeds lie dead.
But I would not walk all alone till I die
Without some life-drunk horns going by.
Up round this apple-earth they come,
Blasting the whispers of the morning dumb:—
Cars in a plain realistic row.
And fair dreams fade
When the raw horns blow.

On each snapping pennant
A big black name—
The careering city
Whence each car came.
They tour from Memphis, Atlanta, Savannah,
Tallahassee and Texarkana.
They tour from St. Louis, Columbus, Manistee,

Like a train-caller in Union Depot

3 From *The Santa Fe Trail—A Humoresque* by Vachel Lindsay. Reprinted by permission of the Macmillan Company, publishers.

They tour from Peoria, Davenport, Kankakee.
Cars from Concord, Niagara, Boston,
Cars from Topeka, Emporia and Austin.
Cars from Chicago, Hannibal, Cairo,
Cars from Alton, Oswego, Toledo.
Cars from Buffalo, Kokomo, Delphi,
Cars from Lodi, Carmi, Loami.
Ho for Kansas, land that restores us
When houses choke us, and great books bore us!
While I watch the highroad
And look at the sky,
While I watch the clouds in amazing grandeur
Roll their legions without rain
Over the blistering Kansas plain—
While I sit by the milestone
And watch the sky,
The United States
Goes by!

Vocal power, variety, and emphasis

The preceding section emphasized the importance of distinct, understandable utterance; here we are concerned with variety and power. You must have sufficient volume of voice to *be heard in the back of the room*. You will need, therefore, to build up the sheer strength and carrying power of your voice. Merely a loud voice, however, is not enough; you must develop control over it so that you can give positive emphasis to your statements. The sound of your voice must show that you are sure of yourself and mean what you say.

Furthermore, through the variations in your voice a great part of your meaning is conveyed. Take a simple sentence like "John stole my watch." Notice the different shades of meaning conveyed by placing the emphasis first on "John," then on "stole," on "my," and on "watch." The first way points out the thief; the second tells what he did; the third calls attention to the rightful owner; and the fourth names the article stolen. All four ideas are contained in the sentence, but the way you say it conveys to your listener which one of the four is uppermost in your mind. The more varied your voice is, the more vigorous and effective will be your remarks.

THE VARIABLE ELEMENTS

The elements of variety which you may develop in your voice are the *rate* at which you speak, the *force* with which you speak, the *pitch* of your voice, and its *quality*. By rate we mean the speed of utterance, that is, the number of syllables uttered per minute. Force is the loudness of utterance, varying from the softest whisper to the full-throated shout. The location of the sound on the musical scale is its pitch; varying the pitch means going up or down on this scale.

Vocal quality was discussed in the preceding section. We shall consider here briefly the ways in which the voice may be varied in rate, pitch, and force, and then discuss the relation of these to emphasis and climax. Remember, however, that no amount of reading about these matters will improve your voice unless you practice, and practice frequently. You will find the exercises at the end of this chapter helpful for this purpose. Use them. Practice the technique of vocal manipulation until your voice becomes strong and flexible.

Rate. The normal speed of utterance for most speakers averages between 120 and 180 words a minute; however, this rate is not obtained by a continuous clock-like regularity. In general, the speed of talking ought to correspond to the thought expressed. Weighty or complex matters should be presented slowly in order that the listener may have time to digest them properly. On the other hand, when you are attempting to describe a rapid sequence of events or a quick cumulation of ideas, your speed should be more rapid. Observe how rapidly the sports announcer talks when he is describing a fast play in a football game; in contrast, notice the slow, dignified rate with which one repeats the Lord's Prayer.

96

A fairly rapid rate is usually essential in narrative—nothing spoils a story so easily as to have it drag; but whenever you wish to drive home an important point or to emphasize some major fact, the rate of your speaking should be reduced materially.

Variation of rate, however, involves more than mere speed or slowness, for the rate of speaking depends on two elements: *quantity,* or the length of time used in the actual utterance of sound within a word, and *pause,* or the length of time spent in silence between words. Besides affecting the general rate, quantity and pause in themselves help to convey meaning.

Quantity varies primarily to suit the mood or feeling expressed. Beauty, solemnity, dignity, peacefulness, serenity, and the like call for long quantity in expression. If you say with sharp staccato quantity the beginning of Lincoln's famous address at Gettysburg, "Four score and seven years ago, our fathers brought forth on this continent a new nation, . . ." the result is obviously absurd; such sentiments require sustained tones. On the other hand, excitement, wit, gayety, surprise, vivacity, and the like require the use of short quantity. Imagine listening to the following play-by-play account of a basketball game given in a slow drawl: "Jones passes to Schmidt—he's dribbling down the floor—back to Jones—back again to Schmidt—over to Lee—and it's in! Another basket for. . . ." Like the game itself, such a description needs snap; short quantity provides it. Notice that vowel sounds are usually longer than consonant sounds; and that some consonants and vowels are longer than others. The word "roll," for example, contains sounds that are intrinsically longer than those in "hit." In this way many words suggest their meaning by the very duration of the sounds in them. Skillful speakers know this and use such words, either consciously or because of an unconscious sensitivity to these values, to help convey their feelings.

Pause is primarily an intellectual device serving to punctuate the spoken thought. Just as commas, semicolons, and periods separate written words into thought groups, so pauses of different length separate the words in speech into meaningful units. Haphazard use of pause, therefore, may be just as confusing to your listeners as the injudicious use of punctuation would be to the reader. Be sure that your pauses come between thought groups and not in the middle of them.

Pauses may also be used for emphasis. Placed immediately before or after an important statement, they serve to suggest to your audience, "Let this idea sink in." A pause just before the climax of a story sometimes helps increase suspense. A dramatic pause, longer than the usual one, used at the right moment, may express the depth of the speaker's feeling much more forcefully than any words could. On the other hand, do not stop vacantly just to let the time pass; concentrate on the thought you are trying to emphasize. Thoughtful pauses are dynamic; empty ones are merely silly.

One fault in speaking is so common—and so serious—that it should have special attention here. Many speakers, even speakers of long experience, have an annoying habit of filling pauses with "and-uh." A speech thus punctuated loses much of its effectiveness.

Pitch. Just as singers' voices differ, some being soprano or tenor and some contralto or bass, so do people vary in the normal pitch level at which they speak. The wisest plan is to talk in one's normal pitch range; otherwise there is danger of straining the voice. The pitch level at which we choose to speak carries a very definite impression to the audience. Ordinarily, a pitch that is continuously high suggests weakness, excitement, irritation, or extreme youth, while a lower pitch level suggests assurance, poise, and strength. For that reason, your customary pitch should normally be in the lower half of your natural range; but your voice must not remain there all the time—break away and come back. Nothing improves the animation and vivacity of speech so much as effective variation in pitch. Be particularly careful when you are applying increasing degrees of force not to let your voice get out of control, going to a higher and higher key until it cracks under the strain. If you notice tension, pause for a moment and lower your pitch.

Inflection. Few beginning speakers use enough variation even within their normal range of pitch; they tend to hit one level and stay there. This type of monotony can be avoided and meaning made more clear by developing a flexibility of pitch inflection. In general, an upward step or slide suggests interrogation, indecision, uncertainty, doubt, or suspense; while a downward inflection suggests firmness, determination, certainty, finality, or confidence. Thus if you were to say, "What shall we do about it? Just this:—," a rising inflection on the question would serve to create suspense, while a downward inflection on the last phrase would indicate the certainty with which you were presenting your answer. A double inflection, as when one says, "O o oh!" to express the meaning, "I didn't realize that!" suggests a subtle conflict or contradiction of meaning; it is frequently used to express irony or sarcasm, and to convey all sorts of subtle innuendo. By mastering the use of inflection you will help to make your meaning more clear.

All this does not mean that when you arise to speak you should say to yourself, "This sentence requires a double inflection; I shall raise my pitch on these two words and come down on that one." Such concentration on the mechanics of utterance would destroy the last vestige of communicative contact with your audience. Rather, in private and in class exercises, you should practice the technique, reading aloud selected passages which require pitch inflection, until the habit of flexibility grows upon you. Then, when you speak, these habits will show themselves in the increased variety and greater expressiveness of your utterance.

Melody patterns. In all kinds of speech the rhythm and swing of phrase and sentence weave themselves into a continuous pattern of changing pitch. As the thought or mood changes, this melodic pattern should also change. Sorrow or grief are not well expressed by the quick, lilting melody of playfulness and wit. A monotonous melody pattern, moreover, is just as ineffective as staying in one key all the time. Beware particularly of see-sawing back and forth in a sing-song voice. Avoid also the tendency of many inexperienced speakers to end every sentence with an upward cadence; assertions become questions when so uttered, and even what you are certain of sounds very doubtful. A monotonous downward cadence is almost as bad since it robs you of the power of expressing uncertainty when you want to do so. If you develop flexibility of pitch inflection as suggested in the preceding section, your melody pattern will normally adjust itself to the thought and mood you intend to express, but be on the watch to see that you do not get into a vocal rut, unconsciously using the same melody for everything you say.

Force. The first requirement any audience places on a speaker is that he talk loud enough to be heard easily. In addition, a certain amount of force is required to convey the impression of confidence and vigor in the speaker. Continuing to talk in too quiet a voice may suggest that you are not sure of yourself or that you don't care whether your audience hears you or not. Making your listener strain to hear what you say wears him out; his attention wanders; he moves about restlessly in his seat and wishes the ordeal were over. On the other hand, avoid continuous shouting. This too wears out an audience and dissipates attention. People become quite as bored by a continuous loud noise as by a continuous soft one.

The force with which you speak may be varied in the *amount* of force applied; thus a whisper or an undertone is uttered with a low degree of force, while a shout contains a high degree. On the other hand, you may vary the *manner* in which that force is applied; you may apply the force abruptly and explosively or increase it with a gradual swell.

Force is varied in degree primarily for emphasis. Either by increasing the loudness of a word or phrase or by pointedly reducing its loudness, you may make that word or phrase stand out as if it had been underscored. Moreover, changing the amount of force is an effective way to reawaken lagging interest. A drowsy audience will sit up quickly if you suddenly project an important word or phrase with sharply increased force. Remember, however, that the effect is produced not by the degree of force alone, but by the *change* in it: a sharp reduction is quite as effective as a sharp increase. Silence can awaken a man sleeping in a noisy room.

While you are practicing to develop control of the amount of force you use, you will do well to observe what happens to the pitch and quality of your voice. The natural tendency of most speakers is to raise the pitch whenever they try to increase the loudness. You have probably noticed that when you shout, your voice is keyed much higher than when you speak in a conversational tone. This is because the effort to produce a loud tone tends to increase muscle tension throughout the speaking mechanism; this general tension is apt to produce high pitch as well as more force. Sometimes the tension is so great in the throat as to produce a harsh quality as well. A little practice, however, will enable you to overcome this tendency. Just as you have learned to wiggle one finger without moving the others or to wink one eye without the other, so you can learn also to apply force by contracting the breathing muscles without tightening the muscles of the throat or unnecessarily raising the pitch of your voice. A good way to begin is by repeating a sentence such as "That is absolutely *true!*" Hit the last word in the sentence with a greater degree of force *and at the same time lower your pitch.* When you have mastered this bit of vocal control, say the entire sentence louder, and LOUDER, and LOUDER, until you can shout it without your pitch going up too. Keep a fairly sustained tone and try to maintain a full, resonant quality. By developing control over the degree of force in your voice you will have done much to make your speaking more emphatic and to convey to your audience an impression of reserve power.

The manner in which force is applied generally indicates the underlying sentiments of the speaker. If force is applied gradually and firmly, it suggests deep but controlled sentiment such as dignity or reverence. When force is applied firmly but more rapidly and with a vigorous

101

stroke, it expresses decisiveness, vigor, and earnestness. The sudden and *explosive* application of force suggests violent or uncontrolled feeling; it is associated with extreme anger, sudden fear, and the like. Remember, however, that in speech the form with which force is applied should be the natural response to inner feeling; sheer vocal manipulation is bound to sound artificial and hollow. But only by a certain amount of conscious drill can you develop sufficient flexibility and control over your voice to provide these feelings with a free and easy means of expression.

Emphasis and climax

All forms of vocal variety are useful in providing emphasis. Any change of rate or of force or of pitch serves to make the word, phrase, or sentence in which the change occurs stand out from those which precede or follow it. This is true regardless of the direction of the change. Whether the rate or force is increased or decreased, whether the pitch is raised or lowered, emphasis will result. And the greater the amount of change, or the more suddenly it is applied, the more emphatic will the statement be. Furthermore, emphasis is increased by pause and contrast; the former by allowing the audience to "get set" for the important idea or to digest it afterward, and the latter by making the change seem greater.

Within a word, emphasis is called accent and ordinarily follows the accepted standards of pronunciation. Correct accent is necessary for understanding. Consider the change of meaning produced by shifting the accent from one syllable to the other in the word "refuse." The rules of stress, however, are by no means inflexible when words are used in connected speech. Emphasis and contrast often require the shifting of accent for the sake of greater clarity. For example, notice what you do to the accent in the word "proceed" when you use it in this sentence: "I said to proceed, not to recede." It is apparent, then, that both conventional accent and the requirements of contrast and emphasis influence the placing of stress in words.

Two warnings should be noted: avoid overemphasis, and avoid continuous emphasis. If you emphasize a point beyond its evident value or importance, your audience will lose faith in your judgment; if you attempt to emphasize everything, nothing will stand out. Pick out the things that are really important and give them the significance of utterance they deserve. Be judicious in your use of emphasis.

Frequently a speaker gives expression to a growing thought or feeling that rises steadily in power until it reaches a point where the strongest appeal is made. Such climaxes of thought or feeling require climactic use of vocal expression. Each successive thought unit, whether it is a word, phrase, or sentence, is said with a successive increase in the degree of force, with more rapid rate, with a higher level of pitch, or with any combination of these changes.

Some immature speakers try too many climaxes in one speech. The effect of such procedure is lost by the very repetition; climaxes become too commonplace and are no longer climactic by the end of the speech. One good climax has more power to move an audience than five mediocre ones, frequently more even than five good ones. Save your climaxes for the places where they will be most effective, usually near the end of the speech, or at the ends of really major thought units.

Beware also of anticlimax. If before the real climax has been reached the increases of power begin to lessen or the climactic movement stops, the audience feels let down. Start slowly enough or quietly enough or at a low enough pitch so that you can keep on building till the end has been reached.

In this chapter we have talked about physical behavior and distinctness of pronunciation. We have talked about variety of rate, and of force, and of pitch, and of vocal quality. We have discussed emphasis and climax. Do not expect to master all these techniques in one day or one week. Take time to digest all the ideas explained in this chapter; practice on the material provided for exercise; return to this practice again and again.

problems

1. Say the following phrases, stretching out the first word and exploding the second:

   a. Ready—go!

   b. Company—halt!

   c. Heave—ho!

   d. Now—stop!

2. Repeating the alphabet or counting from one to twenty, perform the following vocal gymnastics (being careful throughout to maintain good vocal quality and distinctness of utterance):

   a. Begin very slowly, steadily increasing the speed until you are speaking as rapidly as possible; then reverse the process.

   b. Begin very softly and increase the force until you are nearly shouting; reverse the process. Then practice shifting from one extreme to the other, occasionally changing to a moderate degree of force.

   c. Keeping the loudness constant, shift from the explosive application of force combined with a staccato utterance to a firm, smooth application of force.

   d. Stress alternate letters (or numbers); then change by stressing every third letter, every fourth, etc.; then change back to alternate letters again.

   e. Begin at the lowest pitch you can comfortably reach and raise the pitch steadily until you reach the highest comfortable pitch; reverse the process. Shift back and forth suddenly from high to low to middle, etc.

3. In the manner suggested, vary the *rate, pitch,* and *force* with which you say the following sentences:

   a. "I hate you! I hate you! I hate you!"

      1. Increase the degree of force with each repetition, making the last almost a shout.

      2. Say the second "hate" louder than the first, and the last one *sotto voce.*

      3. Shout the first statement; then let the force diminish as if echoing the mood.

   b. "I have told you a hundred times, and the answer is still the same."

      1. Make the statement a straightforward assertion, using explosive form.

      2. Speak explosively as though uncontrollably angry.

      3. Speak as with deep but controlled emotion, applying force gradually.

104

c. "The winners are Smith, Cummings, and Jambowski."

1. Insert a long pause after "are" for suspense; then give the names rapidly.
2. Insert pauses before each name as if picking them out.
3. Say the whole sentence rapidly in a matter-of-fact way.

d. "If you come one step nearer, I'll—." End the sentence with the following words:

1. punch your nose!"
2. scream!"
3. never talk to you again."
4. show the picture to you."
5. well, I'm not sure just what I will do."

(See how many attitudes you can make these statements express.)

e. "I certainly feel fine today;—that is, except for my sunburn. Now don't slap me on the back! Ouch! Stop it! Please!" Begin confidently on a low key, successively raising the pitch level until the "Please" is said near the top of your range. Repeat several times, trying to begin lower each time.

4. Practice reading aloud passages from prose and poetry that require emphasis and contrast to make the meaning clear. Vary the pitch, rate, and force in different ways until you feel you have the best possible interpretation of the meaning. The following examples are of the type suggested:

Mark Twain

One of the most striking differences between a cat and a lie is that a cat has only nine lives.

Jonathan Swift

So, Naturalists observe, a flea
Has smaller fleas that on him prey;
And these have smaller still to bite 'em;
And so proceed ad infinitum.

Esau Wood

Esau Wood sawed wood. Esau Wood would saw wood. All the wood Esau Wood saw Esau Wood would saw. In other words, all the wood Esau saw to saw Esau sought to saw. Oh, the wood Wood would saw! And oh! the wood-saw with which Wood would saw wood. But one day Wood's wood-saw would saw no wood, and thus the wood Wood sawed was not the wood Wood would saw if Wood's wood-saw would saw wood. Now, Wood would saw wood with a wood-saw that would saw wood, so Esau sought a saw that would saw wood. One day Esau saw a saw saw wood as no other wood-saw Wood saw would saw wood. In fact, of all the wood-saws Wood ever saw saw wood Wood never saw a wood-saw that would saw wood as the wood-saw Wood saw saw wood would saw wood, and I never saw a wood-saw that would saw as the wood-saw Wood saw would saw until I saw Esau Wood saw wood with the wood-saw Wood saw saw wood. Now Wood saws wood with the wood-saw Wood saw saw wood.

Patrick Henry

Gentlemen may cry, peace, peace!—but there is no peace. The war has actually begun! I know not what course others may take; but, as for me, give me liberty, or give me death!

from PAUL REVERE'S RIDE, *Longfellow*

A hurry of hoofs in a village street,
A shape in the moonlight, a bulk in the dark,
And beneath from the pebbles, in passing, a spark
Struck out by a steed flying fearless and fleet;
That was all! And yet, through the gloom and the light,
The fate of a nation was riding that night;
And the spark struck out by that steed, in his flight,
Kindled the land into flame with its heat.

from The Declaration of Independence

We hold these truths to be self-evident: that all men are created equal; that they are endowed by their Creator with certain inalienable rights; that among these are life, liberty, and the pursuit of happiness. That to secure these rights, governments are instituted among men, deriving their just powers from the consent of the governed; that whenever any form of government becomes destructive of these ends it is the right of the people to alter or to abolish it, and to institute a new government, laying its foundation on such principles, and organizing its powers in such form as to them shall seem most likely to effect their safety and happiness.

from ORATION ON LAFAYETTE, *Edward Everett*

And what was it, fellow-citizens, which gave to our Lafayette his spotless fame? The love of liberty. What has consecrated his memory in the hearts of good men? The love of liberty. What nerved his youthful arm with strength, and inspired him, in the morning of his days, with sagacity and counsel? The living love of liberty. To what did he sacrifice power, and rank, and country, and freedom itself? To the horror of licentiousness,—to the sanctity of plighted faith,—to the love of liberty protected by law. Thus the great principle of your Revolutionary fathers, and of your Pilgrim sires, was the rule of his life—*the love of liberty protected by law.*

from A CHRISTMAS CAROL, *Charles Dickens*

"A merry Christmas, uncle! God save you!" cried a cheerful voice. It was the voice of Scrooge's nephew, who came upon him so quickly that this was the first intimation he had of his approach.

"Bah!" said Scrooge, "Humbug!"

He had so heated himself with rapid walking in the fog and frost, this nephew of Scrooge's, that he was all in a glow; his face was ruddy and handsome; his eyes sparkled, and his breath smoked again.

"Christmas a humbug, uncle!" said Scrooge's nephew. "You don't mean that, I am sure."

"I do," said Scrooge. "Merry Christmas! What right have you to be merry? What reason have you to be merry? You're poor enough."

"Come, then," returned the nephew gaily. "What right have you to be dismal? What reason have you to be morose? You're rich enough."

Scrooge having no better answer ready on the spur of the moment, said "Bah!" again, and followed it up with "Humbug!"

"Don't be cross, uncle!" said the nephew.

"What else can I be," returned the uncle, "when I live in such a world of fools as this? Merry Christmas! What's Christmas time to you but a time for paying bills without money; a time for finding yourself a year older, and not an hour richer; a time for balancing your books and having every item in 'em through a round dozen of months presented dead against you? If I could work my will," said Scrooge indignantly, "every idiot who goes about with Merry Christmas on his lips, should be boiled in his own pudding, and buried with a stake of holly through his heart. He should."

"Uncle!" pleaded his nephew.

"Nephew," returned his uncle sternly, "keep Christmas in your own way, and let me keep it in mine."

"Keep it!" repeated Scrooge's nephew. "But you don't keep it."

"Let me leave it alone, then," said Scrooge. "Much good may it do you! Much good has it ever done you!"

from LIFE ON THE MISSISSIPPI, *Mark Twain*

.... Every town and village along that vast stretch of double river-frontage had a best dwelling, finest dwelling, mansion—the home of its wealthiest and most conspicuous citizen. It is easy to describe it: large grassy yard, with paling fence painted white—in fair repair; brick walk from gate to door; big, square, two-story "frame" house, painted white and porticoed like a Grecian temple—with this difference, that the imposing fluted columns and Corinthian capitals were a pathetic sham, being made of white pine, and painted; iron knocker; brass door-knob—discolored, for lack of polishing. Within, an uncarpeted hall, of planed boards; opening out of it, a parlor, fifteen feet by fifteen—in some instances five or ten feet larger; ingrain carpet; mahogany center-table; lamp on it, with green-paper shade—standing on a gridiron, so to speak, made of high-colored yarns, by the young ladies of the house, and called a lamp-mat; several books, piled and disposed, with cast-iron exactness, according to an inherited and unchangeable plan; among them, *Tupper,* much penciled; also, *Friendship's Offering,* and *Affection's Wreath,* with their sappy inanities illustrated in die-away mezzotints; also Ossian; *Alonzo and Mellissa;* maybe *Ivanhoe;* also "Album," full of original "poetry" of the Thou-hast-wounded-the-spirit-that-loved-thee breed; two or three goody-goody works—*Shepherd of Salisbury Plain,* etc.; current number of the chaste and innocuous *Godey's Lady's Book,* with painted fashion-plate of wax-figure women with mouths all alike—lips and eyelids the same size—each five-foot woman with a two-inch wedge sticking from under her dress and letting on to half of her foot. Polished air-tight stove (new and deadly invention), with pipe passing through a board which closes up the discarded good old fireplace. On each end of the wooden mantel, over the fireplace, a large basket of peaches and other fruits, natural size, all done in plaster, rudely, or in wax, and painted to resemble the originals—which they don't. Over middle of mantel, engraving—"Washington Crossing the Delaware"; on the wall by the door, copy of it done in thunder and lightning crewels by one of the young ladies—work of art which would have made Washington hesitate about crossing, if

108

he could have foreseen what advantage was going to be taken of it. Piano—kettle in disguise—with music, bound and unbound, piled on it, and on a stand near by: "Battle of Prague"; "Bird Waltz"; "Arkansas Traveler"; "Rosin the Bow"; "Marseillaise Hymn"; "On a Lone Barren Isle" (St. Helena); "The Last Link is Broken" .... Frantic work of art on the wall—pious motto, done on the premises, sometimes in colored yarns, sometimes in faded grasses: progenitor of the "God Bless Our Home" of modern commerce. Framed in black moldings on the wall, other works of art, conceived and committed on the premises, by the young ladies; being grim black-and-white crayons; landscapes, mostly; lake, solitary sailboat, petrified clouds, pregeological trees on shore, anthracite precipice; name of criminal conspicuous in the corner. Lithograph, "Napoleon Crossing the Alps." Lithograph, "The Grave at St. Helena." Steel plates, Trumbull's "Battle of Bunker Hill," and the "Sally from Gibraltar." Copper plates, "Moses Smiting the Rock" and "Return of the Prodigal Son." In big gilt frame, slander of the family in oil: papa holding a book ("Constitution of the United States"); guitar leaning against mamma, blue ribbons fluttering from its neck; the young ladies, as children, in slippers and scalloped pantalettes, one embracing toy horse, the other beguiling kitten with ball of yarn, and both simpering up at mamma who simpers back. These persons all fresh, raw, and red—apparently skinned. Opposite, in gilt frame, grandpa and grandma, at thirty and twenty-two, stiff, old-fashioned, high-collared, puff-sleeved, glaring pallidly out from a background of solid Egyptian night. Under a glass French clock dome, large bouquet of stiff flowers done in corpsy-white wax. Pyramidal what-not in the corner, the shelves occupied chiefly with bric-a-brac of the period, disposed with an eye to best effect. . . .

5. Read the following passages with increasing force so as to give the effect of climax:

Duke of Wellington

There is no mistake; there has been no mistake; and there shall be no mistake.

Daniel Webster

Let us cultivate a true spirit of union and harmony . . . let us act under a settled conviction, and an habitual feeling, that these twenty-four States are one country. . . . Let our object be, OUR COUNTRY, OUR WHOLE COUNTRY, AND NOTHING BUT OUR COUNTRY.

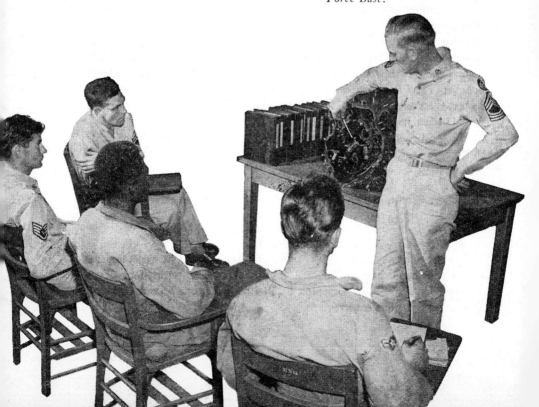

Making good use of visual supporting material, a master sergeant lectures to a group of trainees at Carswell Air Force Base.

Chapter 4 HOW TO SUPPORT

ONE POINT

Many occasions arise in which you want to make clear a single idea or prove but one simple point. Such occasions often come in class discussions, in short reports, in simple instructions, and in arguments. In these situations you do not need a complex structure to make your talk effective. Even when speeches are given primarily to entertain, rather than to explain or persuade, they are usually better if the illustrations, anecdotes, and humor in them are unified by a single point or theme. In fact, the beginning speaker shows wisdom if he starts by limiting himself to single points well supported and leaves the more complex discussions until later. Thus he will avoid hollow abstractions covering a wide range but proving or clarifying nothing; and he will find, when he does later attempt more complex instruction and argument, that the units of his talks will be composed of the same single points strategically arranged.

The first thing to do, of course, is to decide definitely on the point you want to explain or prove. Condense your ideas to a single sentence to be *sure* you have only one point. State it simply: for example, "Always camp downstream from your drinking water supply," or, "A good truck driver must keep relaxed." Having stated your point, stick to it; don't wander off on another topic.

Most people, however, are not quick to understand general statements, bare and undeveloped. Nor will they believe a proposition or act on a proposal without proof or stimulation. You must round out your point with examples that will make it clear and vivid—examples that are concrete and specific.

The forms of verbal supporting material

Roughly speaking, there are seven forms of verbal supporting material which may be used to develop the ideas in a talk:

1. Explanation
2. Analogy or Comparison
3. Illustration (detailed example or story)
   a. Hypothetical Illustration
   b. Factual Illustration
4. Specific Instance (undeveloped example)
5. Statistics
6. Testimony
7. Restatement

Many times, of course, two or more of these may be combined, as when figures are used to detail an illustration, or a comparison is made between two sets of statistics, or the testimony of an expert is used to give weight to a restatement.

The forms of support are the flesh and blood which bring your speech to life. The thought-skeleton of your speech must be there to give it unity and coherence, but it is the meat which you put upon that skeleton that will give it body and warmth and reality for your audience.

As you consider the following explanations of the seven types of material, notice that the first three (explanation, comparison, and illustration) are primarily useful in making an idea clear and vivid, while

112

the next three (instances, statistics, and testimony) have the function of establishing and verifying its truth or importance. Restatement, of course, serves for emphasis.

1. EXPLANATION

A complete explanation often involves the use of several of the other forms of supporting material. In fact, Chapter 6 will be devoted entirely to speeches the main purpose of which may be to explain. The term as here used refers to a simple explanation or definition and not to any such detailed development. *It is a simple, concise exposition, setting forth the relation between a whole and its parts or making clear an obscure term.* In the following example, notice how the late Justice Brandeis makes clear what is meant by a "profession":

> The peculiar character of a profession as distinguished from other occupations, I take to be these: *First.* A profession is an occupation for which the necessary preliminary training is intellectual in character, involving knowledge and to some extent learning, as distinguished from mere skill. *Second.* It is an occupation which is pursued largely for others and not merely for one's self. *Third.* It is an occupation in which the amount of financial return is not the accepted measure of success.[1]

Another example of this type of material is the explanation of academic freedom by Professor William G. Carleton:

> The social sciences, by their growing maturity, have earned the right to academic freedom. And what is academic freedom? It is not the right to irresponsible utterance. It is the right to publicize the truth, as trained men see the truth in a particular stage of its development, after years of study and thought and research, without fear of reprisal, without fear of the loss of job or of opportunity for professional advancement. Of course the trained specialist may be wrong. He may even make a fool of himself. But when men are afraid to dare, when they are afraid to make fools of themselves, creative thought languishes and dies.[2]

1 From "Business—A Profession," by Louis D. Brandeis, printed in *Modern Speeches*, edited by Homer D. Lindgren (Crofts, N. Y., 1926), p. 106.
2 From an address before the Florida Council of Social Sciences, Nov. 3, 1949. Printed in *Vital Speeches*, Vol. XVI, pp. 144-145.

In neither speech from which the examples cited above were taken did the speakers content themselves with explanation alone. In every case the idea was amplified by the use of one or more of the other types of material. Explanation is a good beginning for making an idea clear; it is rarely adequate by itself. Be careful, also, not to make an explanation too long and abstract. Many an audience has been put to sleep by a long-winded explanation full of abstract details. *Make it simple; make it brief; make it accurate.*

2. ANALOGY OR COMPARISON

By this term is meant the pointing out of similarities between that which is already known, understood, or believed and that which is not. It is connecting the known with the unknown. For example, Thomas Edison is reported to have explained the operation of electricity in a telegraph as being "like a Dachshund long enough to reach from Edinburgh to London; when you pull his tail in Edinburgh, he barks in London." [3] Tyler Dennett, former president of Williams College, quotes a Massachusetts statesman as having once described the difference between a democracy and a dictatorship as follows:

> It is the difference between a raft and a yacht. On the yacht you are safe if you have a good captain as dictator. On a raft your feet are wet all the time, but you never sink. [4]

Again, Mr. Justice Robert H. Jackson, addressing an audience of college deans, used the following comparison:

> In the north country the final test of a man is whether he can safely guide a canoe through "white water," as they call the swirling and rushing rapids. The world has an overabundance of those who paddle pretty well in still water. The world cries for men who can navigate "white water." [5]

Likewise, when Col. Lawrence Kwong was asked why the Chinese Nationalists so often maneuvered into battle position and then sur-

3 From *Thomas Alva Edison* by Francis Rolt-Wheeler (Macmillan, N.Y.), pp. 90-91.
4 From "Democracy as a Factor in Education," *Vital Speeches*, May 15, 1937, p. 461.
5 Printed in *Vital Speeches*, Vol. IV, December 15, 1937, p. 150.

rendered without fighting, why there had been no pitched battle in the defense of Shanghai, he said rather dryly:

> Well, in a game of checkers you maneuver for position. Eventually there comes a time when it's obvious that one side is going to win and one side is going to lose. When that time comes, it's perfectly pointless for the victor to get up and shoot the other man dead.[6]

A similar technique was used by Abraham Lincoln in an oft-quoted analogy, directed by him against those who were criticizing his conduct of the Civil War. The newspapers had been full of the exploits of Blondin, a famous tight-rope walker. Lincoln used this fact to emphasize the precarious position of the government:

> Gentlemen, I want you to suppose a case for a moment. Suppose that all the property you were worth was in gold, and you had put it in the hands of Blondin, the famous rope-walker, to carry across the Niagara Falls on a tight rope. Would you shake the rope while he was passing over it, or keep shouting to him, "Blondin, stoop a little more! Go a little faster!" No, I am sure you would not. You would hold your breath as well as your tongue, and keep your hands off until he was safely over. Now the government is in the same situation. It is carrying an immense weight across a stormy ocean. Untold treasures are in its hands. It is doing the best it can. Don't badger it! Just keep still, and it will get you safely over.

It will be observed from these examples that the principal function of the comparison or the analogy is to make an idea clear and vivid. For this purpose it is an excellent tool and deserves to be widely used. Sometimes, however, it is used as a method of proof. For example, the successful operation of a municipal electric light plant in one city is used to prove its advisability in another city of a similar size. As proof, the comparison is relatively weak since so many conditions may vary between the two places. At best it indicates only a high degree of probability. If proof is required, it is best to follow a comparison or analogy with a number of the other forms of supporting material.

6 Reported by Frank H. Bartholomew of the United Press. Printed in *Vital Speeches of the Day*, Feb. 1, 1950, p. 251.

3. Illustration

A *detailed narrative* example of the idea or statement to be supported is called an illustration. It is the story of an incident used to bring out the point that you are trying to make. Sometimes an illustration relates the results which have been obtained from the adoption of a proposal which the speaker advocates; sometimes it describes in detail an individual example of the general conditions the speaker wishes to emphasize. Note two principal characteristics: *the illustration is narrative in form—it tells the story; and the details of the story are vividly described.*

There are two principal types of illustration: the hypothetical and the factual. The former tells a story which *could* have happened or *probably will* happen; the latter tells what *actually has* happened.

a. The *hypothetical illustration* is an imaginary narrative. It must, however, be consistent with the known facts. It must be reasonable. The following is an example:

> Let's put ourselves in the other fellow's place. If you got no satisfaction out of your job as employer, if you had no pride in the sense of accomplishment, if you didn't feel yourself a vital part of a dynamic organization, all the pay you would get would be money. Take away all those things that make up your compensation, and every one of you would demand that your pay be doubled, because money would be all that was left.
>
> Out in your shop a man comes to work at 7 A.M. He doesn't know too much about his job and almost nothing about his company or how his work fits into it. He works 8 hours and goes home—with what? His pay and nothing more. Nobody (except the union steward!) took much if any notice of him. Nobody complimented him if he did do well because nobody except a foreman *knows* whether or not he did well, and he realized *that* fact. Nobody ever flattered him by asking his opinion about something. In millions of cases nobody ever told him the importance of his work.
>
> At night he goes home to his family and neighbors—unimportant with nothing to boast about or even talk about. And the union calls a meeting to discuss a grievance—that workman can get up on his feet and sound off while people listen, he can be an officer with a title, he can boast to his family and friends how he "gave those big shots of the company what-for!" A strike

vote is exciting!—Being a picket is important!—He gets looked at and talked about; he wears a badge!

Again let's be honest. If you and I were in that worker's situation, wouldn't we do pretty much what he's doing?[7]

The principal use for the hypothetical illustration is to make an abstract explanation more vivid and concrete. It is a particularly useful tool for explaining a complicated plan. Instead of merely outlining the details, you take some hypothetical person, yourself or a member of the audience, and put him through the process of operating the plan.

For making a point clear the hypothetical illustration is good; for proof, however, it is of doubtful value.

b. The *factual illustration* is a story describing in detail a specific event. As such, the factual illustration is very effective. Described in detail, the incident is made clear and vivid; the illustration carries conviction. Note the effect of the following from a speech on "The Two-Party System of Government" by Gov. Thomas E. Dewey:

> When I visited Berlin last May I found that the American Military Government officials had already very kindly worked out a calendar for me, including one "must" visit to Mayor Ernst Reuter, the elected Oberburgermeister of the Western Sector of the City.
>
> Upon arriving at the City Hall I was surprised to find several thousand people waiting quietly in front of the building. Our party was met by Mayor Reuter and as soon as we sat down in the reception chamber with other members of the City Government, he volunteered the answer to my unspoken question. "I appreciate your coming here so much," he said. "You can see how much it meant to those thousands of people outside. It is a very important lesson for our people to see that a man can be defeated for the highest office in his country and still receive the full honors of his country—and also to see him still alive."
>
> Of all the vivid impressions of my most recent European visit, this is one of the most vivid. We were in a city divided four ways, occupied by the military forces of four nations and blockaded by the Russians who surround it. This courageous German liberal was almost pitifully eager to have

7 From "Effective Leadership for Better Employee Relations," a speech by Charles J. Stilwell. Printed in *Vital Speeches*, December 15, 1947, p. 157.

the people of his city see with their own eyes how it is possible for people to disagree fundamentally with those in charge of their government and still remain out of concentration camps and escape the firing squad.

It seems strange to us that this simple fundamental of free government should be such a novelty. Yet it exists in a steadily diminishing portion of the world today.[8]

There are three considerations which you should keep in mind when you are choosing a factual illustration to support an idea. First, is it clearly related to the idea? Its point should be obvious. Second, is it a fair example? An audience is quick to notice unusual circumstances in an illustration, and if you seem to have picked only the exceptional case, the examples will be less convincing. Third, is it vivid and impressive in detail? The primary value of an illustration is the sense of reality which it creates. Be sure that your illustrations are *pointed, fair,* and *vivid*.

4. SPECIFIC INSTANCE

In developing an idea you may need to give specific instances. These are condensed forms of the factual illustration. They are undetailed examples. Time may not allow you to relate a large number of detailed illustrations, but in order to show the widespread nature of a situation or the frequency of an occurrence you will often need to mention a number of instances, each showing your point to be true:

The most remarkable developments in communications have come in the past fifty years. In 1887, Heinrich Hertz unlocked the secret of the elusive wireless waves. In 1901, Marconi proved that these waves could be used as a means of communication. By 1912, the Government was making definite assignments of frequencies and in 1920, KDKA in Pittsburgh went on the air as the first commerical station. By 1930, the radio spectrum had been extended and services assigned above 50,000 kilocycles. The Federal Communications Commission is now considering the problem of assigning frequencies as high as 30,000,000 kilocycles.[9]

8 Printed in *Vital Speeches*, Vol. XVI, June 1, 1950, p. 489.
9 From "American Radio after the War," by Paul A. Walker. Delivered before the Third Annual Radio Conference. Printed in *Vital Speeches*, December 15, 1944, p. 151.

118

Sometimes instances are presented with less exact detail than was used in the preceding example:

But I am persuaded that the most important thing that happened in Britain was that this nation chose to win or lose the war under the established rules of parliamentary procedure. It feared nazism, but did not choose to imitate it. . . . I remember that while London was being bombed in the daylight, the House of Commons devoted two days to discussing conditions under which enemy aliens were detained on the Isle of Man. Though Britain fell, there were to be no concentration camps here. I remember that two days after Italy declared war an Italian citizen, convicted of murder in the lower court, appealed successfully to the highest court in the land, and the original verdict was set aside. There was still in the land, regardless of race, nationality, or hatred, representative government. Equality before the law survived.[10]

The use of specific instances adds strength and comprehensiveness to an idea. They provide excellent proof, especially if they follow a detailed illustration which makes the idea clear.

5. STATISTICS

Statistics are figures used to show the proportion of instances of a certain kind, to show how many or few or great or small they are. Statistics are useful in covering a great deal of territory in a short time. When judiciously used, they are impressive and convincing.

During the past 100 years we have developed under free enterprise the most comprehensive, efficient, and dependable railroad plant in the world. Last year, the railroads moved freight over 700 billion ton-miles, as compared with 447 billion in 1929. The average haul was 403 miles. For every man, woman, and child, they moved a ton of freight about 600 miles in 1880, and over 4,500 miles in 1947. During the next 24 hours, the railroads will move 1,800,000,000 ton-miles of freight, equal to 1 ton for a distance of 12½ miles for every man, woman, and child in the United States. And, in the same 24 hours, nearly 2,000,000 passengers will ride an average of 60 miles.[11]

10 From "Farewell to England," a speech given by Edward R. Murrow over the Columbia Broadcasting System on March 10, 1946, and printed in *Talks*. By permission of Edward R. Murrow and the Columbia Broadcasting System, Inc.
11 From a radio talk by Ambrose W. Benkert, Director of the M. & St. P. Railroad. Printed in *Vital Speeches*, Vol. XV, Aug. 15, 1949, pp. 664-665.

Notice in the example just given that the speaker was not satisfied merely to give figures, but that he compared them to one another. Numbers by themselves are abstract; they must be made vivid and graphic by comparison with those things which are familiar to us. Note how another speaker made understandable the small size of an electron. He had first given it as a decimal fraction which was too small for his audience to conceive. Then he said:

> If an electron were increased in size till it became as large as an apple, and a human being grew larger in the same proportion, that person could hold the entire solar system in the palm of his hand and would have to use a magnifying glass in order to see it.

Statistics are powerful proof when they are effectively and honestly used, but you must be sure that they are made understandable to your audience. For this reason it is well to use approximate numbers when you are presenting large figures. Say "nearly four million" rather than "3,984,256." If precision is important, write the figures on a blackboard or chart or hand out a mimeographed sheet. Moreover, note that the term "figures" is much easier to pronounce than "statistics," and though the two terms are not exactly synonymous, most audiences will understand what you mean if you say, "Figures compiled by the Treasury Department show that. . . ."

6. Testimony

Frequently an audience which will not take your word alone will be convinced or impressed by the statement of someone else. The statement of someone else used to support the ideas of the speaker is called testimony. The following is an example:

> The sixth and final argument which I wish to propose briefly has been stated most convincingly by Henry Ford II in his address at the annual dinner of the Yale University Alumni. He emphasized this point: "There is no substitute for competition. Competition in a world of freedom and opportunity has put the tremendous driving power into our national economy and made

120

us strong. It is the force of competition which has made our country today the hope of the world."[12]

The use of a man's testimony must be governed by a measurement of his reliability and of his reputation with the audience. Ask yourself these questions about him:

1. Do his training and experience qualify him to speak with authority on this subject? Is he an expert in this field?
2. Is his statement based on first-hand knowledge?
3. Is his opinion influenced by personal interest? That is, is he prejudiced?
4. How will your hearers regard his testimony? Is he known to them? Do they respect his opinions?

General Chennault uses testimony to meet these requirements:

> For nearly 10 years I have lived face to face with communism in Asia and its permanent goal of world domination, whatever its temporary shifting tactics. Since I am considered an alarmist and a dangerous man for persisting in my warnings I was much encouraged to read in the Washington Times-Herald yesterday an International News Service story of the views of that other American officer who has lived the closest to Communist tactics. That is Gen. Lucius Clay, an officer whose integrity and capacity I know every member of this committee and of Congress appreciates. I have a copy here of the story which many of you may have read. As the story reads, General Clay warned that the west should be wary of any agreement with Russia because the fixed objective of communism remains world domination through revolution. The story goes on quoting General Clay verbatim:
>
> "The Communist Party and the Communist world movement has a fixed objective. That objective is world domination through revolution. It is a long-range objective. That objective will never change because if it did communism would die. However, the intensity of effort can go through many changes."[13]

If you had diphtheria, you would not ask a bus driver to prescribe a treatment; nor would you ask someone who had never been out of a

12 From an address by the Very Rev. Paul C. Reinert, S. J., President of St. Louis University. Printed in *Vital Speeches*, Vol. XVI, April 1, 1950, p. 374.
13 From testimony before the Senate Armed Services Committee by General Claire Chennault, May 3, 1949. Printed in *Vital Speeches*, Vol. XV, pp. 469-470.

small town to describe traffic in New York. It is doubtful how much weight you would give the testimony of a salesman on the quality of the goods he gets a commission for selling. These same requirements must be met by authorities whom you quote. Be particularly careful about using big names merely because they are well known.

7. RESTATEMENT

Restatement gains its strength from the power of repetition. Advertisers realize this power and spend millions of dollars to say the same thing many times over in magazines, on billboards, and over the radio. The biggest danger lies in the monotony which mere repetition has. Restatement is not mere repetition: *restatement consists of saying the same thing, but saying it in a different way.* Observe the restatement at the end of the analogy quoted from Lincoln:

> . . . The government is in the same situation. It is carrying immense weight across a stormy ocean. Untold treasures are in its hands. It is doing the best it can. Don't badger it! Just keep still and it will get you safely over.

By restating an idea in more familiar terms or more vivid language you can frequently increase its power.

These, then, are the seven forms of verbal supporting material. Fill your speech with them. Avoid abstract, unsupported statements. Amplify your statements by using explanation, comparison, illustration, instance, statistics, testimony, and restatement.

The use of visual supporting material: maps, diagrams, pictures, and models

So far we have discussed only the *audible* materials used to explain or prove a point—what you can *say* about it. Equally important, sometimes even more so, are the *visual* materials you can use to *show* what

122

you mean. These visual materials include maps, diagrams, charts, pictures, small working models, and even demonstrations with full scale equipment. For instance, if you were explaining how to use a complicated camera, your instructions would be much clearer if you took an actual camera, showed your listeners the parts that require adjustment, and demonstrated by actually using the camera in typical "shots." Sometimes equipment for demonstration is not available or is too big to bring into the room where the explanation is to be made. Small scale models are very useful here. Model airplanes, for example, are being widely used to teach aerodynamics. Likewise, in explaining a flood control project, you will find a large map of the area very helpful. The operation of a gun or machine and the assembly of its various parts can often be made more clear by large diagrams which show the important pieces. Statistical data can often be made clear by column graphs and "pies"— circles cut into segments to show proportions. Pictures, including lantern slides and moving picture film, are extremely useful also.

There are three important things to remember when you use visual aids in a talk. First, be sure you do not stand between your audience and what you show them. There is a strong tendency to turn your back when you point to the map or diagram, and in doing so to stand directly in front of it. Be careful to stand a little to one side as you point to the visual material, and talk to the listeners before you. Second, be sure to use only those visual materials that are closely related to the point you are presenting, and refer only to those parts of the map or picture important to your point. Avoid the temptation to explain all details in the diagram or model unless these details are necessary to make your point clear. Third, be sure your visual material is large enough to be clearly seen. Use fewer words and large, heavy print; avoid narrow spider-web lines; use vivid colors instead of pastels.

Visual materials help prove a point by making more vivid the facts you present. They are almost indispensable for explanatory talks. Whenever possible in the latter type of talk, then, *show* your listeners what you

Visible material can show what you mean

"One picture is worth a thousand words." This is also true for public speakers. Visual aids present information, and the best ones present it with greater clarity than words alone can. To be an effective means of explaining a point, however, they must be clearly related to the point being discussed, and they must be large enough and so placed before the audience that each person can easily see and understand them.

Notice the visual aids used in the speaking situations shown on these two pages. Each has an interest value in itself, and each contributes to an understanding of the speaker's point.

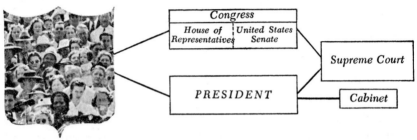

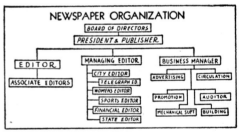

A large audience will be able to see and understand the chart above better than the one to the right because it has fewer parts and a much simpler organization.

mean (in addition to *telling* them by means of illustrations, comparisons, and the like).

The use of supporting material to explain

How, then, does one assemble supporting material in a short talk to explain a single point? Briefly, you first state the point simply, then

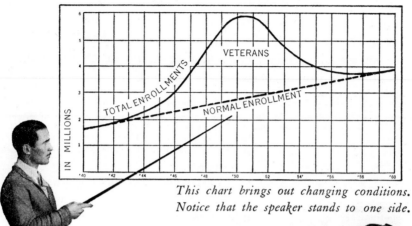

This chart brings out changing conditions.
Notice that the speaker stands to one side.

This speaker is using models to show his audience something of microscopic size. He is Dr. William Parrish, a crystallographer, who built these models to illustrate the difference between the regular structure of a metal crystal and the irregular structure of glass.

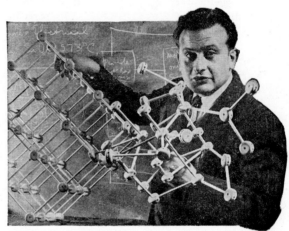

you bring in the supporting material, and finally you restate the point explained. This arrangement can be outlined as follows:

1. State your point in a simple sentence.
2. Make it clear—
     a. by explanation, comparison, and illustration.
     b. by using maps, diagrams, pictures, or models.
3. Restate the point you have made clear.

125

Under 2 above, sometimes the audible and visual materials are presented separately and sometimes together. That is, sometimes you will tell your listeners and then show them; sometimes you will show them while you are telling them. The following outline for a short talk illustrates how supporting material may be assembled to explain a point:

WHAT IS DEMOCRACY?

(Statement) I. The essence of democracy is the control of government by those governed.

(Explanation) A. This means that the people have final authority to:
1. Make the laws under which they live.
2. Select public officials to administer laws.

(Hypothetical Illustration) B. Suppose a group of students were to plan a party in the democratic way.
1. They would meet together for a discussion of it.
2. They would decide where and when it would be held.
3. They would agree how much each should contribute to the cost.
4. In case of disagreement, they would reach a compromise or abide by the vote of the majority.
5. One of them would be selected to collect the money and pay the bills.
6. They might select another person or a

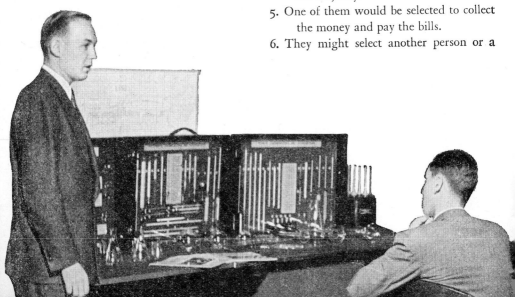

small committee to arrange for the entertainment, etc.

7. Each student would have some part in deciding how the party would be run.

(Comparison with B)

C. If, however, one student took it upon himself to decide all these questions—even to dictating the program of entertainment and how much each one should pay for it—the party would not be *democratic,* regardless of how efficiently it might be run.

(Comparison of Specific Instances)

D. Compare these actual cases:

1. In New England, local government is based on town meetings.
   a. All qualified residents are allowed to speak and vote directly on current problems.
   b. Public officials are selected by vote of the citizens.

2. Indiana cities are governed by representatives of the people.
   a. City ordinances are made by the city council whose members are elected by the voters.
   b. Administrative offices are held by elected officials.

3. In Norway and Poland, under German occupation in 1943, city government

Here is a group of engineering salesmen of the Standard Oil Company of New Jersey listening to an informative talk by an instructor of the company. With the aid of laboratory testing equipment and petroleum samples, he is explaining how various petroleum by-products are formed and how they may be used.

was controlled chiefly by *gauleiters*.

a. These men were chosen by the Nazis, not by the people they governed.

b. They enforced Nazi laws and issued orders over which the people of Norway and Poland had no control.

(Diagram)   E. This diagram will show why the first two examples just cited are democratic while the third was not. (Arrows show the direction of governmental control.)

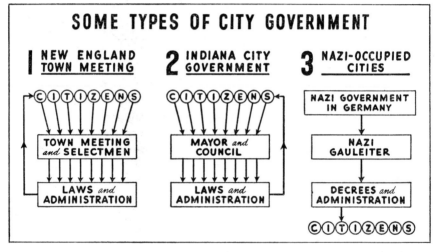

SOME TYPES OF CITY GOVERNMENT

1 NEW ENGLAND TOWN MEETING — **2 INDIANA CITY GOVERNMENT** — **3 NAZI-OCCUPIED CITIES**

(Restatement)   II. Democracy, as Lincoln said of the United States, is government "by the people."

The use of supporting material to establish proof There are two common methods of assembling supporting material to establish the proof for a statement. They may be called the *didactic* method, and the method of *implication*.

128

THE DIDACTIC METHOD

The didactic method is similar to that used to explain a point, as outlined above. It consists of stating your conclusion first, then presenting the proof, and finally restating your conclusion. This is perhaps the clearest and most obvious method of assembling your proof. It can be outlined as follows:

1. State your point.
2. Make it clear by explanation, comparison, or illustration.
3. Support it by additional factual illustrations, specific instances, statistics, or testimony.
4. Restate your point as the conclusion.

THE METHOD OF IMPLICATION

The method of implication consists of presenting the facts first, from which the inevitable conclusion that must be drawn is the point you wish to make. You state the conclusion at the end, *after* the evidence to support it has been presented. This method, sometimes called the "natural" method of argument, coincides more nearly with the way by which we reach conclusions when we are uninfluenced by another person. For this reason, though not quite so clear or so easy to use as the didactic method, the method of implication is sometimes more persuasive. It avoids making your listeners feel that you are pushing something down their throats. It is, in fact, almost the only method to use with people who are hostile to the point you wish to present. An outline of this procedure follows:

1. Present an analogy or illustration which *implies* the point you wish to make.
2. Present additional illustrations, instances, figures, and testimony which point inevitably to this conclusion without stating it.
3. Show how these facts lead unavoidably to this conclusion; use explanation if necessary.
4. Definitely state your point as a conclusion.

Study carefully the sample outline for the following speech. (Note that the *didactic* method has been used. By omitting the first statement, this outline would illustrate the method of *implication*.)

TRAFFIC LAWS

(General Statement)   I. There is a need for better traffic regulation.

(Hypothetical Illustration)   A. Suppose you had an experience like this:
1. You parked just at the end of a parking zone.
2. Someone else pushed your car out of the zone.
3. You were arrested and fined.

(Factual Illustration)   B. Son of the Mayor of Fort Bend, Illinois, was stopped eighteen times but not arrested.
1. Officer stopped the car.
2. Began argument.
3. Discovered boy's identity.
4. Apologized and released him.

(Specific Instances)   C. There are many similar cases:
1. Elmer Jay interrupted an unmarked funeral procession in Sheboygan, Wisconsin.
2. Henry Black violated six traffic rules in Lansing, Michigan, without being given a penalty.
3. Frequent double-parking occurs in downtown sections of Lafayette.

(Statistics)   D. Figures show the extent of traffic law violation:
1. 300,000 motorists were arrested in New York last year.
2. One million dollars were paid in fines by New York motorists.
   a. This is more than the total paid in all England, Scotland, and Wales.
   b. This amount would buy over a thousand new automobiles.

130

(Testimony)	E. Prevalence of this condition is recognized by experts.
	1. Testimony of R. L. Burgess, special investigator for *The American Magazine,* who traveled 8000 miles through cities in twenty-one states:
	"There is ample justification for a growing bitterness among our millions of car-owners who have come to resent and ridicule an outrageous system of traffic law enforcement which violates almost every American principle of justice and equity."
	2. Each day's papers provide new statements of alarm.
(Analogy)	F. It would be almost as easy for an American to eat with chopsticks as to keep track of the traffic regulations of neighboring cities.
(Restatement)	II. Traffic reform is an urgent American problem.

NOTE: Many one-point speeches will not require so many different forms of support as were used above. Most one-point speeches are briefer. This sample was chosen to show how a number of different types of support might be combined.

The use of supporting material to entertain

At times your audience may require entertainment along with your more serious explanation or proof, and there are occasions when your sole purpose may be simply to amuse and entertain your audience. Supporting material for the entertaining speech is assembled around a central theme in much the same way as when your purpose is to explain or prove a point seriously.

The items of supporting material to be used, however, will be chosen for their entertaining value rather than for their clarity or substance, and

"He calmly interposed: 'Many a damn fool would have swallered that.'"

"He had a lusty appe Eating did not inte with his talking."

will be presented less to secure a basic understanding of the subject than to provide interesting diversion. Careful explanation is omitted in favor of lively description and novel fact. Humorous anecdotes and tales of your own or of someone else's experiences, gossip about unusual or important people and events, exaggerated descriptions, puns, irony, and unexpected turns of phraseology—all will serve to illuminate the point you are making and should be used generously.

Do not rely on "canned" jokes. Let one story or observation lead naturally into another, each serving to bring out the point around which your talk is built. See that your tales are to the point. And remember that however much people may like froth, they do not like froth alone. Underlying your jollity, though never completely quelling it, should be a central theme a little more substantial—some sentiment of loyalty or appreciation for the group addressed or the subject discussed.

The talk, then, will consist of a series of illustrations, stories, anecdotes, and humorous comments, following one another in rapid order and developed around some central idea. The following is a simple way to arrange the material for such a talk:

1. Tell a story, anecdote, or illustration.
2. Point out the essential idea or point of view expressed by it, around which you intend to unify the details of your speech.

Members of the Texas State Folklore Society listen to J. Frank Dobie, authority on the folklore of the Southwest, tell some "tall tales" about Sam Houston and the early days in Texas. Notice how, by facial expression and gesture, Mr. Dobie practically enacts his story. The technique, of course, is effective in any talk for entertainment.

Sam Houston was for President..."

" 'He's nothing but a damned vegetarian,' old Sam Houston bellered."

3. Follow with a series of additional stories, anecdotes, and illustrations, amplifying or illuminating this central point. Arrange these items in the order of increasing interest or humor.

4. Close with an unusual restatement of the central point which you have illuminated.

By developing your talk in this way, you will not only provide your audience with entertainment, but also preserve a unity of thought by which people can remember it. The brief outline below illustrates how one student developed an entertaining speech in this way by humorously developing a central point:

A TOAST TO THE APPLE

(Statement)   I. The apple should be our national fruit.

(Biblical Illustration)   A. Adam and Eve started our life of joy and confusion because of an apple. (Retell the story.)

   B. Apples saved the lives of our favorite childhood characters.

("Literary" Examples)   1. The third little pig in the *Three Little Pigs* was saved from the wolf by an apple.

   2. Alex in the *Bear Story* was saved from starvation by eating the apples growing on the sycamore tree.

(Ditto)   C. Apples are the symbol of our early education.

   1. "A was an apple pie; B bit it; C cut it."

   D. Apples enter into our courtship songs.

(Musical Instances)   1. We sing to her, "I'll Be with You in Apple Blossom Time."

   2. We commemorate the event with, "In the Shade of the Old Apple Tree."

   3. We warn her, "Don't Sit Under the Apple Tree with Anyone Else But Me."

   E. Our own health may depend upon an apple.

(Testimony)   1. As the proverb says, "An apple a day keeps the doctor away."

(Specific Instance)   F. Johnny Appleseed is rightfully a national hero.

(Restatement)   II. So here's to the apple—our national fruit!

When you stand up to speak, remember that you cannot encourage enjoyment in others unless your own manner suggests that you are enjoying yourself. Be genial and good-natured, but beware of appearing as though you are forcing yourself. Do not put on the sickly grin of the lad who was bound he would laugh harder the more he was thrashed. On the other hand, stay clear of the scowling determinations of the overzealous reformer. As Mr. Dooley put it, "Let your spakin' be light and airy." Be quick and alert, lively and animated; above all, don't let your speech drag.

The short speech which follows illustrates the method suggested above for assembling supporting material primarily for entertainment.

The Babies[14]

We have not all had the good fortune to be ladies. We have not all been Generals, or poets, or statesmen, but when the toast works down to the babies we stand on common ground, for we have all been babies. It is a shame that for a thousand years, the world's banquets have utterly ignored the baby, as if he didn't amount to anything. If you will stop and think a minute—if you will go back 50 or 100 years to your early married life and recontemplate your first baby—you will remember that he amounted to a good deal, and even something over. You soldiers all know that when that little fellow arrived at family headquarters you had to hand in your resignation. He took entire command. You became his lackey—his mere body-servant, and you had to stand around, too. He was not a commander who made allowances for time, distance, weather, or anything else. You had to execute his order whether it was possible or not. And there was only one form of marching in his manual of tactics, and that was the double-quick. He treated you with every sort of insolence and disrespect, and the bravest of you didn't dare to say a word. You could face the death storm of Donelson and Vicksburg, and give back blow for blow, but when he clawed your whiskers, and pulled your hair, and twisted your nose, you had to take it. When the thunders of war were sounding in your ears you set your faces toward the batteries, and advanced with steady tread, but, when he turned on the terrors of his war-whoop, you advanced in the other direction, and mighty glad of the chance too. When he

14 Delivered by Mark Twain at a banquet given by the Army of the Tennessee to their first commander, General U. S. Grant, November 1879.

called for soothing sirup, did you venture to throw out any side remarks about certain services being unbecoming an officer and a gentleman? No. You got up and got it. When he ordered his pap bottle and it was not warm, did you talk back? Not you. You went to work and warmed it. You even descended so far in your menial office as to take a suck at that warm, insipid stuff, just to see if it was right—three parts water to one of milk—a touch of sugar to modify the colic, and a drop of peppermint to kill those immortal hiccoughs. I can taste that stuff yet. And how many things you learned as you went along! Sentimental young folks still take stock in that beautiful old saying that when the baby smiles, it is because the angels are whispering to him. Very pretty, but too thin—simply wind on the stomach, my friends. If the baby proposed to take a walk at his usual hour, 2 o'clock in the morning, didn't you rise up promptly and remark, with a mental addition which would not improve a Sunday-school book much, that that was the very thing you were about to propose yourself? Oh! you were under good discipline, and, as you went faltering up and down the room in your undress uniform, you not only prattled undignified baby-talk, but even tuned up your martial voices and tried to sing!—"Rock-a-by baby in the treetop," for instance. What a spectacle for an Army of the Tennessee! And what an affliction for the neighbors too, for it is not everybody within a mile around that likes military music at 3 in the morning. And when you had been keeping this sort of thing up two or three hours, and your little velvet-head intimated that nothing suited him like exercise and noise, what did you do? You simply went on until you dropped in the last ditch. The idea that a baby doesn't amount to anything! Why, one baby is just a house and a front yard full by itself. One baby can furnish more business than you and your whole Interior Department can attend to. He is enterprising, irrepressible, brimful of lawless activities. Do what you please, you can't make him stay on the reservation. Sufficient unto the day is one baby. As long as you are in your right mind don't you ever pray for twins. Twins amount to a permanent riot. And there ain't any real difference between triplets and an insurrection.

Yes, it was high time for a toast to the masses to recognize the importance of the babies. Think what is in store for the present crop! Fifty years from now we shall all be dead, I trust, and then this flag, if it still survive (and let us hope it may), will be floating over a Republic numbering 200,000,000 souls, according to the settled laws of our increase. Our present schooner of State will have grown into a political leviathan—a *Great Eastern*. The cradled babies of today will be on the deck. Let them be well trained, for we are going to leave a big contract on their hands. Among the three or four million cradles now rocking in the land are some which this Nation would preserve for ages as sacred things, if we could know which ones they are. In one of these cradles the unconscious Farragut of the future is at this moment teething; think of it, and putting in a word of dead earnest, unarticulated, but perfectly justifiable profanity over it too. In another the future renowned astronomer is blinking at the shining milky way with but a liquid interest, poor little chap! and wondering what has become of that other one they call the wet-nurse. In another the future great historian is lying—and doubtless will continue to lie until his earthly mission is ended. In another the future President is busying himself with no profounder problem of state than what the mischief has become of his hair so early, and in a mighty array of other cradles there are now some 60,000 future office-seekers, getting ready to furnish him occasion to grapple with that same old problem a second time. And in still one more cradle, somewhere under the flag, the future illustrious Commander-in-Chief of the American armies is so little burdened with his approaching grandeurs and responsibilities as to be giving his whole strategic mind at this moment to trying to find out some way to get his big toe into his mouth—an achievement which, meaning no disrespect, the illustrious guest of this evening turned his entire attention to some fifty-six years ago; and if the child is but a prophecy of the man, there are mighty few who will doubt that he succeeded.

problems

1. In the speeches printed in the Supplement find effective examples of each of the seven forms of supporting material discussed in this chapter.
2. Write short examples (relying on your experiences) of four of the seven forms of verbal supporting material.
3. Prepare an outline for a short talk explaining one point clearly. State the point; amplify it with explanation, analogy or comparison, and illustration; use maps, diagrams, or models if possible; restate the point in closing.
4. Prepare an outline for a talk proving one point, using at least five different forms of supporting material.
   a. Make the outline conform to the *didactic method*.
   b. Revise it to conform to the *method of implication*.

5. Prepare an outline for a short talk to entertain by tying together a series of illustrations, stories, anecdotes, and humorous comment around one central point; use the method described in this chapter.

6. With the outline worked out above in Problems 3, 4, or 5 as a basis, prepare to give a five-minute one-point talk to the class.

7. Prepare a short talk answering an argument made previously by some other member of the class. Do two things:
   a. Point out any weakness, insufficiency, or lack of reliability in the support offered by the other speaker for his point.
   b. Present your own supporting material—show that it is strong, sufficient, reliable.

8. Make a similar talk answering an argument found in a magazine article or a speech heard outside of class.

Chapter 5 HOW TO ARRANGE

AND OUTLINE

RELATED POINTS

In the previous chapter we have discussed the substantial content of which speeches are built. And we have seen how this material may be grouped around a single point or idea to give it support. Most speeches, however, contain more than one point, and we are now ready to consider how to put these points together in a clear and logical manner. We shall see how to arrange the main points in a speech together with their subordinate points and supporting material, and how they may be written down in outline form.

Types of arrangement When you arise to speak, nothing will help you to remember what you have planned to say quite so much as having the points in your speech arranged in a systematic sequence so that one point leads naturally into the next. Moreover, your audience will follow your thoughts more easily and grasp them more firmly if the pattern of your speech is clear. It must be evident to you and to your listeners that you are not wandering aimlessly from point to point, but that your ideas are closely related to one another and that they are marching forward to completeness in a unified and orderly manner. There are several ways of arranging the points in your speech to accomplish this result.

TIME SEQUENCE

Begin at a certain period or date and move forward or backward from that. (Be careful not to reverse the order once you have started.) For example, weather conditions may be discussed by considering in order the conditions which exist in the spring, summer, fall, and winter, respectively; methods for refining petroleum, by tracing the development of the refining process from the earliest attempts down to the present; or the manufacture of an automobile, by following the process on the assembly line from beginning to end. Here is an example of this arrangement:

THE EARLY HISTORY OF TEXAS
  I. Until 1822, Texas was under Spanish colonial rule.
 II. From then till 1835, Texas remained a part of the Mexican Republic.
III. For the next ten years, Texas was an independent nation.
IV. In 1845, Texas became one of the United States.

SPACE SEQUENCE

Arrange your material from east to west, north to south, from the bottom up, from the center to the outside. Thus, the density of population may be discussed on the basis of geographical areas; the plans of a building may be considered floor by floor; or the layout for a city park may be explained by proceeding from the front to the rear. The following shows this type of sequence:

PRINCIPAL AMERICAN DIALECTS

  I. Eastern dialect is spoken chiefly in New England.
 II. Southern dialect is heard in the former Confederate States.
III. General American dialect is common west and north of these two areas.

140

Cause-effect sequence

Discuss certain forces and then point out the results which followed them, or describe conditions or events and then point out the forces which caused them. Thus, one might first describe the surrender of the Japanese in 1945 and second explain the causes of their defeat. A speech on the relationship between war and inflation might be arranged in the following manner:

WAR BRINGS INFLATION

I. Economic inflation has occurred after every major war.
   (A, B, C, etc.—cite examples.)
II. The causes of postwar inflation are these:
   (A, B, C, etc.—list and explain causes.)

Problem-solution sequence

Many times, your material can best be presented by dividing it into two major sections: the description of a problem (or related problems) and the presentation of a solution (or solutions) to it. Thus one might describe the problems involved in building the Alcan Highway to Alaska, and then explain how the problems were solved. Again, this type of arrangement may be applied to problems facing the immediate audience; for example, one might discuss with the members of the senior class the problems of securing suitable employment and then suggest one or more ways of solving this problem. It is even possible to apply this method to discussions of future contingencies: for example, one could outline the problems to be faced by the American school system after twenty more years of increasing population and then present suggested solutions to these problems. When this type of sequence is used with a multiple problem or solution, each of the two main divisions of your discussion must itself be arranged in an orderly way; for this purpose one of the other sequences may be used. In a speech on the control of crime, one speaker employed this method as shown in the following outline:

  I. Our criminal problem is becoming serious.
     A. The crime rate has increased.
     B. Serious offenses are more common.
     C. Juvenile crimes have become alarming.
 II. We must meet this problem in three ways:
     A. We must begin a crime-prevention program.
     B. Our police force must be strengthened to insure arrests.
     C. Our court procedure must be freed from politics.

SPECIAL TOPICAL SEQUENCE

Certain types of information are already cataloged in divisions with which the audience is familiar. For example, financial reports are divided traditionally into assets and liabilities, or into income and expenditure. Some organizations are divided into departments; a talk on the organization of the United States Government, for instance, would naturally be divided into three sections: the legislative, the executive, and the judicial branches. Whenever a partition is already established in the information or argument you are about to present, usually the best method is to follow that partition. Moreover, one's points sometimes consist of a series of qualities or functions of the thing he is discussing; or one may wish to present a series of parallel "reasons why" or "basic objections." Such a series cannot always be arranged easily in a time or space sequence and a special topical sequence should be used. Thus, one might have a series of points like this:

DEMOCRATIC GOVERNMENT IS BEST
  I. It guarantees legitimate freedom to the individual.
 II. It reflects the will of the majority.
III. It deepens the citizen's feeling of responsibility.

Likewise, one's points may be arranged to answer a series of questions already known to be uppermost in the minds of the audience. It would be folly to diffuse the answers to these questions by adopting a different partition of the subject. We shall see how such an arrangement can be used when we develop a detailed outline for a speech on "National Parks" later in this chapter.

The fact that one of the above methods has been chosen for the main topics does not prevent the use of another method for the subordinate points. On no condition, however, shift from one method to another in the order of the main points themselves. The following outline will illustrate the proper way to combine two or more methods:

THE CARE OF AN AUTOMOBILE

I. The Lubricating System.
   A. Every 1000 miles:
      1. Change the oil in engine pan.
      2. Grease front steering spindle.
      3. Grease universal joint.
      4. . . . etc.
   B. Every 2000 miles:
      1. Change grease in the steering gear.
      2. Change grease in the clutch bearing.
   C. Every 5000 miles:
      1. Pack the transmission with grease.
      2. Pack the differential with grease.
II. The Cooling System.
III. The Fuel System.
IV. The Electrical System.
V. The Running Gear.

Notice that the *special topical sequence* is used throughout in the main points, that the *time sequence* is used in A, B, and C, and that *space sequence* is used in the minor points, 1, 2, 3, etc.

Phrasing main points

Both for clarity and for emphasis, the wording of the main points in your speech is important. While the illustrations, arguments, and facts which you present will constitute the bulk of your speech, it is the statement of main points which ties these details together and points up their meaning. Good speakers take particular pains to phrase these main points in such a way that the meaning will be clear, persuasive, and easily remembered by their listeners. To achieve this result, four characteristics of good phrasing should be kept in mind: conciseness, vividness, motivation, and parallelism.

Conciseness

State your points as briefly as you can without sacrificing their meaning. Use the fewest words possible. Boil it down! A simple declarative sentence is better than a complex one. Avoid using a clumsy modifying phrase or distracting subordinate clause. State the essence of your idea in a short sentence which can be modified or elaborated as you present the supporting material, or phrase your point as a simple question to which your detailed facts will provide the answer. Thus, "Our state taxes are too high" is better than "Taxes in this state, with one or two exceptions, are higher than the present economic conditions justify." The latter statement may present your idea more completely than the first, but it contains nothing that your supporting material should not make clear anyhow, while its greater complexity will make it less crisp and emphatic.

Vividness

Wherever possible, use words and phrases that are colorful and provoke attention. If the wording of your main points is dull and lifeless, you cannot expect them to stand out and be remembered. Since they *are* the main points, they should be phrased so that they *sound* that way. They should be the "punch lines" of your speech. Notice how much more vivid it is to say, "We must turn these rascals out!" than to say, "We must remove these incompetent and dishonest men from office." Remember, of course, that vivid phrasing can be overdone. The sober presentation of a technical report at a scientific meeting does not require the colorful language needed at a political rally; on the other hand, neither does it justify the trite and sterile jargon too often employed.

144

Motivation

Whenever possible, word your main points so that they appeal to the interests and desires of your audience. Review the discussion of audience analysis and motivation in Chapter 2 and try to phrase your main points in accord with your analysis. Remember that you will not be speaking merely about something, but *to* somebody; your main points should *appeal to each person* in the audience. Instead of stating, "Chemical research has helped to improve medical treatment," say, "Modern chemistry helps the doctor make you well." Rather than saying, "Travel by air is fast," why not say, "Air travel saves you time."

Parallelism

Try to use the same sentence structure and a similar type of phraseology in each of a series of main points. Since these points represent coordinate major units of your speech, word them so they sound that way. Avoid unnecessary shifts from active to passive voice or from question to assertion. Where possible, use prepositions, connectives, and auxiliary verbs which permit a similar balance, rhythm, and direction of thought. Instead of wording a series of main points thus:

I. The amount of your income tax depends on the amount you earn.
II. Property tax is assessed on the value of what you own.
III. You pay sales taxes in proportion to the amount you buy.

Phrase them like this:

I. The amount you earn decides your income tax.
II. The amount you own controls your property tax.
III. The amount you buy determines your sales tax.

Note, indeed, that a part of each statement in the series above was repeated, while the rest of the statement changed from point to point. Such repetition of key words is often done to intensify the parallelism.

Parallelism, then, together with conciseness, vividness, and motivation, will help to make your main points stand out as you state them.

Arranging sub-points and supporting material

Consider next how the sub-points and supporting material may be arranged to give the internal structure of your speech orderliness and substance.

SUBORDINATING THE SUB-POINTS

A string-of-beads discussion, in which everything seems to have equal weight—tied together as it usually is by "and-uh," "and next," "and then," "and so"—lacks vigor and soon gets tiring. If you emphasize everything, nothing will seem prominent. Regardless of how well you have chosen, arranged, and worded your main points, they will not stand out unless your sub-points are properly subordinated to them. Therefore, at the start try to avoid listing sub-points as if they were main points, and avoid listing under a main point items that have no direct subordinate relation to that point. Here are a few of the types of items that are commonly subordinate in character:

Parts of a whole. Frequently the main point concerns an object or a process which consists of a series of component parts; these parts then constitute the sub-points under it. Or sometimes the main point expresses a summation, the sub-points of which state the items which add up to that summation. Thus the grip, shaft, and head may be the parts of a golf club; or the number of churches in England, Scotland, Ireland, and Wales may be cited as sub-totals of the sum for the British Isles.

Lists of qualities or functions. When the main point deals with the nature of something, the sub-points often list the qualities which constitute that nature. If the main point suggests the purpose of some mechanism, organization, or procedure, the sub-points may list the specific functions it performs. Thus timbre, pitch, intensity, and duration may be the qualities under which the nature of sound is discussed; the objective of a police department may be made clear by discussing a list of its duties or functions.

146

Series of causes or results. If the cause-effect sequence is used for your main points, you will often find that neither cause nor effect is single. The series of causes and results will then constitute the series of sub-points. Even when other types of sequence are used for main points, a list of causes or results often forms the sub-items of a major point. In this way, the causes of a crop failure might be listed as drought, frost, and blight.

Items of logical proof. In an argumentative speech, the sub-points should always be such that they provide logical proof of the main point they support. Often they consist of a series of reasons or of the coordinate steps in a single process of reasoning. When this is done, you should always be able to connect the main point and sub-points with the word "because" (main point is true, *because* sub-points are true) and, in reverse, you should be able to use the word "therefore" (sub-points are true, *therefore* main point is true). An example of this type of subordination is this: Strikes and lockouts are wasteful, because (*a*) workers lose their wages, (*b*) employers lose their profits, and (*c*) consumers lose the products they might have had.

Illustrative examples. Many times, the main point consists of a generalized statement for which the sub-points provide a series of specific illustrative examples. This method is used both for exposition and for argument, the examples constituting, respectively, clarification or proof. The general statement that fluorine helps reduce tooth decay might have as its sub-points a series of examples citing the experience of those cities which have added fluorine to their drinking water.

These are by no means all the types of subordinate items, but these common types should serve to illustrate the general principle of subordination. Remember also that the same principle applies to further subordination under sub-points. In longer and more detailed speeches you may have sub-sub-points and even sub-sub-sub-points! Be careful not to become too intricate and involved in this process, but however far you go, keep your subordination logical.

ARRANGING COORDINATE SUB-POINTS

Usually, there are two or more sub-points under every main point in your speech. While these are subordinate to the main point, they should be coordinate with each other. In what sequence, then, should they be arranged? The answer is simple: list them according to one of the types of arrangement listed at the beginning of this chapter. Choose whichever sequence—time, space, causal, etc.—seems most appropriate. You may want to use one sequence for the items under one main point and a different sequence for those under another, but do not shift from one to another in the same coordinate series. Above all, be sure you do employ some systematic order; don't crowd them in haphazardly just because they are subordinate points.

SUPPORTING SUB-POINTS

The importance of supporting material was emphasized in Chapter 4. The general rule should be, *never make a statement in a speech without presenting at least one item of support to clarify, illustrate, or prove it*. Too often, speakers think that if they have set down sub-points under every main point, they have done enough. The fact is, however, that one can subdivide points all day without doing any more than add detail to the *structure* of the speech. The *substance* of it lies in the figures, illustrations, facts, and testimony introduced. Within reasonable limits, the more you have, the stronger that point in your speech will be.

We have now considered the principles and some of the methods for logical and coherent arrangement of the ideas in a speech. Even with a thorough grasp of these principles and methods, however, there are few persons who can sit down with a mass of material at hand and work out the details of a speech in their minds. Some orderly method must usually be followed for setting these ideas and facts down on paper; the method used by most speakers is that of constructing outlines, a method particularly effective because it serves to throw into bold relief

148

the structure as well as the content of the speech. Noting first the requirements of good outline form, we shall then see how to go about preparing an outline which sets forth in orderly fashion the main points, the sub-points, and the supporting material.

Requirements of good outline form

The amount of detail and the type of sequential arrangement used will depend on your subject, your analysis of the situation, and your previous experience in speech composition. But regardless of these factors, any good outline should meet certain basic requirements:

Each unit in the outline should contain but one item or statement. This is essential to the very nature of outlining. If two or three items or statements are run together under the same symbol, the structural relationship does not stand out clearly. Notice this difference in the following example:

Wrong

I. Our city should conduct a campaign against the thousands of flies that infest the city every year, breeding everywhere and buzzing at every kitchen door, because they spread disease by carrying germs and contaminating food, and because they can be eliminated easily by killing them with DDT and preventing their breeding by cleaning up refuse.

Right

I. Our city should conduct a campaign against flies.
   A. Thousands of flies infest the city every year.
      1. They breed everywhere.
      2. They buzz at every kitchen door.
   B. Flies spread disease.
      1. They carry germs.
      2. They contaminate food.
   C. Flies can be eliminated easily.
      1. Widespread use of DDT kills them.
      2. Cleaning up refuse prevents their breeding.

The items in the outline should be logically subordinated. Those statements or facts that are listed as sub-points under larger headings should really be subordinate in meaning and not of equal or greater importance. Moreover, nothing should be included as a sub-point unless it has some direct connection with the main point under which it comes. Each subordinate point should directly and logically support or amplify the superior point under which it stands.

Wrong
    I. Radio is a direct benefit to humanity.
        A. It has saved many lives at sea.
   II. It makes easier the spreading of news.
 III. Present broadcasting methods are not as good as they might be.
        A. There are too many stations cluttering the air.
            1. Programs are becoming worse.
            2. There are too many crooners, high-pressure sales talks.
            3. There are too many "soap operas."
        B. This is true even though a great many criminals have been tracked down by means of radio.

Right
    I. Radio is a direct benefit to humanity.
        A. It has saved many lives at sea.
        B. It makes easier the spreading of news.
        C. It has aided in tracking down a great many criminals.
   II. Present broadcasting methods are not as good as they might be.
        A. There are too many stations cluttering the air.
        B. Programs are becoming worse.
            1. There are too many crooners.
            2. There are too many high-pressure sales talks.
            3. There are too many "soap operas."

The logical relation of the items included should be shown by proper indentation. The greater the logical importance of a statement, the nearer to the left-hand margin should it be started. Moreover, if a statement is greater than one line in length, the second line of it should be indented exactly the same as the first.

Wrong

I. Shortening the college course to three years is not necessary.

    A. Provision is already made for students who are unable to spend four years in college.

    B. Other parts of one's educational career can be cut short with less loss than would result from this proposal.

        1. The grade school course could be shortened.

        2. The preparatory-school course could be shortened.

        3. The course in professional school could be made shorter.

Wrong

I. Shortening the college course to three years is not necessary.

A. Provision is already made for the students who are unable to spend four years in college.

B. Other parts of one's educational career can be cut short with less loss than would result from this proposal.

1. The grade school course could be shortened.

2. The preparatory-school course could be shortened.

3. The course in professional school could be made shorter.

Right

I. Shortening the college course to three years is not necessary.

    A. Provision is already made for the students who are unable to spend four years in college.

    B. Other parts of one's educational career can be cut short with less loss than would result from this proposal.

        1. The grade school course could be shortened.

        2. The preparatory-school course could be shortened.

        3. The course in professional school could be made shorter.

Some consistent set of symbols should be used. One such set is exemplified in the outlines printed in this chapter. But whether you use this set or some other, do not change in the middle of the outline. Items of the same logical importance should have the same type of symbol, and those which differ in their logical importance should *not* use that same type. Thus:

Wrong
    I. There is a need for better traffic regulation.
        II. Figures show the extent of traffic-law violations:
            A. 300,000 motorists were arrested in New York last year.
            2. One million dollars was paid in fines last year by New York motorists.
                1. This is more than the total paid in all England, Scotland, and Wales.
                a. This amount would buy over a thousand new automobiles.

Right
    I. There is a need for better traffic regulation.
        A. Figures show the extent of traffic-law violations:
            1. 300,000 motorists were arrested in New York last year.
            2. One million dollars was paid in fines last year by New York motorists.
                a. This is more than the total paid in all England, Scotland, and Wales.
                b. This amount would buy over a thousand new automobiles.

In addition to these four requirements which apply to all types of outlines, there is an additional requirement that applies to the final draft of a complete and finished outline. *All the main points and all the sub-points should be written down as complete sentences.* Only by doing so can you be sure that the meaning of each point and its relation to the other points is completely clear.

How to prepare an outline

We turn now to the actual process of getting an outline down on paper. Our objective is to develop in outline form a logical and usable framework for the ideas we intend to present in the speech itself. Our outline should obey the principles of orderly arrangement and logical completeness discussed earlier in this chapter and its form should fill the requirements just listed above. Obviously, one does not arrive at this result in one sudden step: he does not stare thoughtfully into space for a period of time and then begin writing down an outline in finished and final form. An outline, like the speech it represents, grows, develops, and becomes more definite in a series of orderly stages. While the details of this process may vary from person to person, the basic procedure is the same. Your work will move along more easily and systematically if you follow it. In brief, this process is as follows:

I. Select and limit the subject of your speech.
   A. Phrase your general topic.
   B. Consider your purpose and the limiting factors of time, audience, and occasion.
   C. Restate your topic to fit these limits.
II. Develop a rough draft of your outline in the following way:
   A. List, in rough form, the main points you expect to cover.
   B. Rearrange these main points in some systematic sequence.
   C. Insert and arrange the sub-points under each main point.
   D. Note the supporting material to be used under each point.
   E. Check your rough draft: see whether it covers your subject and fits your purpose. (If not, revise it or start over with a different sequence of main points.)
III. Recast the outline into final form:
   A. Rephrase the main points to make them concise, vivid, parallel, and motivated.
   B. Write out the sub-points as complete sentences.
      1. Check them for proper coordination.
      2. Check them for subordination to the main point.
   C. Fill in the supporting material in detail.
      1. Check support for pertinence.
      2. Check support for adequacy.
   D. Recheck the entire outline for:
      1. Good outline form.
      2. Coverage of subject.
      3. Accomplishment of purpose.

Now let us see how this process might be applied to develop a finished outline.

SELECTING AND LIMITING THE SUBJECT

Suppose you had decided to talk about our national park system at a luncheon club. Your general topic, then, would be:

OUR NATIONAL PARK SYSTEM

But before proceeding with your outline you will need to limit this topic somewhat. A review of Chapter 2 at this point would suggest that you ought to consider your listeners' interest in civic affairs generally and in particular their curiosity about interesting places to visit. Accordingly, your purpose should be to inform them both about the federal management of these parks and about the interesting features in the parks themselves. Since only thirty minutes is allowed you for the speech, however, only a brief discussion of the origin and history of park management can be included and your description of the parks must necessarily be limited to a few of the most representative ones. Knowing the interest of such an audience in money matters, you may decide to include some discussion of park finance. You restate your topic thus:

OUR NATIONAL PARK SYSTEM

(Limited to a brief description of its origin, management, and finance, and to some facts about typical parks.)

Only your general topic would be announced to your audience, of course, as the title of your speech; but the entire statement included within parentheses would appear on your outline to indicate the limits you have set.

DEVELOPING THE ROUGH DRAFT

While deciding on the limits of your subject, you will already have selected in broad terms the main topics to be covered in your speech.

154

Now set these down in rough form to see how they may be modified and fitted in sequence. At this stage your list may be in a form something like this:

1. Origin and History of Park System.
2. Federal Management of the Parks.
3. Representative Parks.
4. Method of Financing the Park System.

This list covers what you want to say, but the sequence is doubtful and the subject matter of the points overlaps. A time sequence could be used for the whole speech, bringing in the parks as they were acquired and discussing for each period the changes in management and financing methods; but this would result in too much repetition and might subordinate the ideas which should be emphasized. After considering several other types of arrangement you might finally decide on a special topical sequence based on the questions you know will be of interest to your audience, namely:

1. How did the National Park System develop?
2. How is it financed?
3. What interesting features does it contain?

Under this arrangement, the history of the park system and the governmental agencies involved in its management can be included in discussing the first point and greater emphasis can be given to the points of greater interest.

Your next step will be to phrase these points roughly as answers to the questions listed above and to insert the sub-points under each of them. In this way you can test the sequence you have tentatively chosen; you can see whether it "hangs together" when the details are added. After inserting and arranging your sub-points, make rough notations under each to indicate what supporting material can be used to illustrate and amplify them. When you have done this, your rough draft will look something like the sample reproduced on the next two pages.

155

OUR NATIONAL PARK SYSTEM
(Limited to a brief description of its origin, management, and finance, and to some facts about typical parks.)

I. National Park System developed as U.S. expanded
  A. Early documents imply authority
    1. Declaration of Independence
    2. Constitution
  B. First parks established after Civil War
    1. Yosemite
    2. Yellowstone
  C. President authorized in 1906 to establish national monuments
    1. Federal Antiquities Act
  D. Parks controlled by special agencies since 1916
    1. National Park Service
      a. Authority
      b. Function
    2. Special commissions
      a. National Capital Park Planning
      b. Commissions to conserve shore lines
  E. Coordination of national and state parks — 1936
    1. National Park Service and State agencies
    2. Federal funds for construction, not maintenance

II. National Parks financed from various sources
  A. Direct appropriation of Federal Funds
    1. Source is tax money
      a. 1949 data
    2. Money is used for:
      a. Maintenance
      b. More park areas
  B. Indirect aid from other agencies
    1. U.S. Forest Service
      a. Nursery stock
      b. Fire fighting
    2. Tennessee Valley Authority — lakes and parks
    3. Special public work agencies
      a. C.C.C. cleared forests
      b. W.P.A. and C.W.A. construction
      c. F.E.R.A. funds
    4. Professional assistance from other agencies
      a. Government Printing Office
      b. Bureau of Mines
  C. Fees collected in Parks:
    1. Entrance fees
    2. Licenses for fishing and camping
    3. Hotel concessions

D. Special Gifts add facilities
   1. John D. Rockefeller, Jr. - Smoky Mountains
   2. Railroads - Grand Canyon

III. Representative parks contain interesting features
  A. Acadia - Maine coast - beautiful
    1. Describe coastline: islands, harbor, mountains, lakes, etc
  B. Great Smoky Mountains - Tenn./N.C. - varied
    1. High mountains of East U.S.
    2. Mountain folk
    3. Plant life: figures on variety
  C. Grand Canyon - Arizona - impressive
    1. Great canyon (data on size)
    2. Colorado river erosion (million tons/day)
    3. Kaibab forest
  D. Yellowstone - Wyoming - natural marvels
    1. Geysers: Old Faithful, etc.
    2. Hot springs
    3. Petrified forests
    4. Wild life refuge: bison, elk, bear, beaver
  E. Glacier - Montana - mountain wonders
    1. Geological phenomena - glaciers, etc.
    2. Native Indian settlements
    3. Fishing: streams and lakes

Now examine your rough draft carefully. See whether it covers all the points you want to include. Note whether you have thrown it out of balance by expanding unimportant points too greatly or by skimping on the more important items. Ask yourself whether it is likely to accomplish its purpose with the audience for which it is designed. Check your supporting material thoroughly to see that you have enough examples, facts, and quotable references throughout; if not, seek out what you lack. If you are now satisfied with your outline in the rough, you are ready to recast it into final form.

This phase of your preparation will consist mainly of improving your phraseology and of filling in details. Write out your points as sentences which exactly state your meaning, and see that your outline form meets the requirements listed on pages 149 to 152. As you do so, you may discover errors in logical sequence or weakness of support in some places. These should be corrected as you go along. If your rough draft has been carefully prepared, however, this revision should not be difficult.

Your work in this revision will be speeded if you do it in the order suggested on page 153. Begin with your main points. Rephrase them so they make your meaning clear and vivid. Then taking each main point in turn, restate the sub-points under it, checking coordination and subordination carefully. As you do this, fill in the supporting material in more complete detail, testing it for pertinence and adequacy. When you have done this in detail for each part of the outline, go back and review the outline as a whole: check its form, its coverage of the subject, its adaptation to your purpose. Perhaps by this time your revision will look like this:

OUR NATIONAL PARK SYSTEM

(Limited to a brief description of its origin, management, and finance, and to some facts about typical parks.)

I. Our Park System developed as our country grew.
   A. Early American documents implied federal authority for parks.
      1. This concept was broadly stated in the Declaration of Independence.
         a. "All men are endowed with certain inalienable rights . . . among these are Life, Liberty, and *the pursuit of Happiness.*
         b. "To secure these rights, governments are instituted among men."
      2. This broad concept was reaffirmed in the Constitution:
         a. The preamble lists as one function of the government "to promote the general welfare."
         b. Article I, Section 8, gives Congress power to "collect taxes . . . and provide for the general welfare."

B. As the Civil War ended, Congress established the first national parks:
   1. In 1864, Yosemite Valley was granted to California "to be held for public use, resort, and recreation."
   2. In 1872, Yellowstone National Park was created as a "pleasuring ground for the benefit and enjoyment of the people."
   3. In 1880, Yosemite Valley was declared a National Park.
C. In 1906, Congress delegated authority to the President for establishing national monuments.
   1. The Federal Antiquities Act authorized the President to designate "objects of historic or scientific interest" as national monuments.
   2. The Secretary of the Interior was authorized to accept the land on which such objects were situated.
D. Since 1916, special agencies have controlled the national parks.
   1. The National Park Service was created in 1916 as an agency of the Department of the Interior.
      a. It controls the national parks, monuments, and reservations.
      b. Its function is dual:
         i. To conserve scenery and wild life.
         ii. To facilitate recreation.
   2. Special commissions have been created for special purposes.
      a. One example is the National Capital Park and Planning Commission created in 1924.
         i. Its purpose was to provide parks and playgrounds in and around the District of Columbia.
         ii. It was authorized to obtain land for this purpose.
      b. Another example is the creation in 1930 of commissions to conserve the beauty of shore lines for recreational use.
E. In 1936, coordination of national and state parks began.
   1. Congress authorized the National Park Service to cooperate with state agencies in a study of this program.
   2. Federal funds were promised for aid in the construction but not in the maintenance of state projects.

II. Our national parks get revenue from varied sources.
A. Direct appropriations from federal funds go to the Park Service.
   1. This money comes from the taxes we pay.
      a. For 1949, the National Park Service requested $16,894,150.
      b. This equals about 12¢ per capita.

159

2. These funds are spent for two purposes:
   a. To improve, maintain, and operate existing parks.
   b. To acquire land for more park area.

B. Indirect aid comes from other government agencies.
   1. The United States Forest Service has contributed.
      a. It has provided nursery stock.
      b. It assists in forest-fire control.
   2. The Tennessee Valley Authority has created lakes and parks.
   3. Public works agencies spent large sums for the national parks.
      a. The Civilian Conservation Corps worked in the forests.
      b. The Work Projects Administration and the Civil Works Administration aided construction projects.
      c. The Federal Emergency Relief Administration provided some funds.
   4. Many other agencies provide professional assistance.
      a. The Government Printing Office is one example.
      b. The Bureau of Mines is another.

C. Fees collected in the parks help finance the program.
   1. Visitors to the parks pay entrance fees.
   2. Campers and fishermen pay special fees in certain parks.
   3. Hotels and restaurants pay for concessions.

D. Special gifts often add to park facilities.
   1. John D. Rockefeller, Jr., helped develop Great Smoky Mountain Park.
   2. The Santa Fe and Union Pacific Railroads helped in developing the Grand Canyon National Park.

III. Our parks have many unique points to interest you.
   A. Acadia National Park, on the Maine Coast, is very beautiful.
      1. Its coastline is dotted with wooded islands.
      2. Deep harbors are flanked by rocky bluffs.
      3. Mountains are found beside inland lakes.
   B. The Great Smoky Mountain National Park, on the Tennessee-North Carolina border, is refreshingly varied.
      1. It contains the highest mountains in the East.
      2. Early American culture still exists in isolated mountain settlements.
      3. No area in the East displays so great a variety of plant life.
         a. There are over 1300 types of trees and shrubs.
         b. There are 1700 species of fungi.
         c. Botanists have listed 330 mosses and 230 lichens.

160

C. The Grand Canyon National Park, in Arizona, is impressive.
   1. The great canyon itself is awe inspiring.
      a. It is 217 miles long.
      b. It is over a mile deep.
      c. It is 1 to 15 miles across.
   2. The Colorado River demonstrates its power of erosion.
      a. It looks small compared to the canyon.
      b. Yet it carries down one million tons of sand and silt each day.
   3. The Kaibab Forest provides cool contrast.
D. Yellowstone National Park, in northwestern Wyoming, contains many natural marvels.
   1. The geysers are world famous.
      a. Old Faithful Geyser is noted for its regularity.
      b. Other geysers are remarkable for size and variety.
   2. Many types of hot mineral springs are scattered through the park.
   3. Two petrified forests contain fossils of ancient trees.
   4. The wild-life refuge is one of the largest in the world.
      a. There are herds of bison and elk in their natural state.
      b. Several types of bear roam wild.
      c. Beaver and other small animals are plentiful.
E. Glacier National Park, on the Montana-Canadian border, is a mountain wonderland.
   1. Mountain geology is strikingly displayed.
      a. Active glaciers may be seen at work.
      b. Cliffs and lakes show the effect of wind, water, and snow.
   2. Native Indian settlements may be visited.
   3. Fishing is unsurpassed.
      a. The mountain streams are filled with trout.
      b. Cold mountain lakes abound in other game fish.

Fitting the beginning and end to the main structure

Generally, you will want to develop the main points of your speech in considerable detail before working out a method of starting and finishing it; otherwise the beginning and the end may stand out as separate and disconnected pieces. Strive, instead, to fit them smoothly to the principal content of your speech so that the whole is closely knit. Regardless of whether the main points are arranged in time or space sequence or in any of the other methods suggested in this chapter, you will need to lead your audience into that sequence and tie it together for them at the end. Thus, you must add a section to the start and finish of your outline. For the present these sections may be marked off separately on your outline and labeled "Opening" and "Close," or "Beginning" and "Ending," or "Introduction" and "Conclusion," depending on the terminology which is familiar to you. The structure of your outline should then appear somewhat like this sample:

<pre>
   Opening   I. _____
                   A. _____
Main substance   I. _____
                   A. _____
                II. _____
                   A. _____
                      1. _____
                      2. _____
               III. _____
     Close   I. _____
                   A. _____
                   B. _____
                   C. _____
</pre>

Thus, an opening section for the speech on "Our National Park System," outlined in this chapter, could be arranged like this:

Opening
    I. Did you know you owned property from Maine to California?
       A. You are part owner of some beautiful islands on the coast of Maine.
       B. You own one 140-millionth part of the biggest canyon in the world.

C. You even own large herds of bison, elk, and moose!
II. As a citizen, you are part owner of our National Park System.
A. As a taxpayer, you help pay for it.
B. As a traveler, you can enjoy its facilities for recreation.
III. Businessmen should be particularly interested in the country's largest recreational enterprise.
A. The story of its expansion is an interesting one.
B. The present size and variety of the parks are surprising.

The concluding section of this outline, summarizing its main points and relating them to the audience, could be arranged like this:

Close

I. Remember that you are part owner of our National Park System.
A. The Park Service operates the parks as the agent of your government.
B. A few cents a year in taxes from each of you provides the millions to finance the park system.
C. Your parks are filled with beauty and novelty worth visiting.

In the next two chapters we shall somewhat modify this plan of outlining as we study the adaptation of speech structure to the psychology of the audience. As we do so, we shall use a better set of terms to mark off the sections of a speech, terms which reflect their psychological functions. But we shall see that the beginning and ending and the logical structure of a speech may easily be adapted to the normal patterns of human thought and action, while retaining the unity and coherence which result from careful outlining as explained above.

A final word of advice is here in order. Arranging and outlining the substance of a speech is not child's play which can be casually tossed

163

off in a few odd moments. Time and effort are required to do it well. Allow yourself the time and exert the effort; the resulting clarity and force with which you speak will more than compensate you. Remember too that there is a certain knack to outlining which develops with experience. If you have not done much of it in your study of written composition or elsewhere, outlining will be newer to you and will take more time to learn. As you do more of it, your skill will increase and with it the speed at which you work. Begin now by carefully outlining every speech you make in class.

problems

1. For each type of arrangement (time sequence, space sequence, etc.) discussed in this chapter, select a subject for which such an arrangement would be suitable; then arrange the main points for a speech on each subject in the proper sequence.

2. Rephrase the main points on one (or more) of the topics chosen for Problem 1 so that they exemplify conciseness, vividness, motivation, and parallelism.

3. Prepare an outline of the main and sub-points covered in one of the speeches printed at the end of this book and criticize this outline with regard to coordination and subordination.

4. Arrange with a classmate to criticize each other's outlines for your next speeches with reference to the requirements of good outline form listed on pages 149 to 152.

5. Try arranging in a different type of sequence the material contained under one of the main points of the speech on "Our National Park System" outlined in this chapter. (Or better, try outlining the entire speech in a different manner.) Can you improve it? What difficulties did you encounter?

6. After listening to some good speaker, make a rough-draft outline of the principal substance of his speech. Examine this rough draft critically as if you were yourself expecting to develop a speech on this topic.

7. For your next class speech, develop an outline following the procedure recommended on page 153.

Chapter 6 HOW TO DEVELOP

TALKS TO INFORM

OR INSTRUCT

O ne of the primary functions of speech itself is to provide an avenue for the transfer of knowledge. By means of speech one man is able to give others that which he has acquired by his own experience. This is the problem of the official who has to explain to his staff the applications of a new law or regulation. This is the problem of the teacher who must lecture to his class in physics about a laboratory experiment or the engineer who has to show his workmen how to operate a new machine. The ability to present information in an understandable fashion through public speech is therefore important, and this chapter will consider the technique involved.

Types
of informative talks
S ituations requiring the extended presentation of information are frequent; to enumerate all the occasions at which this necessity arises is impossible. There are, however, three types of informative talks which occur most frequently:

REPORTS

Experts are often engaged to make special investigations and to report their findings. Such reports are often submitted in written form, but the occasion frequently arises for an oral explanation. Teachers, fraternal representatives, and businessmen present reports at conventions and later report their experiences and the information they have obtained to their colleagues back home.

INSTRUCTIONS

Men in charge of work often have to inform their subordinates how it is to be done, particularly when the work is different from the tasks previously performed or when it is of a special nature. For convenience, instructions are often given to the entire group of workers rather than to individuals. Experience has shown that written instructions, while good, are often misunderstood unless first explained orally and demonstrated.

LECTURES

Men and women are often called upon to tell of their experiences and knowledge to groups other than those with which they are directly associated. Four or five such talks are given every week at the luncheon clubs of nearly every American city. The teacher must explain his subject to the class he is instructing. Club meetings, conventions, extension classes—at all these and others, speeches of information are presented, offering people the opportunity of learning about other men's affairs. At all such occasions, it behooves a speaker to present his facts in an interesting and understandable fashion.

Purpose: to secure understanding The one outstanding aim of the informative talk is *to secure a clear understanding of the ideas presented*. Do not mistake the informative talk as an opportunity to show off how much you know. You are not engaged in mental gymnastics to see how much you can "get off your chest" in a given length of time, but in an attempt to help others get a firm grasp on certain fundamental facts. This does not mean that you need to be dry as dust. People absorb information more easily when it is made interesting. Hence, a secondary purpose of such a talk is to create an interest in the information. But although this secondary purpose is important, it must never be made the primary object. Too often the speaker rambles from one interesting point to another without connecting them in any clear fashion. Remember that your principal duty is to make the conclusions of your report clear, to have your instructions understood, or to insure a proper grasp of the content of your lecture.

Organization: conforming to thinking process

We saw in Chapter 4 how material may be grouped around a single point or idea to give it support. In Chapter 5, we saw how several such points could be arranged logically; we are now ready to concern ourselves with the method of putting these points together so that the combined whole will result in clear understanding.

First of all, we must remember that a speaker must not develop his points too rapidly. He must lead the thoughts of his listeners naturally rather than force them arbitrarily. The structure of a talk, then, must conform to the thinking process of the listener.

Hence the talk which aims to present instruction or other informative material should not ordinarily plunge right into the midst of it but should prepare the listener's mind. It should include two rather short but very important preliminary steps: (1) *getting attention* and (2) creating interest in the subject by *demonstrating to the listener his need to know* about it. Unless these two preliminary steps are taken, the listener is apt to say to himself, "What has that got to do with me? Why should I listen carefully? Why should I try to remember that stuff?"

You must answer these questions briefly but effectively before you go on if you want your talk to do the most good. You will then be ready for the third and principal step in the talk, that of (3) *presenting the information or instruction itself.* We shall see as we move ahead that this third step will occupy about nine-tenths of the talk and that it, in turn, must be divided into sections that can be easily grasped and summarized at the end. For the present, however, fix in mind these three steps:

1. GETTING ATTENTION AT THE BEGINNING
2. DEMONSTRATING THE NEED TO KNOW
3. PRESENTING THE INSTRUCTION OR INFORMATION ITSELF

Let us turn now to see how each of these steps may be developed.

GETTING ATTENTION AT THE BEGINNING

Attention must be maintained throughout your talk, of course; but in the beginning step *gaining attention is your main task.* The need for novelty, vividness, and personal vigor is nowhere greater than at the beginning of the speech. But mere attention is not enough for you to secure in this step; that attention must be favorable, and it must be attention directed toward the main ideas of your talk. There are several methods by which this result can be obtained:

1. *Reference to the subject or problem*
2. *Rhetorical question*
3. *Startling statement*
4. *Humorous anecdote*
5. *Illustration*

1. *Reference to the subject or problem.* When you are sure that your listeners already have a vital interest in the problem or subject you are to discuss, it is often enough merely to state it and then plunge directly into the next step. The very speed and directness of this approach suggest movement and alertness. For example, a speaker began his talk to a group of college seniors by saying, "I'm going to talk to you men tonight

about jobs: how to get them, and how to keep them." Notice the brevity and forthrightness of this attention step. Do not make the mistake, however, of beginning all speeches this way. Only when you are sure that the subject itself is of vital interest should you use this method alone.

2. *Rhetorical question.* Often a speech may be opened by asking a question which the audience will be impelled to answer in their own minds, thus beginning active thought on the subject of the speech. A student discussing the fire hazards of the building in which his class was being held began by asking, "What would you do if a fire should break out downstairs while I am talking and the stairway should collapse before you could get out?" Questions of this kind are especially effective if they impinge upon some vital concern of the audience or set forth some unusual or puzzling problem.

3. *Startling statement.* A third method, called the "shock technique" by H. A. Overstreet,[1] consists of jarring the attention of the audience into life either by a statement of some startling fact or by an unexpected phrasing of your opinion. Eugene E. Wilson began a commencement address to graduates at Worcester Polytechnic Institute in this way:

> Today man-made law is in conflict with natural law. Paradoxically, just at the moment when natural science is unlocking the secrets of the physical world, social science is in a flat spin; just as the engineer has created the material things that give promise of an abundant life for the human race, politicians have thrown social orders violently into reverse; individual freedom is giving way to slavery; fear is triumphant over hope. This is a problem to challenge every thinking person, especially the engineer.[2]

Again, Alfred E. Smith began a speech before the New York League of Women Voters by saying, "I have repeatedly said that the State of New York to a certain extent is the victim of its own growth."[3] Whether

1 Overstreet, H. A., *Influencing Human Behavior* (Norton, N. Y., 1925), p. 120 ff.
2 From *Vital Speeches*, Vol. XIII, November 1, 1946, p. 61.
3 *Modern Speeches*, edited by Homer D. Lindgren (Crofts, N. Y., 1926), p. 490.

startling statements are used as the sole method of developing the attention step or whether they are combined with other methods, surprising and unusual phrasing serves an important part in catching hold of the audience. Very often an apt quotation phrased in a striking manner will serve this purpose.

4. *Humorous anecdote.* A funny story or experience often sends a speech off to a good start. To be effective, however, it must be in good taste and to the point. Nothing is worse than the habit some speakers have of telling a joke which has nothing to do with the speech and then shifting abruptly to the subject. The audience will listen to the joke, but their attention is not directed by it to the speech proper. Moreover, be sure, if you use this method, that the anecdote is really funny. If it falls flat, you will be in a poor position. In the example given below note how skillfully the short humorous anecdote leads into the subject:

> On December 31 I completed twenty years in university administration. This reflection causes me some pangs. Lord Northington said in 1765, when the gout caught up with him, "If I had known that these legs of mine were to carry a lord chancellor, I would have taken better care of them when I was a lad." If I had known that this head of mine was to be used by a university president, I would have tried to get some education when I was at Yale. One of my predecessors often talked about education as a substitute for experience. I have substituted experience for education. Still, twenty years is twenty years. The range of data I have examined over so long a period, illuminated by the earnest tutoring you have given me, entitles me to certain conclusions about universities in general and this one in particular.[4]

5. *Illustration.* The example given on page 117 shows how a talk can be started with an illustration giving the facts of an event in some detail. In addition to actual incidents taken from life, stories obtained from literature and hypothetical illustrations describing possible events may be used. In this way the attention of the audience is focused by the story interest and directed toward the main discussion by the point of the illustration. Be sure the story has interest in itself and that it is

4 From ''The University in War and Peace,'' by Robert M. Hutchins. Delivered at a University of Chicago Trustee-Faculty dinner, January 13, 1943. Printed in *Representative American Speeches: 1942-1943*, XVI, 236.

connected to the main idea. The chances that an illustration or story will gain attention are twice as good as those of any other method listed above.

These are the principal ways of gaining attention at the beginning of a speech. Sometimes one method alone is used; sometimes two or more are combined. Note how Robert J. Havighurst, after beginning with rhetorical questions, continued his opening remarks before the National Congress of Parents and Teachers with a series of striking statements:

> Can people like ourselves *do* anything about the family? Or is the destiny of the family as an institution determined by the blind working of social forces, over which we have no power?
>
> The family stands eternal and impregnable in human history, like the rock of Gibraltar, and yet the family is also vulnerable and evanescent. It has a "here today, gone tomorrow" aspect. The lifetime of an individual family is seldom more than fifty years, reckoning from its beginning in marriage to its ending with the death of the people who married. The family consists literally of *what we do* as family members. Every man and woman who marry and start a family take the destiny of the family in their hands. The family is the fleeting product of their passions, needs, habits and aspirations. The family is as old as human life on this planet and as young as this afternoon, when John and Jane got married.[5]

When you are sure that the subject of your speech in and of itself is of considerable interest to the audience, you can frequently save time by going immediately into it. When you do, you will attract attention by reference to your theme. When the audience is not vitally concerned with the subject, however, or when people are unaware of the importance of the subject to them personally, use a startling statement or an unusual illustration at the very beginning of your speech in order to focus their attention. Almost always a "reference to the subject" is inserted with whatever other method is employed. Remember always that gaining attention is only a means to an end and not the end itself. Be sure that your attention step leads naturally into the subject.

5 From *Vital Speeches*, Vol. XIV, July 1, 1948, p. 565.

Demonstrating the Need for the Information

Although it should be short, the demonstration-of-need step is exceedingly important. Many a speaker has failed because he assumed that his audience would be eagerly waiting to seize the pearls of knowledge as they fell from his lips. Unfortunately, this is not often the case. You must show that the information you are about to present will be valuable to your listeners; people must be made to feel a need for it. Suggest how your information will help them prevent injuries, or save money, or do their work more easily, and they will listen to you. Develop this part of the speech as follows:

1. *Statement:* Point out the importance of the subject and the need to be better informed upon it.

2. *Illustration:* Tell of one or more incidents to illustrate the need.

3. *Reinforcement:* Employ as many additional facts, examples, quotations, etc., as are required to make the need more convincing and impressive.

4. *Pointing:* Show the direct relation of the subject to the well-being and success of your audience. (See the "Need to Know" step in the sample outline on page 175 ff.)

You will notice how similar this development is to the structure of the one-point talk described in Chapter 4. In fact, most need steps, if taken by themselves, are one-point speeches: they point out the one thing—need. Develop your need step, therefore, just as you would a one-point talk.

Presenting the Information Itself

You are now ready to present to your listeners the actual information or instruction itself. This step will be the longest part of the speech to inform—from three fourths to nine tenths of it. In it will be included the information for which the preceding step pointed out a need. Briefly, this part of the speech usually involves: (1) *Initial Summary,* (2) *Detailed Information,* and (3) *Final Summary.*

The *initial summary* consists of a brief preview of the information you expect to present. This preview may consist of an enumeration of the main points around which you expect to group your facts, or it may be a homely example containing the simple element of your idea. In this way you make clear the direction of your discussion and help your audience get a clear picture of it in advance. For example, an athletic director once began an explanation of the organization of athletic activities on his campus as follows:

> In order to make clear the organization of our athletic activities, I shall discuss first, the management of our intercollegiate sports; second, our intramural system; and last, the class work in physical education.

Obviously the enumeration of main points in this initial summary should parallel the order in which you intend to take them up, or you will give your listeners a false lead. Properly used, the initial summary acts as an excellent guidepost.

Next the *detailed information* is presented. The main points mentioned above are each considered in turn, and the detailed facts and explanations related to them are grouped around them in orderly fashion. Here you must exercise the greatest care with regard to the clarity of organization. You will find the methods discussed in Chapter 5 quite convenient for the orderly arrangement of your information; review thoroughly the "types of arrangement" (time sequence, space sequence, cause-effect sequence, problem-solution sequence, and special topical sequence) discussed in that chapter.

The fact that one of these methods of arrangement has been chosen for the main topics does not prevent the use of another method for the subordinate points. However, on no condition shift from one method to another in the order of the main points themselves. You must be sure at all times that your speech moves along in a definite direction.

The *final summary* consists of a recapitulation of the main points discussed, with the inclusion of whatever important conclusions you have made clear in relation to them. The final summary is similar to the initial summary in structure, but it is usually not quite so brief. It serves to tie together the information you have presented in order to leave your listeners with a unified picture of it. The following example of a final summary was used by the athletic director quoted earlier:

> From what I have said, you can readily see that the three main divisions of our athletic system are closely related to one another. The intercollegiate sports serve as the stimulus for interest in developing superior skill as well as a source of revenue for financing the rest of the program. Our intramural system extends the facilities for physical recreation to a large part of our student body—three thousand last year. And our physical education classes not only serve in training men to become the coaches of the future, but also act in systematically building up the physical endurance of the student body as a whole and in giving corrective work to those who have physical defects. The work of these three divisions is well organized and complete.

The system of arranging the main body of instruction or information, then, may be outlined as follows:

1. *Initial Summary:* Briefly state the main points in advance.
2. *Detailed Information:* Discuss and explain the facts pertaining to these main points in the order given.
3. *Final Summary:* Restate the main points presented, together with any important conclusions developed.

If presented in this way, the information will be clear and coherent.

A fourth element is sometimes needed in this part of the speech, namely, *definitions of important terms.* There is no fixed point at which these should be introduced. They are most frequently given either just before or just after the initial summary when they relate to the whole body of information to be presented. When they are related only to some one part of the information, they are introduced at the point where the use of the term defined becomes necessary. Frequently, no definition of terms is needed at all. Be sure, however, that all technical terms you use are understood by your listeners.

By now you should have presented your information and secured an understanding of it. The general aim of your speech should be accomplished. Ordinarily, the final summary of main points and the conclusion mark the end of the speech. (There are times, however, when you may wish to encourage further interest and study of the subject you have been discussing—in a sense, to actuate as well as inform. In this event, suggest to your audience how valuable this knowledge will be to them. Then close quickly by suggesting that they make a further study of the matter. Give them one or two sources of further information or call attention to instruction books they already have.)

The following sample outline will illustrate how to organize material in a talk for instruction or information.

Taking Care of Your Roads[6]

(Speech made before Lafayette Optimist Club by Professor Ben Petty, Director of Indiana Road School for County Highway Superintendents)

(Getting Attention)

I. It is a pleasure to be back with old friends.

II. You have asked me to talk on roads, a subject in which I am extremely interested.

(The Need to Know)

I. Most businessmen are too busy to investigate the facts about roads.

II. Yet you use the roads, and *pay* for them.

  A. Indiana spends fifty million dollars a year this way.

  B. Most of this money comes from license fees and gasoline taxes.

III. You ought to be sure this money is spent wisely.

(The Information Itself)

I. Preliminary summary: To understand road expenditures, you must grasp the distinction between three kinds of roads: township roads, county roads, and state roads.

  A. Township roads have local importance.

    1. These are under the control of township trustees.

      a. These men are too busy with other duties.

      b. They rarely understand the road problem.

6 This outline was made by the author while listening to Professor Petty speak.

2. The expenditure for these roads is large.
   a. In this township $29,000 is spent per year—$157 per mile.
   b. Other townships spend similar amounts.
3. Township roads should be taken over by the county.
   a. The larger unit offers better organization.
   b. The county has better equipment.

B. County roads provide for intermediate traffic.
   1. There are 239,000 miles of these roads in the state.
   2. They are controlled by County Highway Superintendents.
      a. These men are political appointees.
      b. It is important for you to see that the right man gets this position in your county.
         i. He will spend $179,000 in this county this coming year.
         ii. The quality of road maintenance is in his hands.
   3. Traffic has increased on these roads in twenty years:
      a. There used to be twenty-five horse-drawn vehicles per day.
      b. Now, 1000 high-speed autos, trucks, and busses use them.
   4. Upkeep cost is $296 per mile—90¢ a day.
   5. There has been a marked improvement in the management of the roads in this county under your present superintendent.
C. State roads handle the through traffic.
   1. During the past ten years, traffic on state roads has increased greatly.
      a. Passenger cars have increased to three times their previous number.
      b. Trucks have increased four times in number.
   2. Yet these roads are less important to your local community than the local roads.
      a. The function of local roads is to make them feeders for state roads.
      b. Most local business comes to town on local roads.
   3. The real purpose of paved state roads is to concentrate the heavy traffic and save the more important local roads.

(Final Summary)

II. Remember that *all* your roads are important.
    A. You call township and county roads secondary.
    B. You should call them *primary*.
       1. Because of better county and township roads, you can travel more easily in Indiana than in any other state.

176

2. Brief illustration from personal experience.
C. Your state roads serve to keep traffic off these primary local roads.
D. Your roads require more of your attention.

From the sample outline above, you will observe that the organization of a talk to inform or instruct will have a skeleton structure somewhat like this:

Subject:_____ : Purpose_____

(Getting Attention)

I. (Opening statement)_____
  A. (Support) _____
    1, 2, etc. (Details)_____
  B. (Support) _____
II. (Statement or restatement)_____

(The Need to Know)

I. (Statement of need)_____
  A. (Main supporting statement)_____
    1, 2, etc. (Support)_____
  B. (Main supporting statement)_____
  C, D, etc._____
II. (Pointing statement relating to audience)_____
  A, B, etc. (Support)_____
III. (Summary statement)_____

(The Information Itself)

I. (Statement of subject, including
preliminary summary)_____
  A. (Statement of first main
  division of subject)_____
    1. (Support) _____
      a. (Detail) _____
      b. (Detail) _____
    2. (Support) _____
  B, C, etc. (Statements of other main
  divisions of subject)_____
II. (Summary statement)_____
  A, B, C. (Recapitulation of main points)_____

When you begin outlining such a talk of your own, a good way to proceed is to lay out a copy of the skeleton plan presented above and then fill in the main points and supporting material in terms of your own subject matter.

The choice
of effective
supporting material

The arrangement of main points in the structure of a talk giving instruction or information should now be clear to you. Consider more carefully now the material used to fill in that structure. Just as supporting material is needed to give substance and clarity to *one* point (see Chapter 4), so must illustrations, comparisons, demonstrations, and the like be used to develop *each* of the main points in the longer informative talk. In fact, the main body of such a talk will consist of a series of one-point talks following one another in systematic fashion. Notice in Professor Petty's talk how each of the three sections—township, county, and state roads—is really a one-point talk; taken together the three form a coordinated explanation of the larger subject, the road system of the state as a whole. It would be wise at this point for you to review Chapter 4 thoroughly, especially those parts dealing with the use of supporting material to explain points.

Holding
the listener's interest

No matter how clearly organized your talk is, however, or how well developed with explanatory material, it will fail to do the job unless your audience listens with close attention. Listening to someone talk is not easy; drowsiness comes readily, especially after a heavy meal or strenuous exercise. You must take pains, therefore, to choose material that will hold your listeners' interest.

Attention is a great deal like electricity: we don't know exactly what it is, but we do know what it does and what conditions bring it about. A baseball fan is sitting in the bleachers. The count is three and two. The pitcher wraps his fingers round the ball, winds up, and sends a hot one sizzling over the plate. The umpire bawls out, "Strike three; yer out!" Only then does the spectator lean back, take a long breath, and notice what has been going on about him: the man behind him who has all this time been thumping him on the back, the sack of peanuts he dropped, the threatening clouds that have suddenly come up, the hornet buzzing around his ankles. What has happened? We say his attention was focused on the game. Those things to which he was paying attention controlled his entire thought and action, forcing everything else into the background. It has been said that *what holds attention, controls action*, and that without attention speaking is absolutely useless. Certainly the most influential speakers have been those who have gripped the attention of their audiences.

How, then, can we capture the attention of an audience and hold it? A great deal depends upon the way in which the speaker talks, upon his platform manner and his voice. The reputation of the speaker and his prestige will also help determine the degree of attention accorded him. But we are here concerned with the speech content. What type of things that a speaker can say will command the attention of his audience? The qualities of subject matter which capture the spontaneous attention of an audience may be called *the factors of interest*. They are:

1. *Activity or Movement*   6. *Suspense*
2. *Reality*   7. *Conflict*
3. *Nearness*   8. *Humor*
4. *Familiarity*   9. *The Vital*
5. *Novelty*

These qualities, of course, overlap and frequently combine in a single statement or example, but consider them first separately.

1. *Activity.* If you were at a football game and one player was sitting on the bench while another was running with the ball, which player would you look at? The moving one, of course. Your speech likewise must move. Stories of action in which something happens have this quality. Instead of describing the structure of a machine, show how it works—get the wheels turning.

Your talk as a whole should also move. Nothing is so boring as a talk that seems to get nowhere. Make the movement of your speech clear to your audience by indicating when you have done with one point and are about to move on to the next; and don't spend too much time on one point—don't elaborate the obvious.

2. *Reality.* The earliest words a child learns are names of objects and of tangible acts related to them. This interest in reality persists throughout life. The abstract proposition $2+2=4$ may be true, but it holds little interest. Instead of talking abstract theory, talk in terms of people, events, places, tangible circumstances. Use pictures, diagrams, and charts; tell what happened to Dr. Smith when he fell out of the boat; use all the forms of support possible; make your descriptions vivid. And remember particularly that individual cases are more real than general classifications. Instead of saying, "A certain friend of mine—" call him by name. Instead of camp, say *what* camp or *what kind* of camp.

3. *Nearness.* A direct reference to someone in the group, to some object near at hand, to some incident which has just occurred, or to the immediate occasion for which the talk is being made will usually get attention. A reference to some remark of the preceding speaker has the same effect. The next time your listeners start dozing while you are speaking, try this on them: use a hypothetical illustration in which you name one of them as the supposed chief character. The name will wake up not only that person but everyone near him as well.

4. *Familiarity.* Some things which are not near at hand are still familiar to us because of the frequency with which we meet them in

180

our daily lives. Thus, knives and forks, rain, shaving, classes, and a host of other common objects and events become closely built into our experiences. Because of this very intimate connection with ourselves familiar things catch our attention. We say, "Ah, that is an old friend." But as with old friends, we become bored if we see too much of them and nothing else. The familiar holds attention only when it is brought up in connection with something unfamiliar or when something about it that we had not noticed before is pointed out. Thus, stories about Lincoln and Washington are interesting because we feel familiar with their characters; but we don't like to hear the same old cherry tree or rail-splitter stories about them unless the stories are given a new twist.

5. *Novelty.* An old newspaper proverb has it that when a dog bites a man, it's an accident; when a man bites a dog, it's news. We pay immediate attention to that which is new or unusual. Airplanes fly daily the hundreds of miles from Chicago to New York, but there is nothing in the papers about them unless they crash.

Be careful, however, not to discuss things whose novelty is so profound that they are entirely unfamiliar. Remember that your audience must know what you are talking about, or attention will be lost. A balanced combination of the new and the old, of the novel and the familiar brings the best results.

There are two special types of novelty: the novelty of *size* and that brought out by *contrast*.

a. Size. Objects that are extremely large or extremely small attract our attention. People are often startled into attention by large figures, especially if they are much larger than commonly supposed or than numbers with which they are familiar. In an address given at the University of Virginia Henry W. Grady remarked, "A home that cost three million dollars and a breakfast that cost five thousand are disquieting facts." Notice that mere size alone will not always attract attention, but *unusual* size. Reference to a truck costing five thousand dollars or a bridge worth three million would hardly have been striking. The New Yorker pays no attention to the great height of the sky-scrapers, but the newcomer may get a cramp in his neck gazing up at the Empire State Building.

b. Contrast. How much more compelling the facts mentioned by Grady become when he throws them in contrast with others: "Our great wealth has brought us profit and splendor, but the status itself is a menace. A home that cost three million dollars and a breakfast that cost five thousand are disquieting facts to the millions who live in a hut and dine on a crust. The fact that a man . . . has an income of twenty million dollars falls strangely on the ears of those who hear it as they sit empty-handed with children crying for bread."[8]

6. *Suspense.* A large part of the interest which people have in a mystery story arises from the uncertainty of its solution. If the reader were told at once who had killed the murdered man and how and when the deed was done, the rest of the book would never be read. An effective advertisement began in this way: "The L. J. Smithson Co. had experienced a high accident rate for two years, but last year accidents were cut over ten per cent." Immediately you wonder, "How did they do it?" Few people go to see what they think will be a one-sided foot-ball game; the result is too nearly certain. The suspense of an evenly matched game draws a crowd. Hold the attention of your listeners by pointing out results the cause of which must be explained (like the example mentioned above), or by calling attention to a force the effect of which is uncertain. Keep up the suspense in the stories you use to illustrate your points. Mention some valuable information that you expect to divulge later on in your talk but that first requires an understanding of the immediate point. Make full use of the factor of suspense, but remember two things: (*a*) Don't make your point so very uncertain that the listeners lose all hope of solving the riddle; give them a large

8 From an address before the literary societies of the University of Virginia given by Henry W. Grady, June 25, 1889.

enough taste to make them want to know more. *(b)* Make sure the situation is important enough that the suspense matters.

7. *Conflict.* The opposition of forces compels attention. In a sense, conflict is a form of activity, but it is more than that—it is a clash between opposing actions. In another sense it suggests uncertainty, but even when there is little doubt of the outcome the very conflict draws some attention. Dog fights, election contests, the struggle of man with the adverse elements of nature and disease—all these have the attraction of conflict in them, and people are interested when you describe them. Controversial issues are of more interest than those agreed to. Disagreement with a group will bring more attention than agreement, though it is sometimes dangerous. A vigorous attack upon some enemy force—crime, graft, a personal opponent, or military foe—will draw attention without that risk. Describe a fight, show the opposition between two forces, or make a verbal attack yourself, and people will follow you with interest.

8. *Humor.* Laughter indicates enjoyment, and people pay attention to that which they enjoy. Few things will hold the attention of listeners as well as a judicious use of humor. It serves as relaxation from the tension which other factors of attention often create and thus prevents fatigue while still retaining control over the thoughts of the listener. Funny anecdotes and humorous allusions serve to brighten many a talk. For the present let us be content with two requirements for its effective use: *(a)* *Relevancy,* beware of getting off the point being discussed; *(b)* *Good taste,* avoid humor at occasions where it would be out of place, and avoid particular types of humor which would offend the specific group before you. Do not use jokes about race or religion unless they are in good taste.

9. *The Vital.* People always pay attention to those things which affect their life or health, their reputation, property, or employment. If you can show a man that what you say concerns him or his family, he will

consider your discussion vital and will listen intently. Even the danger to someone else's life attracts attention because we tend to identify ourselves with others. If the other eight factors of attention are important in speech, this one is indispensable. If your comments concern the vital problems of your audience, they will listen.

These nine factors of interest should be **your constant** guide in the selection of material with which to develop **your talk.** The application of these factors of attention can best be **illustrated** by examining the text of an effective talk. Analyze the following:

"Here Comes Trouble, Out of China"[7]
THE FALL OF SHANGHAI

By FRANK H. BARTHOLOMEW, *Vice President, United Press Associations*
Delivered before the Economic Club of Detroit, Michigan, December 5, 1949

I would like to give you a brief description of what it is like when a great city falls to the Communists—Shanghai, sixth largest city in the world, and the richest prize that ever went under the Red flag.

I got into Shanghai right after Nanking fell and landed at the Lunghwa Airport. It was a scene of the utmost confusion of wealth in panic—that's the only way I can describe it. In the course of my job as a reporter I have seen strife and turmoil and warfare in a good many lands and different situations, but never anything like Lunghwa. It seemed as though the entire population of Shanghai were thronging the airport; rich Chinese carrying all the portable wealth they could bring with them—the women were bedecked with jewels, servants were carrying small trunks, which obviously contained coins or jewelry; all possible portable wealth—paintings, all that sort of thing; rich silk robes were stacked up in mounds, guarded as best they could be by various members of the families who were attempting to evacuate. The public announcer system was a babel of shrieking Chinese. The control tower was fighting with aircraft which were stacked up waiting to come in.

When a plane would land there would be a tremendous rush to get aboard. Nobody had tickets, reservations, or even inquired what its destination was. The idea was just to get aboard, put your goods aboard. I never saw anything

7 Abridged from *Vital Speeches*, Vol. XVI, February 1, 1950. By permission of Mr. Bartholomew.

to equal it. All planes were involved: Pan-American, Northwest Airlines, of the American flag; and then Chennault's line, and the China National Airways.

I had a great deal of trouble in getting through this crowd myself, into Shanghai, naturally, and in getting through customs. One of the difficulties was that while they were appraising my very modest effects, a portable typewriter and a Valpack with a few shirts, the rate of exchange had risen so rapidly that I couldn't buy enough Chinese dollars there to pay the customs. But my troubles were a mere nothing to those of an Australian newsreel photographer who was with me and who was assessed twenty-million dollars duty on his raw film. Well, that staggered me, but that was my first time into Shanghai. We borrowed the twenty-million dollars from the Northwest Airlines (God Bless Them!) and bailed this fellow out of customs. I think the actual cash equivalent was nine or ten dollars, but it does take a lot of bills.

We got on a rickety bus and started into Shanghai, and about a mile down the road we came to a road block of Nationalist soldiers. They had built an amazing fence. It was about eight feet high, built of peeled poles, and it seemed to run in each direction as far as the eye could see. And at this opening where the narrow road went through the fence were two machine guns in position.

Sentries unloaded our bus at gunpoint, and everyone was asked to produce identification papers. Outside of the Australian and myself, the rest of them aboard were Orientals, and they had all sorts of trouble, because no matter what sort of document they exhibited, a tremendous argument ensued and many of them were hauled off to the guardhouse. I only had my passport and I didn't propose to risk that with any sentry, and the Australian was in the same position, so we simply made motions that we possessed nothing, and he very smilingly nodded for us to go ahead. Having no papers there was no trouble. After we got started, a bilingual Chinese on the bus said that the main trouble back there was that the sentries not only couldn't read English, they couldn't read Chinese either, so every time they got a document this terrific babble of argument broke out as to what the document probably said.

About this fence. Later on I followed it for more than 20 miles with an American military observer. It semi-circled Shanghai and represented the Nationalists' idea of the defense of the city against an artillery bombardment. The American military observer said, "Well, Bartholomew, there you see the net result of all our effort down the years to teach military strategy and tactics to the Chinese. They listen, they are very apt, and appreciative, and understanding, and the first time the pressure is on, what happens? They remember that their ancestors were protected by the Great Wall of China, and there isn't time to go in for masonry, so they do the next best thing and build a wooden fence."

We proceeded into Shanghai through the unbelievably fertile rice fields that surround the city. China is a land of tremendous fertility both as to crops and people. Regardless of the impression we get in this country of the results of the drought and the famine, it takes a tremendous fertility to support the most populous nation of the globe, of course.

Going into the city proper we passed the automobile salesrooms, and I want to tell you there were some rare bargains offered. If you think competition is beginning to develop in the sale of automobiles manufactured in this magnificent city of yours, you should have been there with me and seen new Buicks offered for $300 and other cars in proportion. The idea was that they take your $300, and sell you the automobile, and then you could figure out how to keep it away from the Communists. There were no roads leading out of Shanghai. The communists had the city encircled, and had the Nationalists backed up against the sea and the Yang-tze River. That gave me a real touch of claustrophobia. I knew there was real trouble when automobiles could be purchased for $300. . . .

I have painted a picture of pandemonium in this great city of six-million, but I had better try to set it back into its true perspective and balance, because actually all the panic and dismay and turmoil was confined to about 15,000 Europeans, including Americans, and 500,000 Chinese who owned the wealth of the city—the great buildings along the Bund, which would remind you of Chicago's lake front, the electric power, tramway and telephone systems—in all, the possessors of the wealth in the wealthiest city in the Orient. I came to realize, in the weeks that followed, that the remaining five and one-half million people in Shanghai were more or less apathetic to the developments of the war, but they had a great and immediate concern with getting enough to eat for themselves and their families.

To give you an idea of Chinese thinking, the city council of Shanghai was called into executive session on the last day of April, with the Com-

186

munists almost up to the wooden fence. We sent reporters over because it was a closed meeting. The deliberations went on for four or five hours; finally, I got a phone call back from one of our men. He said, "They have just decided to effect daylight saving May 1."

I came to realize, also, that the Chinese has very little patriotism in the sense that we understand it. He is essentially and above all things a trader and a merchant. He has a strong sense of obligation, but it's channeled to his immediate family—to his wife and his children—to see that they are fed and properly housed. It seemed to me that he had little feeling of responsibility for the ills of his neighbors, and almost none at all for his nation. I'm referring now to the rank and file of the Chinese; to the millions who make up China, and not to the educated level that is in distress now. . . .

The Nationalists had occupied all the great buildings on the Bund by now and had set up anti-aircraft batteries on the roofs. Troops were quartered in the great hotels, including Sir Victor Sassoon's magnificent Cathay House. Across the street at the Palace Hotel I saw a whale of a commotion going on. A company of soldiers from the country—cavalry—were insisting on marching into the lobby and bringing their steeds in with them to be quartered, and the manager was doing his futile best to separate the men from the horses, but he lost. . . .

However, there was a more serious aspect to it. The preparations for the defense of Shanghai were intense. Military telephone wires were strung everywhere—across the streets, blockading, cutting off traffic; there were barbed wire entanglements at almost every corner; sandbagged machine gun emplacements; tanks were rumbling through the city; foot soldiers marching and counter-marching; commissary units and all of that. The police went around executing suspected traitors wherever they found them by the simple process of making them kneel and then pistoling them through the back of the head. That was going on all over Shanghai.

The sky every night was ablaze with tracer shells of artillery and the rumble of guns was coming continuously closer.

But what the opposing armies were shooting at was more than I could find out. With the American military observer I went through the wooden fence and out into the country-side between the armies, almost to the sentries and the advanced units of the oncoming Red Army. We certainly saw plenty of artillery and heard plenty of shooting, but I never saw a shell pass overhead and I never saw anything or anyone hit, except by police or sentries. I can't tell you today whether they were shooting blanks, shooting up into the air or whether both armies were made up exclusively of the world's worst marksmen.

There were rumors in Shanghai that the defending army was negotiating with the property holders to sell out and depart—that they were negotiating a bribe not to defend the city. Had a real artillery battle been precipitated it would, of course, have reduced the Bund to rubble. I don't know whether these stories are true or not, but strange things happen in the Orient and in all I saw of the war in China I have yet to observe a man get shot except by execution.

Sunday night the British Consulate circulated a mimeographed letter urging all British nationals to make their way "by any means"—which meant on foot—to the seaplane base at Lunghwa, seven miles outside the city, and to prepare for evacuation by the Royal airforce. Each Britisher was allowed to take exactly 20 pounds of luggage.

I went out on that grey morning to watch the British depart and admired the businesslike way in which the evacuation was accomplished by Short-Sunderland flying boats, with R.F.C. crews. . . . The British were away by noon—Britishers who had lived all their lives in Shanghai, and who had to abandon their homes and fortunes on 10 hours notice—and the weather began to close in.

Then the Communists marched down to one end of the field and captured the outer homing beacon. That was enough for Pan-American Airways. They dispatched their last planes northward to Tokyo, and cleared the field and their part of it. With the station manager and field personnel of Northwest Airlines, I decided to wait for the last American plane to arrive and depart, which was a DC-4 from Korea bound for Manila.

It was quite a day, with a lot of things slowly closing in—the Communists marching up the 9,000 foot runway and fortunately taking their time about it; the weather front coming down solidly to remind us that the Navy had taken the GCA apparatus so no instrument landings were possible. This was because, as you know, this is classified equipment and they didn't want it to fall in the hands of the Communists. Finally overhead an American airplane appeared, and it crossed the field and crossed the city and disappeared. I had a rather sinking feeling that we had missed the bus for sure, and I believe it was shared by the Northwest Airlines field personnel because there was a rush up to the control tower to talk the plane in. It turned out that the pilot had been fired on as he was approaching Shanghai, and he simply wanted to go out and circle the field—"case the joint," as we say in the trade—and come back. He brought the plane down just under the weather, and I want to assure you that we were all aboard in very short order—a photographer for the Associated Press, one for the International News Service, a Catholic priest, two nuns, the air field's personnel and myself. The door slammed, the plane was gunned and after the shortest run I've ever seen for a big aircraft, we were climbing steeply over the heads of the soldiers marching in, and over the burning villages suburban to Shanghai proper. At midnight we were in Manila and the Communists were in Shanghai.

Summary of essentials for informative talks

Remember, then, that there are four essential requirements for a talk given to instruct or inform a group:

1. *Clear organization is the first requirement.* To secure clear organization, observe the following rules: (1) Do not have too many main points. If possible, reduce your ideas to three or four principal topics. Then group the remaining facts under these main headings. (2) Make clear the logical relation between your main points. Keep moving in the same direction. Be consistent; don't jump back and forth from one point to another. (3) Make your transitions clear. As you move from one main topic to another, let your audience know about it. When you start talking about China, say so definitely, or your hearers may think that you are still talking about India. If necessary, go so far as to enumerate your points, "First, second, third, etc."

2. *Use concrete data—don't be abstract.* This is the second essential in the content of a speech for information. Not only must your speech have a clear structure; it must be meaty. But there are ways of presenting facts; they may be made dull or interesting, vague or clear. Two things need to be kept in mind. (1) Do not sacrifice clarity for excessive detail.

Nearly every rule has exceptions, but do not endanger the understanding of a rule by too detailed a discussion of the exceptions. Unless extreme accuracy of detail is essential, present statistics in round numbers in order that the smaller digits may not prevent a comprehension of the larger one. Say "a little over two million," rather than "2,001,397." (2) Use charts, graphs, and maps, models, etc., whenever necessary. Oftentimes a point can be more clearly seen than heard. A diagram of a machine will make its operation easier to explain; columns and pied circles make proportions clearer; written tabulations of facts or figures make their explanation more simple. Diagrams or charts of this sort should be put on a blackboard or hung on a standard where the audience can easily see them, or they may be put on paper and distributed.

3. *Avoid dullness by the occasional use of figures of speech and humor.* There is a limit to people's capacity for absorbing facts. The wise speaker recognizes this and relieves the heaviness of his speech by an occasional humorous comment or figure. He also controls the length of his speech to meet his listeners' capacity.

4. *Connect the unknown with the known.* People learn new things by associating them with what they already know. If you are talking to a group of physicians, compare the facts which you are presenting to those things with which their profession makes them familiar. An educator, for example, talking to a group of manufacturers on the

Note how Mr. Dewey's facial expression and use of gesture change as he shifts from a light mood to a serious one. Some of Mr. Dewey's critics maintain that his manner and gestures are too definitely calculated, but the people in this Wisconsin audience seem to be listening intently—even the children. The manner of speaking should emphasize naturally the meaning of what the speaker says. Variety and contrast in the manner of speaking help to maintain interest at a high level.

190

"This country is not finished."

"I've been for Dewey ever since he licked them Spaniards at Manila."

problems of college education, presented his information in terms of "raw material," "casting," "machining," "polishing," and "assembling."

The
manner of speaking

The manner of delivering an informative talk will depend almost entirely upon the subject you are talking about and the audience you are addressing. In general, talk slowly enough to be understood and rapidly enough to hold interest. Too rapid a rate of speech will confuse your listeners; too slow a rate will lose their interest. The more difficult the information is to grasp, the more slowly you should proceed, but on the first sign of inattention speed up a little. If you do these things and have a well-organized and well-developed talk, your instruction should be effective.

problems

1. Make a list of as many devices for presenting information visually as you can remember having seen speakers use. Note *(a)* device, *(b)* whether used separately or simultaneously with oral explanation, *(c)* what type of material was presented visually, *(d)* whether the points were clarified or not, and *(e)* whether attention was distracted from the discussion.
2. Find examples (in speeches, advertisements, articles) of each of the factors of interest discussed in this chapter. Present these to the class, commenting on their effectiveness. Be able to defend your viewpoint.
3. Study carefully the speech on page 292 and write an analysis of it. Answer in your analysis (with proof to support your statements) such questions as
   a. How well did the speaker achieve his main purpose?
   b. What method of organization was used?
   c. What attention-securing devices were used?
   d. Was the choice of supporting material effective?
   e. How was the unknown connected with the known?
4. Select some principle of physics, chemistry, or biology, and plan some method by which it may be connected with experiences familiar to *(a)* farmers, *(b)*

automobile mechanics, *(c)* retail clerks, *(d)* housewives. Write out a paragraph or prepare a one-minute talk calculated to make this point clear to each of these four in turn.

5. Outline and present a talk instructing a group of men how to perform some important task or operation. Follow the suggestions on organization and material given in this chapter.

6. Prepare an informative talk on some historical, literary, scientific, or economic subject not familiar to your classmates. Employ the technique explained in this chapter to interest them and increase their understanding of this subject.

General Eisenhower speaks with authority and prestige; because of his personal integrity, his knowledge of the facts, and a sincere belief in what he says, he is convincing.

This picture shows him appearing before a Senate Armed Services Committee hearing on preparedness proposals in April, 1948.

Chapter 7 HOW TO DEVELOP

TALKS TO CONVINCE

AND PERSUADE

The essential characteristic of a talk to convince and persuade is that it attempts to influence an attitude or to prove something; hence, it is usually filled with motivation and argument supported with fact, figure, and example. You saw how this is managed in simple (one-point) form in Chapter 4. New situations are referred to old beliefs, and evidence is brought to substantiate the speaker's assertions; there is an attempt to establish or change the convictions of the audience or to urge action of some kind upon them. You should be ready now to handle the more complicated persuasive talks that are a necessary part of the social, economic, and political operations of the society in which we live.

Action and belief are closely related. If you suggest a course of action to your superior or to an executive board, you must usually establish belief in your proposal before action is taken. Moreover, a strong belief will usually govern any action, positive or negative, to which it is related. Thus, the belief once held by many Americans that the oceans were too wide for us to be attacked led them to ignore the threat of growing military power in Japan and Germany and to reject various measures for strengthening our defenses. More recently, the belief that we alone possessed the atom bomb led Americans to reduce the production of traditional military weapons. When you talk to convince, therefore, your purpose may be to urge some immediate action, or it may be to urge belief in some principle or point of view which, though calling for no immediate action, may influence decisions in the future. A speaker can, by the use of psychological appeals, sway an audience to an undesirable action. An ethical speaker will feel morally obligated to make sure that the action he advocates is logically sound and desirable in its effect.

Although the actual decision is the thing you seek, an unwilling decision is of little value, for it is often revoked soon after it is made or serves as a barrier to subsequent decisions. You must make the members of your audience *want* to do what you propose rather than feel that they *have* to. For this reason, two subsidiary purposes should be kept in mind: (1) to impress your listeners with a motive for believing, i.e., self-preservation, power, profit, pleasure, or pride; and (2) to convince them of the logic of your proposal, i.e., the relation between cause and effect, theory and practice, and so on.

Analysis of the proposition

Before going further, consider briefly the process of analysis which must precede the actual construction of the speech which aims at conviction. The speaker himself must understand thoroughly the proposition he is going to present if he wishes it to be accepted, and to do this requires a systematic method of analysis. Roughly speaking, there are two kinds of propositions which a speaker may present for approval: propositions of fact or principle, and propositions of policy.

1. *Propositions which draw conclusions of fact.* If you attempted to get an audience to believe that "the Chinese Revolution was inevitable"

or that "traveling by airplane is reasonably safe," you would in each case be presenting a proposition asserting something to be a fact. (Do not make the mistake of thinking that propositions of fact always *are* facts: instead, they are statements which you are testing for factual proof.) The analysis of such a proposition involves two steps:

a. Determine the criteria, or standards, upon which the judgment is to be based. If you were asked to determine a man's height (a proposition of fact), you would immediately look for a yardstick or some other standard of measure which you could apply to him. A similar standard is essential for the more complicated propositions about which you speak. Very often, the difference between the opposing arguments of two people is not in the evidence itself, but in the standards by which that evidence is judged. Thus, in the propositions listed above, the first thing you would have to do would be to decide what standard to use in judging a thing to be "inevitable," "reasonably safe." To set up definite criteria is especially important when you are discussing propositions which assert that something is good or bad, desirable or undesirable, justifiable or unjustifiable. Are these things to be judged on the basis of economic and financial criteria, or upon moral and ethical standards? Often you will find it well to pick out two or three criteria which do not overlap but which cover all the possible bases for judgment. For example, to determine what is the best insulating material for a house, you might consider the following criteria: cost of materials, labor of installation, insulating efficiency, fireproof characteristics, and vermin resistance.

b. Apply these criteria, one at a time, to the evidence, measuring the fact asserted in the proposition by each standard in turn. Just as you stand your small brother against the door and mark his height with a pencil and then measure the height of that mark with the yardstick, so you must do with the proposition of fact. Indeed, if later when you speak you can get your audience to agree with you on the standards

197

for judgment, and then present evidence to show that the proposition measures up to each of these standards in turn, you will find agreement much easier to secure.

2. *Propositions involving approval of a policy or course of action.* If you were urging your audience to approve of the following propositions, you would be dealing with questions of policy: "The United States *should increase* the size of its military forces." "The football team *should be sent* to the Rose Bowl game by airplane." "Government expenditures for public works *should be cut in half*." In each of these instances you would be urging your audience to do something, or to approve of having it done. You would be urging the adoption of a policy or a course of action. The proper analysis of such a proposition requires that you answer four subsidiary questions, each of which involves a proposition of fact and must itself be individually analyzed:

a. Is there a need for such a policy or course of action? Unless some basis for a change from the existing policy or condition can be shown to the audience, they will be hesitant to approve the one you propose.

b. Is the proposed policy or plan a workable one? Unless it will work effectively to meet the existing need, there is not much reason for adopting or approving it.

Even scoundrels and demagogues like Adolf Hitler can use speech to convince and persuade unless their listeners know how to analyze arguments and guard against tricks of emotional appeal. A thorough knowledge of the techniques of analysis, argument, and appeal will help the honest citizen to secure approval for sound policies and to point out the trickery of those who are unscrupulous.

198

c. Are the benefits it will bring greater than the disadvantages? People hesitate to approve projected plans, even though they may correct present bad conditions if the proposal promises to bring with it evil conditions worse than the ones it may correct. The benefits and advantages of a plan must be carefully weighed along with its workability.

d. Is it better than any other plan or policy which could be approved in place of it? Is there some way of meeting the present need which has fewer disadvantages or greater benefits than the one proposed?

When you are proposing a policy or course of action, consider each of these four questions (sometimes called "issues") in relation to it. Determine the criteria upon which they are to be judged, examine the evidence you have collected, and see how the facts lead you to answer them. And remember that these are the questions that you must later answer for your listeners. Sometimes you will have to present proof for all four of them; sometimes your listeners will already agree upon the answer to one or two and you can concentrate your attention upon the remaining ones.

From what has been said about the two types of propositions, you can readily see how important it is for you yourself to have a clear understanding of the proposition. Work out a clear statement of it in a single sentence, and be able to explain it clearly to the audience. Unless you can make your hearers understand clearly *what* you propose, there is very little reason for trying to get them to see *why*. Moreover, you will find it important to have a thorough grasp of the historical background of the subject, and particularly of any recent events which have made its consideration important.

Incidentally, developing the habit of careful analysis as outlined above will make you a more intelligent listener as well as speaker. You will be more apt to note the weak points and appreciate the strong ones in another's proposals, and thus you will be able to arrive at more accurate conclusions.

The main divisions of a convincing talk

Let us suppose a man is suddenly confronted with a problem. He must first direct his attention to it and become conscious of a need to do something about it; then he must select a suitable solution for the difficulty, become convinced of its soundness, its desirability for him; and finally he must act upon it. This process of human thinking is sufficiently uniform that, in spite of variations in individuals, we can well outline the main divisions of a talk so that they will conform rather closely to it. By so doing, we shall make our talks easier to listen to and more convincing.

This form of speech structure we shall call the *motivated sequence:* the sequence of ideas which, by following the normal process of human thinking, motivates the audience to accept the speaker's proposal. Although not a speech, the following advertisement will briefly illustrate the sequence:

> The South Sea Bubble had burst. All England clamored for the punishment of its directors. Parliament re-echoed with angry recriminations. "Sew them in sacks and throw them in the Thames!" cried one indignant peer.
>
> Yet only a short time before, hopes had run high. The fabulous wealth of South America was to make everybody rich. Shares in the South Sea Company had skyrocketed from £100 to £1000. Landlords sold their estates. Clergymen and widows brought their savings to invest in it.
>
> And now these towering castles in the air had crashed. The King's most important ministers were involved in the scandal. There were suicides, sudden deaths, prison sentences, ruin on every side. But the money was gone forever.
>
> ---
>
> Today, or two hundred years ago—speculative frenzy meets one inevitable end. But though "bubbles" burst and fancy prices fall, solid values still endure.
>
> These values rest on *facts*—not guesses. The investor who makes *facts* his guiding principle in the selection of securities has nothing to fear. Prices at times may be temporarily depressed, but in the long run they will adjust

themselves. The chief problem is to get those essential facts that will make possible a true estimate of *value*—current and prospective.

Here is where Standard Statistics Company can be of invaluable assistance to you. The largest statistical and analytical organization in the world today, "Standard" spends millions of dollars every year for the sole purpose of collecting, analyzing, and distributing accurate, unbiased, pertinent, up-to-the-minute *facts*—facts that will make business ventures and investing in securities less hazardous and more profitable for you.

Its staff of nearly one thousand people numbers highly-trained specialists in analyzing security values and financial conditions, as well as field investigators located at strategic points through the country to study industrial and other properties at first hand.

Regularly, the many varied Standard Services go out to an impressive list of clients, including the largest banks and financial houses in North America and Europe, as well as to thousands of individual investors both large and small.

Whether you have a few thousands, or millions, to invest—whether you are interested in stocks or bonds—whether you want to keep posted on the largest corporation reports and dividend declarations or desire sound, authoritative data on commodity price movements, business trends, or general industrial conditions—whatever *your* particular problem may be, there is a Standard Service to meet your individual need. *You may have the facts on your desk when you need them.*

We will gladly give you further information. Simply write us. Address *Standard Statistics Company, Inc., Dept. P-50, 200 Varick St., New York City.*[1]

Notice that five distinct steps were taken in this advertisement: (1) your *attention* was caught; (2) you were made to feel a definite *need;* (3) you were shown a way to *satisfy* this need; (4) you were made to *visualize* the application of this proposal to you personally; and (5) a definite suggestion was made that you *act.* We might outline these five steps in the advertisement as follows:

1 Advertisement of the Standard Statistics Company in the *Saturday Evening Post,* May 10, 1930.

1. *Attention*

   The South Sea Bubble caused a violent financial panic because guesswork had been substituted for knowledge.

2. *Need*

   Today, you as an investor need to know the facts in order to make safe investments.

3. *Satisfaction*

   The Standard Statistics Co. can furnish these facts.

   a. It is well organized and equipped to secure these facts.

   b. Many impressive clients now rely on our service.

4. *Visualization*

   Your particular problems will be more effectively solved by the facts we can place on your desk.

5. *Action*

   Write us.

Observe that the purpose of the advertisement was to secure conviction and action. With a similar end in view, one might use the same outline for a speech, because the minds of human beings operate in much the same way whether confronted with the content of an advertisement or a persuasive speech. An audience must be guided through the same steps. Attention must be diverted from other things and converged on what the speaker has to say; the audience must be made to realize that a need exists; a method of satisfying this need must be presented and shown to be an effective one; the audience must be made to visualize the desirable condition which the solution will create; and they must be given directions on how to act or what to believe.

If this sequence is kept in mind, the method of organizing a speech becomes comparatively simple. In its complete form the motivated sequence consists of five steps:

1. Getting attention
2. Showing the need: describing the problem
3. Satisfying the need: presenting the solution

202

4. Visualizing the results

5. Requesting action or approval

For the sake of brevity, we shall refer to these five steps as (1) *Attention*, (2) *Need*, (3) *Satisfaction*, (4) *Visualization*, and (5) *Action*.

Notice how the sequence of these five steps was used by Leland Stowe in making an appeal for the relief of hungry children overseas:

(1) I pray that I'll never have to do it again. Can there be anything much worse than to put only a peanut between a child and death? I hope you'll never have to do it, and live with the memory of it afterward. If you had heard their voices and seen their eyes, on that January day in the bomb-scarred workers' district of Athens . . . Yet all I had left was a half-pound can of peanuts. As I struggled to open it, dozens of ragged kids held me in a vise of frantically clawing bodies. Scores of mothers, with babes in their arms, pushed and fought to get within arm's reach. They held their babies out toward me. Tiny hands of skin and bone stretched convulsively. I tried to make every peanut count. In their frenzy they nearly swept me off my feet. Nothing but hundreds of hands: begging hands, clutching hands, despairing hands; all of them pitifully little hands. One salted peanut here, and one peanut there. Six peanuts knocked from my fingers, and a savage scramble of emaciated bodies at my feet. Another peanut here, and another peanut there. Hundreds of hands, reaching and pleading; hundreds of eyes with the light of hope flickering out. I stood there helpless, an empty blue can in my hands . . . Yes, I hope it will never happen to you.

(2) Who would say that a child's life is worth less than a movie a week, or a lipstick or a few packs of cigarettes? Yet, in today's world, there are at least 230,000,000 children who must depend upon the aid of private agencies and individuals. From Amiens to Athens, from Cairo to Calcutta and Chungking, millions upon millions of waifs of war still hold death barely at arm's length. Their only hope rests in the private relief agencies which, in turn, depend entirely upon you and me—upon how much we care and what we give.

(3) A world-wide campaign exists as a demonstration that the peoples of the United Nations do care. Our own branch of UNAC is American Overseas Aid—United Nations Appeal for Children, with headquarters at 39 Broadway, New York City. In February, American Overseas Aid makes its appeal to raise $60,000,000 from Americans. That's something to put peanuts forever in their place. Something big enough for every American to want to be in on.

Every penny contributed to American Overseas Aid will help bring food, medical care and new life to millions of child war victims.

(4) If we could hear their voices and see their eyes, countless millions of children, now hungry and diseased or soon to die, would run and play and laugh once more. It only depends on how many of us hear and how many see. Look at their reaching, outspread fingers—and (5) send your contribution to American Overseas Aid, 39 Broadway, New York.[2]

Observe that Mr. Stowe (1) called attention to his subject with a vivid illustration from personal experience, (2) pointed out the need for funds to provide organized relief, (3) explained how American Overseas Aid was organized to meet this need if enough money were contributed, (4) visualized briefly the contrasting results of starvation or relief, and (5) appealed for direct action in the form of contributions from his listeners.

Remember that these five steps are not of equal length, nor are they always in the same proportion. Each situation will demand variations. At times one or more of the steps may be left out entirely because the attitude of the audience does not require it. At other times, one of the steps may need to be stressed and proportionately enlarged. With this flexibility in mind, let us now see how each of these main divisions of a convincing talk may be developed.

Getting attention

Someone has said that too frequently the attitude of a person about to hear someone else give a talk is "Ho-hum!" You must change that attitude at the very beginning if you are going to convince him. The methods of doing so have been described in the preceding chapter. A review of pages 168 to 171 will remind you how startling statements, illustrations, questions, etc., can be used to overcome the "Ho-hum" attitude and direct wide-awake attention to what you intend to say.

2 From ''Peanuts, Children—and You'' by Leland Stowe. Printed in *Bluebook Magazine*, Vol. LXXXVI, February 1948, p. 52. By permission of Mr. Stowe.

There are two kinds of need which may be shown, depending upon whether the purpose of the speech is—

1. *to urge a change,* or
2. *to demand the preservation of present conditions.*

To develop the need step for the first of these purposes you must make the audience dissatisfied with existing conditions in order to convince them that something must be done. A definite problem must be shown to exist. You must show what is wrong now, and just how bad it is. For example, "The number of carburetors being produced in our plant at Littleton is too small, and for lack of them we have had to shut down our main assembly line at Metropolis three times in the last month." If, on the other hand, you intend to urge the preservation of present policies or conditions, you must first heighten your listeners' satisfaction with those conditions and then show what dangers threaten them unless action is taken to avert that danger. For instance, "The influence of the United States has been greatly increased in recent years, but our security may again be seriously threatened unless we maintain a vigorous and consistent foreign policy."

But although these two types of problem differ in the type of need presented, the *structural* development of the need step in each case will be approximately the same. This technique of development, like that described in Chapter 6, is a fourfold one: (1) *Statement*—a definite, concise statement of the nature of the problem. (2) *Illustration*—one or more detailed examples illustrating it. (3) *Ramification*—an enumeration of additional examples, statistical data, testimony, and other forms of support to whatever extent necessary. This additional support shows that the need is an important one, that you are not enlarging on a few isolated cases. (4) *Pointing*—showing clearly the relation of this problem to the people you are addressing. Make them see that the problems discussed affect them personally; otherwise they will say to themselves, "That is too bad, but what has it got to do with me?"

Let us put this method of development in outline form so that we may clearly see its essential structure.

Fourfold Development of the Need Step

1. *Statement:* state the need—
   a) Point out what is wrong with present conditions. (or)
   b) Point out the danger which threatens the continuance of the present good conditions.
2. *Illustration:* tell of one or more incidents to illustrate the need.
3. *Ramification:* employ as many additional facts, examples, and quotations as are required to make the need convincing and impressive.
4. *Pointing:* show its importance to the individuals in your audience.

Although it is usually desirable, you will not always have to use all four items in the development of the need step. The "statement" and the "pointing" should always be made, but the amount of "illustration" and "ramification" will depend upon the amount of detail required to impress the particular audience you address. But regardless of whether you use the complete development or only a part of it, the development of this part of your speech is important; indeed, you will often find that this step is the most important because in it your subject is definitely related to the needs of your audience.

Satisfying the need: presenting the solution

We have said that the satisfaction step has the purpose of getting the listeners to agree that the belief or action you propose is the correct one—of presenting a solution to the problem and proving it is a good one. Five items are involved in the development of this part of your talk: (1) *Statement:* a brief statement of the attitude, belief, or action you wish the audience to adopt. (2) *Explanation:* make sure that your proposal is understood. Often diagrams or charts are useful here. (3)

206

Theoretical Demonstration: show how the solution logically and adequately meets the need pointed out in the need step. (4) *Practical Experience:* actual examples showing where this proposal has worked effectively or the belief been proved correct—facts, figures, and the testimony of experts to demonstrate this conclusion. (5) *Meeting Objections:* forestall opposition by showing how your proposal overcomes any objections which might be raised.

As you saw in the need step, these five items are not all used every time. Nor must the order always be the same as that listed above. Indeed, the "meeting of objections" can be better done if scattered throughout the discussion wherever the individual objections are most likely to arise. The first four items, however, form a convenient and effective sequence for developing the satisfaction step in a persuasive speech:

THE DEVELOPMENT OF THE SATISFACTION STEP

1. Briefly state the belief or action you propose.
2. Explain it clearly.
3. Show logically how it will meet the need.
4. Cite examples from practical experience to show its soundness. Supplement these examples with facts, figures, and the testimony of experts.

If the satisfaction step is carefully developed in this way, it should cause your audience to feel, "He is right; that is a sensible solution."

VISUALIZING THE RESULTS

The function of the next step is to intensify desire. Its purpose is to make your listeners really want to see the belief accepted by everyone or to see the proposal adopted and carried out. The visualization step should project the audience into the future so that they are impressed with an image of future conditions. Indeed, this step might just as correctly be called the "projection" step, for the effectiveness of it is determined by the vividness of the imaginary projection accomplished. This result may be obtained in one of three ways: by projecting a picture of the future that is *positive,* or one that is *negative,* or one that *contrasts the two.*

1. *The positive method.* This consists of describing conditions as they will be in the future if the solution you propose *is* carried out. Do not be abstract about this. Select some situation which you are quite sure will arise in the future. Then picture your listeners in that situation actually enjoying the safety, pleasure, or pride which your proposal will have produced. Project your solution step into your listeners' future.

2. *The negative method.* This consists of describing conditions as they will be in the future if the solution you propose *is not* carried out. Develop it exactly as you would the positive picture, except that you must picture your audience feeling the bad effects of the danger, or the unpleasantness which the *failure* to effect your solution will have produced. Go back to the need step of your speech and select the most strikingly undesirable things and put these into the picture of future conditions.

3. *The method of contrast.* This is a combination of the two preceding methods. The negative method is used first, showing the bad effects of failure to adopt your proposal; then the positive method shows the good results of adopting it. Thus, the undesirable situation is followed by the desirable one in immediate contrast.

Whichever of these methods you use, the important thing to remember is that the visualization step must stand the test of reality. The conditions you picture must be at least probable. You must make the audience virtually put themselves in the picture. Use vivid imagery: make the audience see, hear, feel, taste, and smell. The more vividly real you make the projected situation seem, the stronger will be the reaction of the audience.

The following is an example of the visualization step using the method of contrast between positive and negative projection. It was developed by a student for a speech urging the use of fireproof materials in home construction.

> But suppose you do build your home of the usual kindling wood: joists, rafters, and shingles. Some dark night you may awake from your pleasant sleep with the smell of acrid smoke in your nostrils, and in your ears the threatening crackle of burning timbers. You will jump out onto the cold floor and rush to wake up the household. Gathering your children in your arms you will hurry down the stairs—if they are not already in flames—and out of doors. There you will watch the firemen chop holes in your roof, pour gallons of water over your plaster, your furniture, your piano. You will shiver with cold in spite of the blazing spectacle and the plastic minds of your children will be indelibly impressed with fright. No fire insurance can repay your family for this horror, even though it may pay a small part of the financial loss.
>
> How much better to use safe materials! Then throughout the long winter nights you can dig down under the warmth of your bedclothes to sleep peacefully in the assurance that your house cannot burn, and that any fire which catches in your furnishings can be confined to a small space and put out. No more the fear of flying sparks. Gone the danger to your wife and children. Sleep—quiet, restful, and secure in the knowledge that the "burning horror" has been banished from your home.[3]

REQUESTING ACTION OR APPROVAL

The function of the action step is to translate the desire created in the visualization step into a definitely fixed attitude or belief, or to galvanize it into overt action. There are many methods for developing this last step in the motivated sequence. The following methods are the most frequently used:

1. *Challenge or appeal:* a definite and more or less emphatic appeal to take a specific course of action or to feel or believe in some definite way. Such an appeal should be short and compelling and should contain within it a suggestion of the principal reason presented in the speech

3 From a student speech by James Fulton.

for doing as you propose. Note how this is done in the following example.

> Gentlemen: the City Engineer has placed in the hands of each of you the detailed plans for improving the purity of our water supply; he has shown that the safety of our children and the health of our entire city demand the approval of these plans; the decision can no longer be delayed. I ask you to appropriate the necessary funds here and now.

2. *Summary:* a quick recapitulation of the main points in the need or satisfaction steps, or both, followed by a definite suggestion of the belief or action your listeners are to adopt. For example:

> For three basic reasons patents on atomic energy should be the property of the Federal Government: first, to give our government a free hand in any atomic energy agreements with other nations or the UNO; second, to insure to the people of this country full utilization of all benefits from peacetime development of atomic energy; and third, to prevent private cartels and other arrangements with nationals of foreign countries, which did much to keep us unprepared for war before and at the start of this war.
>
> For these reasons, I believe that the Federal Government should continue to own all patents on atomic energy. International government is not capable of taking over ownership of these patents. It is not able to prevent cartels, and until some unforseeable future, some Utopian ideal, all patents on atomic energy within the United States should remain the property of the Federal Government, to insure international cooperation.[4]

Or again:

> If we wish to preserve the democratic society in which we live and have grown prosperous; if we cherish the stability that comes from a society of law and order; we must have three components to end private warfare on the labor front.
>
> First, we must have a clear consistent labor policy expressed in legislation which would be fair to employers and labor but which would have the public welfare as its objective.

4 From a speech by Margaret Armstrong, printed in the *University Debaters' Annual 1946*, p. 141.

Second, we must have responsible, enlightened labor leaders who are interested in fostering and not in destroying the stability of society in their mad scramble for power, and who are willing to practice democracy in their own unions.

Finally, we need employers who will give more serious thought and attention to their labor problems; who will, by themselves, attempt to acquire equal status in collective bargaining; who will make an effort to clean out the skeletons in their own closets; and who will stand up and say "no" when they are being pressured into something that is morally indefensible, economically unsound, and intellectually dishonest.[5]

3. *Quotation:* a direct statement made by someone else about the central idea of the speech which suggests the attitude or action you want taken. In using a quotation you must, of course, make sure that it comes from some established authority and that the statement is in itself convincing. William C. Bullitt, former Ambassador to Russia, used this method to close a speech on "The Menace to Peace":

From Eastern Germany to China, men have already learned the terrible truth of William Penn's words: "Those people who are not ruled by God will be ruled by tyrants." And we too shall learn that terrible truth in the sweat of slavery, unless we arouse ourselves now and say to our government that we do not ask for privileges but for duties; that we do not want to hear what we can get from our country, but we do want to hear what we can give to our country; that we know an American is a free man or he is nothing; that we, like our forefathers, are ready to face without flinching whatever fate the Lord God may bestow, ready to give all that we have and all that we are to defend the greatest adventure in human freedom that this earth has known— our America.[6]

4. *Illustration:* a telling incident or story which contains the kernel of the idea or suggests the action you wish the audience to accept.

As I was walking toward the library the other evening, I saw a car coming down Sheridan Road at what I considered too fast a speed for so slippery a night. I turned to watch it as it went past, and it began to skid. All the way

5 From a speech by David Scheinman, printed in *Vital Speeches*, Vol. XIII, April 1, 1947, p. 377.
6 Delivered before a joint session of the Texas Legislature, April 27, 1949. Printed in *Vital Speeches*, Vol. XV, p. 485.

around it went, and then, hitting a dry spot in the pavement, tipped over. But it didn't stop. It went all the way over and back onto its wheels again! And then—more slowly—it drove on down the street.

And I said to myself as I turned away, "Thank heaven for the strength of modern automobile bodies." And I say to you now, "Thank heaven for the foresight of the automotive engineers who design those bodies and whose new designs I urge you to approve tonight."

5. *Personal intention:* a statement of your own intention to take the course of action recommended. This is particularly valuable when your own prestige with your audience is high. The most famous example of this method of closing a speech is that used by Patrick Henry: "As for me, give me liberty or give me death!"

The greatest care must be taken in the action step not to let it be too long. Someone has given the three rules of public speaking to be: "Stand up; speak up; shut up!" It is well here to emphasize the final admonition. Clinch your points briskly and sit down.

The motivated sequence, then, consists of five steps which correspond to the natural process of people's thinking. Talks constructed on this basis may not always be successful, but they are more likely to be successful than those that are hastily thrown together.

OUTLINING THE TALK TO CONVINCE AND PERSUADE

If you develop your talk in the manner indicated above, a skeleton plan of it will appear thus:

Subject: _____

Specific Purpose:_____

(*Attention Step*)

I. (Opening statement)_____

   A. (Support) _____

      1, 2, etc. (Details)_____

   B. (Support) _____

II. (Statement or restatement)_____

(Need Step)

I. (Statement of need)_____
   A. (Main supporting statement)_____
      1, 2, etc. (Support)_____
   B. (Main supporting statement)_____
   C, D, etc._____
II. (Pointing statement
   relating to audience)_____
   A, B, etc. (Support)_____
III. (Summary statement)_____

(Satisfaction Step)

I. (Statement of idea
   or plan proposed)_____
   A. (Explanation)_____
      1, 2, etc. (Details)_____
   B. (Main supporting statement)_____
      1. (Support)_____
         a, b, etc. (Details)_____
      2, 3, etc. (Support)_____
   C, D, etc. (Main supporting statements)_____
II. (Summary statement)_____

(Visualization Step)

I. (Statement of negative projection)_____
   A, B, etc. (Support or details)_____
II. (Statement of positive projection)_____

(Action Step)

I. (Statement of action or belief requested)_____
   A, B, etc. (Support or recapitulation)_____
II. (Restatement or appeal)_____

Do not consider the skeleton plan above as a rigid model; it merely illustrates the general structure. The number of main points and the details of support will vary from speech to speech and cannot be determined in advance. On your skeleton plan fill in the main points with statements of the main ideas you expect to present. See that these statements perform the functions required of them in that part of the speech in which they are used; that is, in the attention step see that they are designed to secure attention; in the need step, emphasize the need, and so on. These statements can at first be roughly worded and later revised to a more accurate or vivid phrasing as explained in Chapter 5. An outline for a speech to convince, for example, might be something like the one below:

"THE JURY IS DISMISSED"[7]

(Attention Step)

I. At the end of a jury trial, the judge announces, "The jury is dismissed."
II. Did you ever wonder how much such a trial costs?
    A. The Orpet trial in Waukegan, Illinois, cost $30,000.
    B. The extra cost of jury trials in the United States is enough to cover the whole outlay otherwise required by both state and federal judiciary.
III. You should be interested in knowing whether the jury system is worth this expense.
    A. As taxpayers, you foot the bill.
    B. As citizens, you may be called for jury duty.
    C. As litigants, you may have to depend on a jury's decision.
IV. Perhaps the jury *system* should be dismissed permanently.

(Need Step)

I. There are three essentials for the satisfactory administration of justice.
    A. Disputes should be settled with speed.
    B. The cost should be kept at a minimum.
    C. Decisions should be intelligent and impartial.
II. The jury system fails to meet any of these requirements.
    A. It permits intolerable delays.
        1. In some cases the selection of a jury takes days or even weeks, says J. L. Gillin in his book on criminology.
            a. The selection of a jury for the Calhoun case in California took ninety-one days and the examination of fifteen hundred talesmen.
            b. The selection of a jury for the Shea case in Chicago took ninety-two days and the examination of nearly five thousand talesmen.

7 Student outline by George Lamb; revised by the author.

2. A great deal of time is wasted in unnecessary discussion and emotional appeal, says Judge Michael Arnold.
3. The congestion of our court calendars tells us that our juries are causing delay.
   a. In 1947 the delay for jury trials in the New York County Supreme Court was nineteen months.
   b. Gregory Mason cites many other similar examples in his article in *World's Work*.

B. The jury system is too expensive.
   1. The Proci case in Suffolk County, Massachusetts, cost a sum of $4400.
   2. The $30,000 Orpet case has already been mentioned.
   3. "These are almost daily occurrences in our courts throughout the country," says J. C. McWhorter in the *American Law Journal*.

C. Juries are incompetent to provide intelligent, impartial decisions.
   1. When a panel of jurors is called, the best fitted are excused.
      a. The following are all excused: doctors, dentists, pharmacists, veterinarians, lawyers, preachers, teachers, city officals, engineers, editors, reporters, and others.
      b. The "ideal" juror knows nothing about the facts involved in the case and must avoid reading anything about them.
   2. Juries are notoriously subject to emotional appeal.
      a. A woman need only be beautiful or young to be freed on a charge of murder, says an editorial in the *New York Times*.
      b. The emotional susceptibility of juries is acknowledged by such men as James Kirby, Clarence Darrow, and Harry Elmer Barnes.
   3. Because of their lack of training, juries are almost wholly incompetent to judge the questions that come before them, according to Harry Elmer Barnes.
   4. The incompetence of juries is demonstrated by the fact that many more jury verdicts are appealed and reversed than are those made by judges alone. (Leon Green, in the *American Law Review*.)

III. The failure of the jury system to meet any of the requirements for effective administration of justice requires that we find a substitute.

I. All trials in the United States should be held before a judge or board of judges without a jury.

    A. This proposal means the abolition of the jury system in trials only.

        1. It does not propose the elimination of the grand jury or the coroner's jury.

        2. It refers only to the "petit" jury.

    B. This plan is already operating successfully.

        1. Two-thirds of all civil cases throughout the country are tried before a judge without a jury.

        2. Ninety-five per cent of all civil cases in Baltimore are tried without a jury.

        3. All but five per cent of the cases in the Municipal Court of New York are tried by a judge without a jury.

        4. The jury is rarely, if ever, used in equity courts.

        5. Juries are never used in courts of admiralty, bankruptcy, or probate.

        6. Ninety per cent of all criminal cases heard in the courts of Maryland were heard before judges alone.

    C. The defects of the jury system have been eliminated wherever this plan has been tried.

        1. It has eliminated delay.

            a. Eighty-eight per cent of the cases which came before such courts in Baltimore were disposed of before the end of the term in which they originated.

            b. The number of criminal courts in Maryland has been reduced one third by the substitution of judges for juries.

            c. The amount of time required for a trial has been cut in half in Wyoming by the introduction of the judge plan.

        2. The expense of trials has been cut down.

            a. Juror's fees, from $24 to $60 a day, have been eliminated.

            b. The reduction of time for trials has resulted in a fifty per cent saving in expense in Wyoming, according to E. A. Thomas, writing in the *North American Review.*

            c. Similar savings in Maryland are reported by Gregory Mason in *World's Work.*

        3. Judges make more intelligent and impartial judgments.

      a. They are better trained than juries.
         i. Most judges are graduates of colleges and law schools.
        ii. Their daily experience in court makes them familiar with human nature as it is exhibited in litigation.
     b. The superior training of the judge makes him far more capable of rendering a logical and just decision than a jury, says Sir James Stephan in his *History of Common Law.*
     c. Any danger of prejudice or bias in the judge can be met by removing his jurisdiction over the case.
         i. A change of venue can be secured.
        ii. The case may be appealed to a higher court.
      iii. Flagrant injustice can be met by impeachment.

D. Permission to waive jury trial in favor of trial before a judge has been recommended by special commissions set up to study the criminal problem.
   1. The Missouri Crime Commission makes this recommendation.
   2. The California Commission makes a similar report.
   3. A similar recommendation is included in the report of the Committee on Jurisprudence of the American Bar Association.

II. The proposal to substitute judges for juries in all trials deserves your support.
  A. It has the support of competent authorities.
  B. It meets the three requirements for the satisfactory administration of justice: speed, economy, and intelligent impartial decisions.
  C. It has worked wherever it has been tried.

(Visualization Step)

I. Unless some change is made, the defects of the present system will continue.
  A. You may be involved in a trial by incompetent jurymen.
   1. Days may pass before the trial even begins. (Description of court-room scene)
   2. The decision will more likely be based on emotion than on intelligent justice. (Description of lawyers' appeals)
  B. Whether you go to court or not, you will have to pay the staggering expense of the jury system.

II. The substitution of judges for juries will assure you of speedy, economical, and intelligent justice.

I. The jury system cannot be abolished in a day.
    A. It has existed since the thirteenth century in **England.**
    B. Anglo-Saxons have a sentimental attachment to it.
II. Juries will go only when enough people know the facts about **them.**
III. You can help by telling others why "The Jury Must Be Dismissed."

Of course, not all speeches require as detailed or complete a development as the one outlined above. Many are much simpler, but all should retain the same basic structure.

CHOOSING MATERIAL FOR PROOF

Evidence: To be convincing, it is especially important to avoid generalities and abstractions. Use concrete facts and vivid illustrations. Especially use those facts and incidents which are within the experience of the audience. Incidents which are recent, which have occurred frequently, or which were intensely important at the time when they happened are the most powerful material with which to build up the talk for conviction. You will need to prove nearly everything you say by presenting evidence of its truth or importance. Nowhere is the need for supporting material so urgent as when you try to get others to believe. Go back to Chapter 4 and review thoroughly the types of supporting material described there, especially the use of illustrations, instances, statistics, and testimony.

Sound logical reasoning: Regardless of how detailed and concrete is the evidence which you present, your speech will not carry strong conviction unless your reasoning is sound. A brief consideration of the three most frequently used forms of reasoning is therefore imperative.

1. *Reasoning from example.* This form of reasoning consists of drawing conclusions about a general situation or a class of objects on the basis of examples of that situation or class. For instance, if a housewife were in doubt about the flavor of the apples in a bushel

basket, she would bite into one of them to test its flavor. If it were good, she would reason that all the apples in the basket would taste the same way. Or perhaps, if she were a bit skeptical, she might dig down into the bottom to be sure that the apples in the basket were all of of the same kind. The same sort of reasoning is employed in most of our thinking whether the point at issue is big or little. Scientific experiments, laboratory tests, social trends—all are closely connected with the process of reasoning from example. Reasoning of this sort may be tested by answering the following questions:

a. Are there enough examples for a thorough sampling? One robin does not make a spring; nor do two or three examples of successful operation prove that a plan will invariably work.

b. Are the examples chosen fairly? To show that a thing is true in New York, Chicago, and Boston—all large cities—does not prove it true all over the country.

c. Are there any outstanding exceptions? One well-known example differing from the conclusion you urge will cause doubt unless you can show that it occurred under unusual circumstances.

2. *Reasoning from axiom.* This form of reasoning consists in applying to a specific situation a rule or principle already known or believed to be true. For example, the fact that merchandise can be bought in large quantities for a lower price than in small quantities is generally conceded. When you argue that chain stores save money by buying goods in large quantities, you are merely applying this general rule to the specific instance—the chain store. Reasoning from axiom may be tested as follows:

a. Is the axiom, or rule, itself true? For many years people believed the world flat. Many high-sounding truisms which pass for truth are merely prejudice or superstition. Before applying one, be sure of its validity. Of course, no matter how true a principle may be, if your listeners do not believe it, you cannot base an argument upon it unless you first convince them of its truth.

b. Does the rule apply to the specific situation? There are too many loose applications of perfectly good rules. For instance, to argue that *chain stores* buy goods more cheaply in large quantities on the basis of the principle mentioned above is perfectly valid, but to assume on this basis that *the customer* can buy them *from* every chain store at a lower price is not valid.

3. *Reasoning from causal relation.* Few people today believe in modern miracles. When something happens, we realize that there must have been a cause; and when we see a force in operation, we realize that it will produce some definite effect. On the basis of this relationship between cause and effect a great deal of our reasoning rests. The rate of violent crime goes up, and we hasten to lay the blame on war, on public apathy, on unworthy public officials. We hear that the star on our football team is in the hospital with a broken ankle, and we immediately become apprehensive about the results of Saturday's game. We reason from known effects to inferred causes and from known causes to inferred effects. There is perhaps no other form of reasoning so often used by speakers; nor is there any form of reasoning which may contain so many flaws. The following tests for soundness should be applied to this type of reasoning:

a. Has the cause been mistaken for the result? When two phenomena occur simultaneously, it is sometimes hard to tell which is cause and which is effect. Do higher wages cause higher prices, or is the reverse true?
b. Is the cause strong enough to produce (or to have produced) the result? A small pebble on the track will not derail a passenger train whereas a large boulder will. Do not mistake a pebble for a boulder.
c. Could anything prevent (or have prevented) the cause from operating? A man may have a gun in his hand but if someone has unloaded it, pulling the trigger won't make it shoot. Be sure that nothing prevented free operation of the cause that you assume produced the effect or result.
d. Could any other cause have produced the same result? Three different possible causes were listed above for the increase in violent crime, each one urged by some persons as the *sole* cause. Be sure that you diagnose the situation correctly; don't put the blame on the wrong thing or put all the blame on one thing if it should be divided.

220

e. Does any causal connection exist at all? Sometimes people assume that merely because one thing happens immediately *before* another, they are causally connected. Do not mistake coincidence for cause.

Emotional appeal: While it is true that people are—or should be—convinced chiefly through logical reasoning and evidence, they *act* largely because they *feel* as they do. Even the logical argument itself must reinforce a basic appeal to the desires and motives of your audience. (Review carefully the discussion of motive appeals on pages 48 to 51 in this connection.) As Professor Ormond Drake points out, "The story of the bleeding soldier on the field of battle and the picture of wounded men on stretchers did more to obtain blood donors than all the statistics concerning our blood supply and other evidence supporting logical conclusions put together." The desire to live is always present, but only when we experience something like the crack of lightning as it strikes the near-by tree do we tremble with fear and look actively for protection. Together with logic and evidence, therefore, the speaker must employ vivid description appealing to the basic desires and emotions which underlie his logic. Notice how Henry W. Grady, in his famous speech "The New South," used this method to arouse sympathy and respect for the defeated southern soldier:

> Let me picture to you the footsore Confederate soldier, as, buttoning up in his faded gray jacket the parole, which was to bear testimony to his children of his fidelity and faith, he turned his face southward from Appomattox in April, 1865. Think of him as, ragged, half-starved, heavy-hearted, enfeebled by wounds and exhaustion—having fought to exhaustion—he surrenders his gun, wrings the hands of his comrades in silence, and, lifting his tear-stained and pallid face for the last time to the graves that dot the old Virginia Hills, pulls his gray cap over his brows and begins the slow and painful journey.[8]

An appeal like this is particularly important in the visualization step; in fact, this step should always be descriptive and should carry

8 Henry W. Grady, from an address at the New England Society dinner in New York, December 22, 1886.

strong emotional appeal. Elsewhere in your speech, an occasional vivid example will add a dynamic quality to your argument which sound logic alone will not give. Except in the visualization step, however, do not substitute emotional appeal for logic and evidence—use both. Add a vivid appeal to your logical argument and you will have the essence of an effective persuasive speech: you will say something calculated to secure from your listeners the decision you seek.

The manner of speaking

To recommend any uniform characteristic manner of speech for this type of talk is impossible. Everything depends upon the situation, and these situations vary more widely than for any other type of speaking. Your style of delivery should be adapted to the occasion and to your listeners. In general, however, a straightforward, energetic presentation that suggests enthusiasm without seeming overemotional is the most effective in securing conviction. Of course, if your primary purpose is to arouse strong emotion, a more dynamic delivery is required.

problems

1. Go to hear some speaker and make a key-word outline of his talk while he is giving it. In your room revise that outline into full-content form, putting in all the details you can remember. Submit both outlines to your instructor.
2. Clip five advertisements from magazines and analyze the reasoning used in them. Determine the type of reasoning used and apply the tests for soundness given in this chapter.
3. In a way similar to that suggested in Problem 2, analyze five newspaper editorials.
4. Listen to the broadcast of a persuasive speech; analyze the motive appeals and the methods of arousing emotion employed.
5. Prepare a short talk pointing out the faulty reasoning in some popular argument of the time.

6. Read carefully and analyze Mark Antony's funeral oration (*Julius Caesar*, III, ii, 78 ff.) or Volumnia's speech to Coriolanus (*Coriolanus*, V, iii, 131 ff.), determining the means by which the speaker tried to achieve the desired end. What kinds of reasoning and proof were used? Support your conclusions.

7. Analyze the speech on page 298. Compare and contrast it with the speech you analyzed in Problem 6.

8. Make an analysis of one of the class speeches you have heard recently. Comment on the speaker's manner of delivery, the organization of the talk, and the subject matter used.

9. Work up a talk urging the acceptance of some belief or the adoption of some course of action in which you believe.

*Script writers on the staff of Para-
mount Pictures discuss the story
problems of a film that their company is making.*

Chapter 8 HOW TO

CARRY ON

GROUP DISCUSSION

In Chapter 1 you were shown that classroom discussion is one type of group discussion and you were given some general advice about participation. To some of you, however, the suggestion that preparation for other types of group discussion is necessary or even possible will seem like a new idea. The common reaction of most persons is, "Well, we'll get together and talk it over. We'll probably find some way out of the difficulty." But trusting to luck frequently fails. Usually the person who has done some hard thinking beforehand is the one whose ideas are accepted. Preparation for discussion is possible, and it is necessary. Here we will consider the process in a little more detail.

Two questions naturally arise: First, what aim shall you have in mind to guide your preparation; i.e., what are the types and purposes of discussion and what are the characteristics which make a discussion successful? Second, how may you go about the specific process of preparation; how shall you make ready to carry on the discussion? This chapter will attempt to answer these questions.

Types
of discussion groups

Discussion groups may be roughly divided into four types: study groups, informal committee or executive meetings, formal business meetings, and panel discussions.

STUDY GROUPS

The meeting of a group for the study of some subject or the exchange of information about it is usually quite informal. Often a speech or lecture is given at the beginning, but the bulk of the time is devoted to instruction and the mutual interchange of thoughts. The whole idea is to learn something from the others present. The most common type of study group with which you are familiar is the class (cf. Chapter 1). Conferences offer another example of this type of discussion; people from different departments or areas relate to one another their experiences and outline their varied methods of dealing with common problems. These are but a few of the many possible examples, for there are innumerable occasions upon which people get together with no other object than to exchange ideas.

INFORMAL COMMITTEE OR EXECUTIVE MEETINGS

When the president of an organization calls a meeting of the executive committee, discussion usually takes place: reports are made upon the condition of affairs, and the policies to be followed in the future are talked over and decided upon. The chairman of the fraternity dance committee calls the members together to lay plans for the spring dance. The business manager of the student dramatic organization calls together his assistants to discuss with them the budget for the next play or the details of the coming ticket-selling campaign. The rules committee of the women's self-government association meets to consider problems of social regulation among the women students. These are but samples selected from the many discussions which take place daily on every campus; they are counterparts of similar meetings which occur throughout any modern community.

Formal business meetings

Most organizations have definite and regular business meetings of a more formal sort. In them, specific and often final action is taken and recorded. Elections are held, budgets are approved, by-laws and rules are considered and adopted, contracts are let, and other matters requiring definite and official action are considered. While the rules of parliamentary procedure (to be considered later in the chapter) are occasionally followed in the less formal types of group discussions, they are almost indispensable—at least in a modified form—for the proper conduct of business meetings.

Panel discussions

There are times when a group is too large to engage in effective discussion or when its members are inadequately informed for such discussion to be profitable. In situations of this kind a small group—five to ten individuals—is seated on the platform and conducts the discussion for the larger group. The individuals in this small group, or panel, as it is called, are chosen either because they are well informed on the subject and can supply the facts needed for intelligent discussion or because they are known to represent viewpoints held by a considerable part of the larger group and can act as spokesmen to express these viewpoints. Sometimes the members of the panel are called upon by the chairman in a prearranged order to present the framework of the discussion in a series of short speeches; this may be followed by an open forum in which the speakers answer questions asked from the floor. At other times no speeches are made at all. The members of the panel carry on a discussion among themselves, ask questions of one another, agree and disagree as occasion arises—that is, they speak for the audience and before the audience, but not with the audience. Various combinations and modifications of these procedures are often used, the essential characteristic being that a panel of experts or spokesmen does the talking while the larger group does not participate as a whole.

The most common type of discussion used in radio broadcasting is the panel discussion described above. Often, speakers with sharply differing points of view are asked to present their opinions in short, uninterrupted statements after which they engage in spirited and informal debate upon their differences. This type of broadcast, frequently made from Washington over one or another of the radio networks, brings together congressmen, senators, and administrative officers to discuss current issues. Sometimes a similar, but more formal method is used: The speakers are allowed a longer time for their initial speeches; their answers to each other are more strictly limited in time; and following this the audience in the studio or auditorium is invited to ask questions of the speakers.

Purposes of group discussion

The specific purpose of any one discussion quite naturally depends upon the situation which calls the group together. A broader view of the matter discloses, however, that discussions are usually held either to interchange ideas or to reach agreements.

TO INTERCHANGE IDEAS, OPINIONS, AND INFORMATION

The least a discussion can do is to inform each participant about the opinions of the others on the subject which is considered. In addition, participants exchange information with each other, thus increasing their factual knowledge of the subject. This may be the only purpose of the discussion, as in a study group, but more often the interchange of ideas and information is merely a preliminary to the making of a decision as indicated below. In either event, the expression of divergent opinions is a valuable method of gaining a broader understanding of the problem at hand and of providing a sounder basis for making any decisions that are necessary.

TO REACH AN AGREEMENT OR MAKE A DECISION

In most discussions it is desirable not only to exchange ideas but to arrive at some point of agreement. The attempt is made to compromise differences of opinion and to bring strongly opposing points of view together upon some common basis. Through the give and take of discussion, individual beliefs are modified and a consensus is reached. Usually agreements are reached quite informally, although at formal business meetings decisions are often made by formal balloting.

Making effective discussion possible

If the discussion is to be effective, the individuals taking part in it must be capable of contributing to it, and the conduct of the group as a whole must be so ordered that worth-while discussion is possible.

ESSENTIALS FOR THE GROUP AS A WHOLE

The first essential in group discussion is order. This does not imply great formality; indeed, formality is often undesirable. Order does require, however, that only one person be allowed to talk at a time, that a courteous attitude be maintained, and that some rather definite procedure be followed to prevent the discussion from wandering too far afield. In the second place, a feeling of cooperation must exist. If each person insists on having his own way, little will be done. Members of the group must be willing to discuss points of view other than their own. Instead of criticizing another for the mistakes he may make, each person should try to understand and assist him. In short, the group should always be considered before the individual. Moreover, there must be a willingness to compromise. There are times, of course, when compromise is not desirable; but reasonable compromise hurts no one, and sometimes it is the only way of reaching an agreement or making a decision. If a general desire to "meet the other fellow halfway" prevails, there is likely to be a better feeling in the group and more will be accomplished. Finally, a feeling of accomplishment should exist. Unless a group feels that it is getting somewhere, interest and enthusiasm will diminish. So far as possible, a definite goal should be set and the field of discussion limited before the conference actually begins. The discussion leader or chairman may do a great deal to secure this result, but he is helpless unless he has the cooperation of the group.

Essentials for the Individual

Without doubt, the most important single thing which enables the individual to participate effectively in the discussion is a knowledge of the subject being considered. If you know what you are talking about,

Regular meetings are essential in conducting almost any business. The chief executives of the General Cable Corporation (shown here) combine lunch with their daily business conference. At the head of the table, the president and secretary check the agenda for the day's discussion.

other faults will sometimes be forgiven. Be sure that you are acquainted with the facts around which your discussion is to hinge. The second essential is an acquaintance with the other members of the group. The more you know about them, the better you can judge the value of their remarks and the better secure approval of your own. Equally important is close attention to the discussion as it progresses. Unless you listen to what is going on, you may lose track of the direction which the discussion has taken. Then you are likely to make foolish comments, to require repetition, or to entertain mistaken ideas of the position taken by other members of the group on the question being discussed. Finally, tactful contribution to the discussion itself is desirable. If you keep quiet, you may learn a good deal, but you will not help anyone else in the solution of the problems raised. Yet it is better to be quiet than to say the wrong thing, at the wrong time, in the wrong way. Develop the ability to present ideas tactfully and persuasively at the strategic time.

Taking part in a broadcast discussion on wages and prices are Robert Nathan (left), economist, who defends his "Nathan Report," prepared for the CIO, against the views of Ralph Robey (right), chief economist of the National Association of Manufacturers. The moderator (center) is Dwight Cooke.

The fruitfulness of a discussion depends a great deal on the leader's capacity for rapid analysis. He must be able to see in what direction the discussion is turning, to catch the significant points even when they are buried in superfluous detail, to note essential agreements between points of view even when expressed in words which make them seem divergent, to strip controversial points of unnecessary complexity and thus to narrow the discussion to the basic issues. In short, he needs to be alert, quick-witted, and clear-thinking. Moreover, a good discussion leader must be able to state the results of his analysis clearly and briefly, to make the essential point stand out before the group as clearly as it does in his own mind.

Just as important for the leader is the quality of fearless impartiality. By seeing that minority viewpoints are allowed expression, and by fairness of wording in putting questions and summarizing discussions, he can help maintain a spirit of cooperation and conciliation among members of the group who may differ from one another vigorously. By fearlessness in maintaining this impartiality, even under majority pressure, he is likely to gain respect and support for his leadership. Discussion groups are no different from other groups in preferring leaders who are fair, firm, and decisive. But the keenness of analysis and fearless impartiality of leadership must be judicially tempered with tact both in words and in manner. There is no place as discussion leader for one who is easily irritated or who says things in a way to irritate others. A good rule is always to accept comments and to state them with the most generous interpretation possible; given a comment containing a reasonable argument and a sarcastic connotation, focus the discussion on the former and ignore the latter. And finally, there are times when the leader of discussion needs a stimulating manner in order to encourage participation by the group. Often, especially at the beginning, people are slow to enter into the discussion; there is a hesitancy and caution about starting off. Provocative questions may help, but even more important is an encouraging and stimulating manner in the leader, a manner which suggests the importance of the subject and confidence that the group does have important things to say about it.

Thus far this chapter has presented an explanation of the function and purpose of group discussion and of the essentials for effective discussion in order to make clear the objectives toward which your preparation should work. Attention can now be turned to the process of preparation itself. For the purpose of clarity, the following explanation is divided into two parts: first, general preparation—that required of everyone, including the leader; and second, preparation to lead the discussion—that additional planning required of the chairman or group leader if he is to direct the discussion in an orderly manner to a fruitful conclusion.

General preparation

Just what preparation should be made by the individual who expects to participate in a discussion? What should you do beforehand in order that you may contribute to the best of your ability? Two fundamental things are required: you must study the group, and you must study the problems which are to be discussed by it.

ANALYSIS OF THE GROUP

You may know something about the subject to be discussed, but unless you appreciate the relation between it and the objectives of the particular group which is to talk it over, you will be handicapped. At the very beginning, then, determine the function of the group. Is it brought together merely to investigate, or does it have power to make decisions? What resources are at its command? Next, analyze the larger unit of which this group is a part. Finally, make a detailed analysis of the individuals who compose the group. By doing so, you will know that X is likely to exaggerate and that his comments must be taken with a grain of salt, but that what W says will bear serious consideration.

In particular, answer for yourself as well as you can the following questions: What is the official position of each member of the group? What are each one's personal traits? What knowledge does each one have of the questions to be discussed? What attitude will each individual have toward the proposals you expect to advocate?

ANALYSIS OF THE SPECIFIC SUBJECTS TO BE DISCUSSED

The more you know about the subject under discussion, the better. Don't rely on old knowledge; be sure that your information is up to date. The more specific and ready the information at your command, the better you will be able to take part in the discussion. In all instances you will need substantial facts in support of your ideas.

For each problem you think will be discussed, therefore, make the following analysis: First, review the facts you already know. Go over the information you have acquired upon the subject and organize it in your mind. Prepare as if you were going to present a talk on every phase of the entire subject; you will then be more ready to discuss any part of it on short notice. Second, find out what recent changes have occurred affecting the problem. Bring your knowledge up to date. Fit the new information you acquire into the outline of what you already have. Then note where there are gaps in your knowledge of the subject and search for information to fill them. Third, determine a tentative point of view on the question. Make up your mind as to what your attitude will be. Is $500,000 too much to spend in building a new recreation center? Do you believe that dues should be paid annually or monthly? Stake out rather definitely your position on each question that is to come before the group and have clearly in mind the reasons for that point of view. However, keep your decision tentative; be willing to change your mind if additional facts disclosed in the discussion prove you to be wrong. Finally, examine the effect your idea or proposal will have upon the other members of the group. If you ask yourself what the effect will be on the organization as a whole and on the individuals in it, you will be prepared to meet any objections which may arise or to modify your proposal to meet them. Possibly what you propose will cause someone to lose money or to retract a promise he has made; forethought will prepare you to meet his opposition. The more thoroughly you organize your facts beforehand and relate them to the problem involved and the people who are to discuss them, the more successful and influential will be your participation.

Special preparation to lead the discussion

What has been said so far applies to every member of the group. The one whose duty it is to lead the discussion needs to make some additional preparation. All that has been mentioned in the preceding section applies to him as well as to the other members of the group; but if he is to be a leader in fact as well as in name, he must prepare to lead.

PREPARING THE AGENDA OF THE DISCUSSION

More than anything else, the chairman's duty is to see that the discussion leads to some conclusion. He must keep the discussion from wandering off the point and becoming tangled with nonessentials. He must see that all the necessary decisions are made and that important matters are not left undecided. In preparing to do these things, you will find helpful some such procedure as the one which follows:

1. Make a list of all the items to come up for consideration. Include in this list both important and less important matters—those which need immediate attention and those which can equally well be postponed.

2. Reduce this list to fit the time limit. Determine how much time is available for the discussion, and cross off enough of the less important

items to bring the list within reason. The items that are deleted can then be compiled into a supplementary list which can be used in case the primary items are disposed of in less time than you expect.

3. Arrange in orderly sequence the items to be discussed. Some matters are themselves dependent upon others. Suppose, for example, that the managing board of the college newspaper is meeting to decide upon the size of the editorial staff, but that a proposal is also under consideration for issuing the paper daily instead of weekly. Quite obviously the second item would have to be settled before the first. If you are to lead the discussion efficiently, you must so arrange the items for consideration that there will be no need to double back or jump around from one point to another.

4. Outline the subsidiary questions involved in each major problem to be discussed. Thus, in the proposal to issue the college paper daily, a number of subordinate points will need to be considered: What will be the added cost of printing and distributing? Can enough advertising space be sold to meet this added expense? What will be done about existing contracts based on the weekly plan? Is there enough local news to provide copy for a daily paper? Should an attempt be made to carry national as well as local news? The leader must have such points as these well in mind in order to be sure none of them is overlooked. Indeed, a mimeographed or blackboard outline of these points will often serve to keep the discussion centered on the problem and to keep it moving in an orderly fashion. Detailed suggestions on how to prepare such an outline for the discussion of major problems will be presented a little later (p. 238).

5. Finally, determine the subsequent questions which will arise from any decisions that may be made. For instance, if it is decided to publish the paper daily, a procedure must be agreed upon for getting the approval of the college authorities, a date must be set for the change, and plans must be laid for carrying the proposal into effect. You must

be ready as each decision is reached to lead the discussion on to the next one. Leadership of this sort will make a discussion orderly and productive of results.

DETERMINING THE CAPABILITIES AND ATTITUDES OF MEMBERS OF THE GROUP

Earlier in the chapter, comment was made on the importance of knowing the other members of the group. Although important for every member, this knowledge is doubly so for the leader; his analysis must go even deeper than that discussed before.

Determine the field of each person's special knowledge. Some persons will know more about a particular aspect of the question than anyone else. Keep these special qualifications in mind so that when questions which require a special type of information arise you can immediately call upon the person who can supply it. Take note also of each person's prestige with the other members of the group. If one person is considered an extremist, don't let that person talk too much. An extremist often has good ideas, but they may be rejected merely because he advocates them. Let someone else follow up the points such a person raises so that a more moderate point of view may save the essential idea.

Finally, inform yourself of each person's administrative abilities and special capacities. Groups often make decisions and determine policies but leave them to be carried out by individual members. You can often cause a project to succeed by suggesting the right person.

By outlining the agenda of the discussion and by adapting items to the capabilities and attitudes of those who are to take part, you will have done much as a leader to secure a speedy and thorough consideration of the problems of the group. The person who can do this effectively and tactfully is rare; careful preparation is a long step toward becoming that person.

Outlining
the discussion plan

Too often group discussion is justi-
fiably criticized for wasting time
and getting nowhere. There is undeniable truth in the claim that a
wise individual can think through and solve a problem more rapidly
and efficiently than can a group. Many times, however, the wise individual fails to give sufficient consideration to some phase of a problem
which seems unimportant to him but is of great importance to those
whom his decision affects; such a slip is less likely to happen in group
discussion. Nevertheless, the fact remains that discussion by a group
does take time. In some instances the discussion moves slowly because
the members of the group have not been notified in time to prepare
themselves. The amount of time can be reduced, and the efficiency of
group discussion increased, by careful planning in advance. Delay and
confusion are far less often caused by muddled thinking on the part
of individuals in a group than by the absence of orderly direction.

The discussion plans set up below are designed to make orderly
direction possible. Because the thinking process when individuals join
in group discussion is not much different from that employed in
speaker-audience situations, these plans are based on the same fundamental structure explained in Chapters 6 and 7. Groups as well as individuals need to focus attention, examine their needs, explore the means
of satisfaction, visualize results, and take appropriate action.

A PLAN FOR STUDY GROUPS

Many times the subject matter to be discussed in a study group is
the content of a textbook or parts of it. Occasionally a study outline
or syllabus, prepared by some authority in the given field, has been
chosen as a guide for the discussion. When either of these conditions
exists, you will do well to prepare your discussion plan in fairly close
parallel to the outline of the material which the group has studied. Your

main task will be to devise means of relating the points in that outline to the experiences of individuals in the group and of seeing that the more important facts and principles receive proper emphasis and consideration. Sometimes prepared outlines of this sort are out of date or incomplete. If you feel this to be true, provision should be made in your discussion plan for asking questions at the proper time with the purpose of bringing the missing information or viewpoints into the discussion.

Many times, however, no such ready-prepared outline is at your disposal; or even if available, the outline may not be well adapted to the particular group. The following suggestions should supply a general structure on the basis of which you can prepare a satisfactory discussion plan.

1. *Focusing attention at the beginning.* The attention step may consist of a statement of the subject by the discussion leader, together with one or two illustrative examples showing its general importance or its relation to the individuals in the group.

2. *Determining just what the group needs to know.* A consideration by the group itself of the importance of the subject and a narrowing of the scope of discussion to those phases which seem most important constitute the need step. The following items should be covered:

   a. What importance does the subject have for the group? Why?

   b. Into what major topical divisions may this subject be conveniently divided?

   c. To which of these phases of the subject should the present discussion be narrowed?

     (1) Which topics are of the greatest interest and importance to the group?

     (2) Upon which topics are the members of the group already informed so fully that further discussion would be fruitless?

   d. Summary. A summary, by the leader, of the discussion thus far includes a statement of the list of topics to which the general subject has now been narrowed and an arrangement of these topics in logical sequence for further discussion.

3. *Discussing the information itself.* The next step (satisfaction) should be a thorough consideration by the group of each of the topics chosen in (c) above in the order suggested by the leader. Although not necessarily in this sequence, the discussion of *each* topic should cover at least the following points:

a. What terms need definition? Is there disagreement about the generally accepted meaning? Which definition does the group prefer?

b. What background material needs to be considered—historical, social, geographic, etc.? What are the known facts?

c. What personal experiences of members of the group may serve to illuminate and clarify the discussion?

d. What basic principles or relationships or tendencies seem to underlie this information and these experiences?

e. Summary. The leader should point out what seem to be the essential facts or principles upon which there is general agreement, and indicate upon which points information is still lacking or conflicting.

The leader should then bring up the second topic and lead the discussion, covering points (a) to (e) again on that topic, repeating this procedure till all the topics have been covered.

4. *Final summary.* At the close of the discussion the chairman should make a compressed restatement, pointing out (a) the reasons disclosed by the discussion for considering the subject important and (b) the essential points brought out under each of the main topics discussed. Do not attempt to make this summary exhaustively complete; its purpose is rather to bring together the more important points in such a way that they will more easily be remembered. (Since this plan is for a study group

not faced with a problem requiring action, there is no provision for decisions; cf. the section on deliberative groups below.)

Quite obviously this plan is only a general skeleton; you will need to develop it in more detail for the specific subject to be discussed. Careful study will suggest to you what are likely to be the answers, or at least the type of answers, to some of the questions indicated. You should be sufficiently familiar with the subject yourself to know at least the more important facts or principles which need to be brought out. By thinking through, in the light of your own knowledge of the subject, the plan presented above, you will be able to prepare more specific questions that will bring out information from the group members; and by a proper analysis of the people who are to be in the group, you can often estimate in advance the relative time needed for each of the topics to be discussed. Remember, however, that your function is to steer the group; make your discussion plan sufficiently flexible so that it can be modified to suit the situation disclosed during the discussion itself.

A PLAN FOR DELIBERATIVE GROUPS EMPOWERED TO ACT

Groups of the sort we shall now consider are concerned with more than the exchange of opinions and information: they are faced with situations requiring agreement on courses of action to be pursued. If the group is one which meets regularly, the members may not be aware of the problem prior to the meeting in which it is brought up. More frequently the existence of such problems is known in advance; at times the existence of a serious difficulty or conflict of interests may be the very reason for calling the group together. At any rate, the principal function of a group discussion of this sort is a problem-solving function. The object is to reach a consensus on what to do about something and how do it. The plan which follows will suggest a procedure useful in discussing a single problem; we shall leave till later the planning of discussion involving a series of problems.

241

1. *Focusing attention.* A brief statement by the chairman indicating the reason for discussion and focusing attention on the problem is the first step.

2. *Evaluating the need or problem.* The next step is an examination of the situation, evaluating the scope and importance of the problem, analyzing its causes, determining the essential matters needing action, and setting up the basic requirements for an effective solution. The following sequence of questions is suggested as an aid in evaluating the problem:

a. What is the basic problem, and what is the evidence that action is required?

   (1) How has the problem affected members of the group?

   (2) What other persons or groups or situations does the problem affect, and how?

   (3) Is the situation likely to improve by itself, or will it become worse if nothing is done about it?

   (4) Is the problem sufficiently serious to warrant discussion and action at this time? (If the answer to this question is negative, further discussion is obviously pointless.)

b. What is the background of the problem, and what are its causes?

   (1) Is the problem primarily financial, social, etc.? Is it a problem of materials or of organizations?

   (2) To what extent is the difficulty the result of misunderstandings or emotional antipathies of individuals or groups?

c. What are the chief things in the present situation which demand action? What demands must be met; what desires satisfied?

   (1) On which of these points is the entire group, or a large part of it, agreed?

   (2) What additional things are desired by a substantial or important minority?

d. What satisfactory elements in the present situation must be retained?

242

e. In the light of the answers to questions (c) and (d) above, what are the essential criteria upon which any proposed plan is to be judged? (Review p. 196 ff. on this point.)
   (1) What must the plan avoid?
   (2) What must the plan do?
   (3) What limits of time, material, personnel, etc., must be considered?
f. In addition to the above requirements what supplementary qualities would be desirable but not absolutely essential?
g. Summary. The leader should summarize the points agreed to thus far. Particularly important is a clear statement of the agreements reached in answer to questions (e) and (f), since these requirements will serve as the basic criteria for the proposals considered in the remainder of the discussion. Moreover, a clear understanding and agreement regarding these requirements will serve to make further discussion more logical and will minimize the tendency to attack and defend proposals as personal matters.

3. *Finding a satisfactory solution.* Then follows the consideration of various proposals for meeting the problem, an examination and comparison of their respective advantages and disadvantages, and the attempt to reach agreement on a satisfactory plan. The following procedure is suggested:

a. What are the proposed solutions for the difficulty? (Or, if the group has met to discuss the merits of one previously proposed plan, what alternatives should be considered?)
   (1) Make a list of the proposals, preferably on a blackboard.
   (2) Be sure that each proposal is defined or explained briefly but clearly.
   (3) If the list of proposals is long, group them according to type for initial consideration.
b. Note what elements are common to all proposals and secure agreement regarding the retention of these elements.

243

c. Examine the differences in the proposals in the light of the criteria set up previously (e, above) while evaluating the problem. This may be done in either of two ways:

    (1) Consider each plan (or type of plan) separately; examine it in the light of all the criteria; determine in this way in what respects it is acceptable and unacceptable.

    (2) Consider each criterion separately; determine which proposals best satisfy it.

d. On the basis of this examination eliminate the less desirable proposals and narrow the discussion to those which remain.

e. Examine the remaining proposals to see whether one of them can be revised to eliminate objectionable features or to add desirable ones or whether the better parts of two or more plans can be combined into a new and more satisfactory one. (Because of strong differences of opinion within the group, unimportant points—at times, even important ones—will often need to be compromised.)

f. Summary. The chairman should give a summary of the principal features of the accepted plan as soon as general agreement upon it has been reached.

4. *Visualizing results.* The next step consists of a brief statement, usually by the chairman, of the probable results of the proposal just agreed upon. The object of such a statement at this point is to carry the proposal into imaginary operation and further to emphasize the unity of opinion to which the group has come. In groups which have no power or authority for official action, this statement will normally end the discussion.

5. *Taking action.* In considering methods for putting the proposal into operation, the following points should be noted:

a. Selection of persons to be made responsible for action.

b. Determination of the time, place, etc., when the proposal should go into effect.

244

c. Taking official action (such as appropriating money, etc.) whenever such action is necessary.

(Note: If several divergent methods of putting the proposal into action are suggested, a procedure similar in sequence to that suggested above in the satisfaction step, but usually more brief, will need to be followed in order to secure agreement on the most satisfactory method.)

d. Summary. A brief restatement of the action just taken should be made by the chairman to be sure the agreement is clear. This statement normally ends the discussion.

ADAPTING THE DELIBERATIVE PLAN TO THE QUESTION

The discussion plan suggested above covers the entire process of deliberation from the first analysis of existing conditions to the taking of final action. This entire process is not always required. As H. S. Elliott points out in his book, *The Process of Group Thinking,* "A group may face a question in any one of five stages: (1) a baffling or confused situation; (2) a problem definitely defined; (3) alternatives specifically suggested; (4) a single definite proposal; (5) ways and means of carrying out a conclusion."[1] How much of the deliberative process will need to be included in the discussion plan will depend, then, upon the stage at which the question comes before the group. If a proposed plan has already been approved at a previous meeting, or if the group finds itself in immediate agreement with regard to it, all that needs to be discussed is the method of putting the plan into action. Only the last section, *taking action,* will need to be included in the plan. Likewise, if a need or problem is generally recognized and the group meets to consider the merits of a single definite proposal, the second step in the outline above can be condensed to a brief discussion of the essential requirements for a satisfactory plan, or merely to a summary of those criteria by the chairman, and this can be followed immediately by an examination of the

1 H. S. Elliott, *The Process of Group Thinking* (Association Press, N. Y., 1932), p. 89ff.

proposal in the light of those requirements. The first step in the preparation of a discussion plan, therefore, is to determine at what stage the question is likely to come before the group; you can then prepare your outline to pick up the discussion at that stage. The discussion leader, however, should study the entire outline so that he will be able to adjust his plan if it is necessary.

PLANNING FOR CONSECUTIVE DISCUSSION OF A SERIES OF PROBLEMS

Executive committees, governing boards, and many similar groups are often faced with the necessity of discussing several problems during the same meeting. Some of these problems may be related to one another while others are quite distinct. Obviously, related questions should be discussed together or in immediate sequence, but the order in which unrelated questions should be considered requires some thought by the chairman. Suggestions for arranging the agenda of a meeting of this sort have already been given (see page 235). Together with whatever modifications may be required to conform with the regularly established order of business in the group, those suggestions should guide you in deciding the sequence in which the problems should be arranged for discussion. There remains to be pointed out only the fact that you will need to work out a discussion plan for each of the individual problems on your list, these plans being abridged wherever possible, of course, in the manner previously explained. Your final outline, then, will consist of a series of deliberative discussion plans, modified to suit the stage at which the respective questions will arise, and arranged in logical sequence.

PLANNING FOR PANEL DISCUSSION

The type of plan to be prepared for a panel will depend on the type of discussion desired. If it is to be a series of speeches followed by an open forum, the plan will normally be a simple partition of the topic among the speakers, a different phase of it being assigned to each one. One person, for example, may present the problem, and each of the other speakers may suggest and evaluate a different type of solution; or different persons may discuss the social, political, and economic aspects of the topic being considered. Following these more formal remarks, the meeting may be opened for questions or comments from the audience, the chairman referring the questions to the various panel speakers for reply.

When the speakers on the panel are to participate among themselves, however, in the actual give and take of the type of discussion with which this chapter has primarily dealt, the discussion plan will need to be prepared by the chairman in greater detail. Approximately the same form may be used as if no audience were to be present during the discussion—that is, the plan will be similar to those included earlier in the chapter. If the purpose is to be informative only, the study-group type of plan can be used; if a problem or a proposed course of action is to be discussed, the deliberative type of plan will be better.

Often it is desirable that the speakers run through the discussion in private before their public appearance; such a "rehearsal" often suggests ways by which the discussion can be compressed, less important points omitted, and the whole plan made more coherent. This is the method, by the way, by which many of the panel discussions heard over radio and television are prepared. Because of the very strict time limits on the air, such preparation is essential if the main points are to be covered, but care must be taken to sustain spontaneity by refraining from the use of detailed scripts or set speeches.

Whatever type of discussion plan is used, however, it should provide for the utilization of the specialized information of the panel members. Although no one should be limited in his remarks to his special field of knowledge alone, nevertheless questions relating definitely to that field should at least be directed to him first. Unless something of this sort is done, the very purpose of selecting a panel to conduct the discussion for the larger group in the audience is likely to be defeated.

ADAPTING THE PLAN TO THE GROUP

Your discussion plan must take into account, furthermore, the personnel of the group. The discussion leader dare not be too subjective in preparing his outline; he must not assume that everyone will be logical, clear-thinking, and unemotional. Known prejudices and strong feelings should be considered and an outlet for them planned, together with a means of modifying their firmness or violence. Or, if certain points are not really vital to the essential issue and are likely to arouse bitterness or to waste time in unnecessary controversy, the leader must plan a tactful method of excluding these points from the discussion. If a certain person is known to have considerable prestige with the other members of the group, the discussion plan must be arranged to provide definitely for the consideration of beliefs other than his in order to avoid too hasty an acceptance of one point of view. The plan must be laid, not only to cover the subject, but to direct people in their discussion of it.

None of the suggestions presented in this chapter will take the place of good sense on the part of the discussion leader, or of experience in planning discussion. The better informed you are on the subject or problem to be discussed and the better you know the members of the group whose discussion you are to lead, the better you will be able to outline a plan for that discussion. When your good sense, experience, and the special knowledge you have of the group indicate that a procedure different from that suggested in this chapter would lead to more rapid progress and more fruitful results, do not hesitate to devise a completely different type of plan. In the beginning, however, you will be wiser to follow rather closely the tested procedures suggested in this chapter. These procedures allow sufficient flexibility for nearly any situation.

248

Stimulating and directing discussion

Even though he has thoroughly prepared the agenda and has carefully outlined a suitable discussion plan, the leader still faces the task of stimulating and directing the actual discussion so that the group will feel free to talk, that its attention will be focused on the important problems, and that a profitable conclusion will be reached. To this end, experienced leaders have offered the following suggestions.

GETTING DISCUSSION STARTED

Begin, as suggested earlier, by making a brief statement of the problem to be discussed; point out its importance, especially as it is related to the group members. This statement should be made with vigor and earnestness, suggesting the vital nature of the subject; it should be expressed in concrete terms supported by specific instances, but it should not be so long that it seems to exhaust the subject matter. This statement should, moreover, lead into a series of provocative questions designed to pull members of the group into the discussion. The questions ought not to be too general; they should call for specific answers based on the experiences of individuals in the group. You might ask, for example, "In what way have you, personally, met this problem recently?" Or better, "Mr. Knowles told me that he ran into this problem in the following way: . . . [Briefly describe.] Have any of you had a similar experience, or if not, how did your experience differ?" If such questions fail to provoke sufficient discussion, call on certain individuals by name to relate their experiences or to express their opinions on the problem. Go to the blackboard and start a list—of causes for the existence of the problem, of types of people or groups whom it affects, of terms needing definition, of proposed courses of action, of anything which fits into your discussion outline and calls for enumeration. Curiously enough, people who hesitate to begin a discussion seldom hesitate to add to a list which has been started.

Still another method is to bring out, at the beginning, one or more extreme points of view on the question. You can relay these viewpoints yourself, or better, call on members of the group who have them. Nothing seems to stir a group into active discussion as much as an extreme statement with which to disagree. The danger of this method lies in the possibility of starting a verbal battle which consumes too much time or stirs up personal animosity. Seldom will this much effort be required to get discussion started, because the problem which served to bring the group together is usually provocative enough in itself. But whenever the group lags at the beginning or hits a "dead spot" later in the discussion, the methods described in this section will prove helpful.

KEEPING THE DISCUSSION FROM WANDERING

The tendency of a group to draw away from the central issue can be greatly diminished by writing on a blackboard a skeleton outline of the discussion plan as a whole. When people can see what points are to be taken up and in what order, they are likely to focus their attention on those points and in that order. Unless something really important has been omitted from the outline, the leader can direct attention to the points on it, one after another, and thus keep the discussion steadily progressing. Using this outline as a skeleton, many leaders fill in the details on the blackboard as they are brought up in the discussion, in this way providing continuously for the group a visual record of what has been said. If, in spite of this rather strong suggestion, the discussion takes an irrelevant turn, all that is usually necessary is to call attention to the irrelevancy and refer to the outline. The same is true when someone doubles back to a point already discussed or jumps ahead to a point not yet reached. Of course, the leader must be sensible and fair in this matter: sometimes the fault is in his outline rather than in the speaker who gets away from it. Something important may have been omitted from the outline. In general, however, the leader will do well to hold the group pretty closely to the outlined discussion plan.

250

There will be times when one or two persons in the group begin to monopolize the discussion. Not infrequently such persons really have a great deal to contribute, but quite as often they tend to repeat certain points or to overexpand minor points. When this occurs, the leader should call on other members of the group, by name if necessary, asking them definite questions which will lead the discussion forward and away from the point which has been overdone and from the person who has been talking too much. If the time is drawing near for closing the discussion, a statement of that fact usually has a marked effect in keeping talk from wandering or becoming repetitive. Remember that while the discussion leader does not usually have the right to direct what conclusion is to be reached, he does have the right and the duty to control the direction of the discussion and to keep it centered on the important issues. The ability to do this with tact and firmness is the mark of a good leader.

ARRIVING AT PROFITABLE CONCLUSIONS

If a good discussion plan has been outlined and adhered to without too many digressions, the group will have come a long way toward concluding with profit. The leader may increase the likelihood of this result, however, in two or three ways. As the discussion proceeds, he will notice a number of things upon which most of those in the group agree; these he can bring together at appropriate intervals in brief summaries. In this way he can narrow the discussion to the points not accepted and can attempt to secure agreement upon them. Another way in which the leader may add to the value of the discussion is by calling forth factual information. Many disagreements disappear when the facts are known; the leader can often bring out these facts by adroit questions and thus eliminate needless argument. By this same method, moreover, personal antipathies can be minimized and the discussion kept on a more rational basis. Finally, at the close of the discussion, the leader should summarize the results, placing emphasis on the points of agreement but in fairness indicating any important minority viewpoint. If some things remain unsettled, these should be pointed out, especially if there is to be a later meeting. The tone of this final summary should be judicious, but if it is at all justified, there should be a suggested satisfaction with the outcome.

Evaluating
the opinions of others

One of the greatest differences between a public speech and a group discussion lies in the obvious fact that, in the latter, one person does not do all the talking. During the greater part of the time you will yourself be a part of the audience—you will be the listener. This will be true whether you are the discussion leader or just a member of the group. As suggested earlier, your principal task while you are listening will be to evaluate what the speaker is saying in order that you may weigh his opinions against your own and against those expressed by other members of the group. By asking yourself the following questions you can make your judgment thorough and systematic:

1. Does the training and experience of the speaker qualify him to express an authoritative opinion? Is he an expert in the particular field of knowledge under discussion?

2. Is his statement based on first-hand knowledge? Did he observe the evidence himself, or is he merely reporting a rumor?

3. Is his opinion prejudiced? Is it influenced by personal interest? Does he stand to profit personally from the decision?

4. Does he usually state his opinions frankly without concealment? Does he reveal all the facts known to him, or is he in the habit of concealing facts unfavorable to his cause?

5. Are the facts or opinions presented consistent with human experience? Do they sound plausible? Could they reasonably be true?

6. Are the facts or opinions presented consistent with one another?

If two reports contradict each other, which seems more substantial?

7. What weight will other members of the group give to this person's opinion? Is his prestige so great that the group will agree with him in the face of conflicting evidence? Is he so little respected that he will not be believed unless someone else supports his opinion?

If you ask yourself these questions about each person who participates in the discussion, you will be able to evaluate his remarks more accurately. (Observe, moreover, that these questions will serve in passing judgment not only on the opinions of speakers in group discussions but on those expressed from the public platform or on the printed page.) A running evaluation of the comments made by others in the discussion helps in making a decision and in predicting the reaction of the group to whatever remarks you yourself may make.

Special techniques for securing agreement

In addition to the general suggestions made so far, there are some special devices which can be used in discussion when it is your purpose to secure agreement to something you propose. *You must remember here that you have a high obligation to be right.*

1. *Pull your proposal from another person by suggestion.* Instead of making the proposal yourself, lead the discussion to a position where the actual point is quite obvious and someone else will be likely to make it for you. Maneuver the discussion to the point of considering ways and means. Then suggest that the group catalog (on the blackboard or on paper) all the possible ways in which the result can be brought about. Someone will be likely to suggest your idea as one of the plans. Then, when all the methods have been set down, you may side with the person who proposed your plan. You will now be supporting someone else's proposal rather than putting forward your own, and you can be much more outspoken.

2. *Ask the opinion of another who you know will agree.* Quite often the first few opinions expressed upon a proposal will set the tone for subsequent statements. If the first few persons to speak are quite definite in favoring or opposing a proposition, there is likely to be some hesitation upon the part of others to voice a different opinion. It is a case of getting off on the right foot. As soon as you have made a proposal pick out someone else in the group who you think will agree with you and ask him, "What do you think about it, Mr. Jones?"

3. *Compromise on small points to secure agreement on big ones.* The attitude of dogmatism tends to breed dogmatic opposition. If by giving in on smaller points you can demonstrate that you are willing to be reasonable, you will tend to strengthen your prestige with the group and to reduce its resistance. The principle of reciprocity is quite as applicable here as elsewhere. By supporting another's proposal, or by giving in to it, you tend to create an obligation in him to support you.

4. *Eliminate doubtful points from your proposal.* Frequently the opposition to a proposal arises not from any objection to its central idea, but from dislike of some part only, such as the date when it is to be applied or the method of application. If it is impossible to secure a compromise on points of this sort, they may sometimes be eliminated from the proposal entirely and left for later decision. Frequently such points can even be dropped without sacrificing the strength of the plan. Shrewd persons have been known to include points of this kind purposely in order to draw the fire of opposition away from the central plan to minor points which may easily be discarded.

Throughout the entire discussion, however, remember that the fundamental object should be to arrive at the best possible decision or to secure the most accurate information. Do not engage in it merely to "win points" or to prove the other fellow wrong. If you prepare carefully in advance, outline a systematic plan for the discussion, and judiciously stimulate and direct the discussion itself, the results obtained will be more sensible and the time consumed will be reduced.

Parliamentary law for informal groups

The formality with which discussion is carried on depends largely upon the type of organization holding the meeting. Legislative assemblies follow a detailed and somewhat complicated set of rules, while many informal study groups employ very few rules if any at all. In order that the discussion may be orderly, however, most groups follow either by formal regulation or by tacit consent certain rules of order which have come to be known as "parliamentary law," because of their origin in parliamentary bodies. For a detailed list of these rules, a complete manual such as *Robert's Rules of Order* should be consulted. For the average group, however, less detailed procedure is required. This section contains only a brief outline of those rules that are followed almost universally, even in less formal groups.

THE CHAIRMAN

Sometimes the president of the organization or the chairman of the committee has already been chosen, in which case he automatically becomes the presiding officer. When no such officer has been selected, the first duty of the group is that of electing a chairman or a president from among its members, after nominations have been made, by a majority vote.

The most important duty of the chairman is to preserve order. He must see that only one person is allowed to speak at a time. Speakers are required to address the chairman and be recognized by him before speaking in order to avoid a general confusion. In addition, the chairman has certain appointive powers, such as the naming of sub-committees and minor officers. In the less formal groups the chairman is allowed to enter the argument and to vote on proposals which are presented for decision; in fact, as explained in the preceding chapters, he often exercises a vigorous leadership in the discussion. In more formal bodies, however, he is limited to the duties of presiding.

Order of business

Nearly every organization has a regular order of business which is followed at each meeting. When no such predetermined order exists, the following one—or such parts of it as fit the business of the group—may be used:

1. Roll call.
2. Minutes of the last meeting—to be read, corrected, and approved.
3. Settlement of unfinished business left over from the last meeting as indicated in the minutes.
4. Committee reports; action upon their recommendations.
5. Consideration of new items of business.
6. Determination of the time and place of the next meeting, unless this is regularly established.
7. Adjournment.

Sometimes a problem arises which is so important that it is made the special order of business for the next meeting. When this is done, the regular order of the next meeting is modified to give this special problem precedence, and all other matters are omitted or postponed. Occasionally the advance prediction of the importance of some question is impossible. When a matter of this kind, requiring immediate attention, arises it may be considered in advance of its regular place in the order of business by the vote of two thirds of the group.

Introducing the subject

At times the subject or subjects for the discussion have been settled in advance; the group may be a committee whose duty was specified by the authority which created it, or the subject may be introduced as a report of a sub-committee. Usually, however, the specific proposal is introduced by a "motion" made by some member of the group. The proper form for introducing a motion is to say, "Mr. Chairman, I move that. . . ." A second person must usually support the introduction of a proposal in order to prevent the consideration of matters which interest only one person. To second a motion, you should say, "Mr. Chairman, I second the motion," or simply, "I second the motion."

Until a motion is made and seconded, no one is allowed to discuss it. After a motion has been made and seconded, no other subject may be discussed until the motion has been disposed of.[2] Too much emphasis cannot be placed on this latter point, for unless this rule is followed the discussion is likely to wander about and no decision be reached.

LIMITING THE SUBJECT

The motion may be limited or modified in two principal ways: by a division of the question, and by amendment.

1. *Division of the question.* Sometimes a motion which contains two questions is made. For example, the motion that "this organization rent an office in the Student Union Building for six months beginning tomorrow" contains the question of the *place* of the proposed office, and the *duration of time* for which the office is to be rented, as well as the question of renting an office at all. When a motion of this kind is made, any member of the group may ask the chairman to divide the motion into two or more parts so that each part can be discussed separately. The chairman has the authority to do this if no one objects. If someone does object or the chairman refuses to divide the question, a motion for division may be made and may be passed by a majority vote.

2. *Amendment of the motion.* There are times when the general idea contained in the motion is satisfactory, but some part of it is undesirable or not clearly stated. The motion can then be changed by striking out or adding certain words to it. In order to do this a "motion to amend" is required, which must itself be seconded and passed by a majority vote before it may become a part of the original motion. The proper form for proposing an amendment is the following: "Mr. Chair-

---

2 For a discussion of privileged, subsidiary, and incidental motions, some of which may be injected into the discussion at any time, see *Robert's Rules of Order Revised* (Scott, Foresman, Chicago, 1951).

man, I move that the motion be amended by striking out the words ('six months') and by inserting the words ('one year') so that the motion will read ('this organization shall rent an office in the Student Union Building for one year')." The motion to amend may itself be amended or discussed, but it must be voted upon before the main question is decided. If the motion to amend is approved, the discussion returns to the original motion *as amended;* if the amending motion fails, the discussion returns to the original form of the main motion.

There are two requirements which the motion to amend must meet to be recognized by the chairman. First, it must be germane; that is, the amending motion may modify the original motion but must not change its meaning entirely. To strike out the whole motion and substitute one having an entirely different central idea is not allowed by the method of amendment. Second, it must embody a real change. Merely to change the motion from an affirmative to a negative statement of the same thing is not permissible. The following example will indicate a proper use of amendment:

a. *Original motion*—"that an expenditure of $500 be authorized for repairing the clubhouse roof."
b. *Amendment*—"that the sum of $1000 be substituted for $500; and that the words 'and completely re-covering' be inserted after the word 'repairing' in the motion."
c. *Motion as amended*—"that an expenditure of $1000 be authorized for repairing and completely re-covering the clubhouse roof."

DISCUSSING THE SUBJECT

The motion before the group at the time may be discussed by any member, but the discussion must be limited to that motion until it is disposed of in some way. The chairman has the right to stop any member who violates this rule and to give the floor to someone else. As soon as the motion has been settled or disposed of, discussion on it must stop unless a formal motion to reconsider it is made and approved. A motion "to reconsider" must be presented by someone who voted with the majority but who wishes to change his vote, and a majority must favor reconsideration. Except in this special case, disposal of a motion automatically stops discussion upon it.

There are, moreover, certain types of motions which cannot be discussed at all but must be put to a vote at once. The most important of these are the following:

1. Motions to call for the regular order of business.
2. Motions for the "previous question."
3. Motions to "lay on the table."
4. Motions for adjournment. (Usually, but not always.)

DISPOSING OF MOTIONS

There are three principal ways to dispose of motions: by a vote on the motion, by a motion to postpone or lay on the table, and by reference to a committee.

1. *Vote on the motion.* Usually the vote on the main motion comes about of its own accord. When the important points have been discussed, the group automatically seems to become ready for a vote. When the chairman senses this attitude on the part of the group, he may suggest a vote, and if there is no objection, the vote is taken. There are times, however, when the attitude of the group toward the proposal is sharply divided, and the discussion continues vigorously even after all the important things have been said. At such times, a motion to the effect that the discussion be stopped and a vote taken is necessary. Such a motion is called a motion for the "previous question," and is made as follows: "Mr. Chairman, I move the previous question." The motion for the previous question cannot be discussed; it must be voted on at once, and it must receive a two-thirds vote for adoption. If it is adopted, the discussion on the main motion must cease and a vote on the main motion be taken

at once. (In less formal groups, this result is obtained merely by calling out "Question!" If there is no objection, the chairman puts the pending motion to a vote at once.)

2. *Motion to postpone or to lay on the table.* The principal effect of a motion to postpone, or to lay the proposition on the table, is to remove the proposal from discussion for the time being in order to allow a consideration of more important matters. A motion which has been postponed or laid on the table may be called up for discussion at a more convenient time and finally disposed of then. The motion to postpone is made by saying, "Mr. Chairman, I move the question be postponed indefinitely," or ". . . postponed until . . . [a definite time]." To lay a proposal on the table, simply say, "Mr. Chairman, I move the question be laid on the table." The motion to postpone or to lay on the table may be made at any time during the discussion, is undebatable, and can be adopted by a majority vote.

Note, however, that unless a definite time is set for reconsideration of a motion which is postponed or laid on the table, the chances are that it will be forgotten or that the pressure of other matters will prevent its being brought up again and considered finally. In fact, the motion to postpone indefinitely is often used to defeat a proposal politely without making the members of the group commit themselves definitely upon it; indeed, a "motion to reconsider" is required to revive discussion of it. Moreover, this motion is often used to test the strength of the support or opposition which the proposal has in the group; a person's vote on postponement shows his attitude toward the proposal itself without the necessity of a final decision.

3. *Referring the motion to a committee.* A motion to refer the proposal to a committee may be made at any time during the discussion and, if adopted by a majority vote, has the effect of removing the main motion from discussion and passing it on to the committee indicated. There are sometimes standing committees to which the motion may be referred;

if not, the chairman may be authorized to appoint a special committee, or a special group may be named in the motion itself. The proposal may be passed on to a committee without instructions, or the committee may be instructed to investigate and report back to the group, or it may be authorized to take final action.

This means of disposing of questions under discussion is especially valuable for handling minor questions on which the group does not wish to spend time for detailed consideration. Sometimes, moreover, no one in the group at the time has adequate information on the subject to justify a final decision, and by instructing a committee to investigate and report, that information can be assured for future consideration.

The form for stating a motion to refer to committee varies with its detailed intent. A few of the forms frequently used are the following: "Mr. Chairman, I move that the question be referred to the . . . committee," or "to the . . . committee, with instructions to report at . . . [a definite time]," or " . . . committee, with power to act." When a special committee must be set up to consider the proposal, provision for creating that committee must be included in the proposal as follows: "Mr. Chairman, I move that this question be referred to a committee of . . . members to be appointed by the chair," or " . . . members, namely, Mr. . . . , Miss . . . , Mrs. . . . , [etc.]," the remainder of the motion continuing as indicated above.

ADJOURNMENT

When the business of the meeting is concluded and no one addresses the chairman for further discussion, the chairman may close the meeting by simply declaring it adjourned. Sometimes, moreover, a fixed time for adjournment has been determined before the group meets; in this event, when the time arrives, the chairman is required to declare the meeting adjourned unless a motion is passed definitely extending the discussion beyond that limit. At any time during the discussion, a motion may be adopted by majority vote fixing the time for adjournment. In any of these situations, when the time arrives, the chairman merely announces, "I declare the meeting adjourned."

If no fixed time has been set, the meeting may be ended at any time by the adoption of a motion to adjourn. This motion may be introduced at any place in the discussion and may be adopted by a majority vote. No discussion upon it is allowed, and it must be voted upon at once—unless adjournment would have the effect of disbanding the group entirely with no provision for reassembling, in which case the motion to adjourn loses its privileged character.

When no definite provision has been made for a future meeting of the group, a motion to fix the time for reconvening takes precedence over a motion to adjourn. This is called a motion "to fix the time to which to adjourn." This motion may be discussed (usually) or amended, and must be decided by a majority vote before the motion to adjourn is itself put to a vote. Unless this is kept in mind, business is often left unfinished with no provision for ultimate settlement.

MODIFYING THE RULES OF ORDER

Because of the small size or informality of the group, not all of the rules listed above may be necessary. Parliamentary procedure is for the purpose of speeding up the orderly conduct of business; it must never be employed with such unnecessary detail and dogmatism that it merely formalizes and complicates the discussion of the group. To follow the rules slavishly in small groups is frequently a waste of time rather than a help. On the other hand, larger meetings frequently require the application of parliamentary rules in all their detail—much greater detail than that presented in this chapter. Sometimes the situation requires the adoption of special rules not listed even in manuals of parliamentary procedure, but fitted to the peculiar needs of a particular group. Apply the rules of parliamentary law as fully as required to preserve order and to expedite business, but only to that degree.

262

problems

1. Outline a discussion plan which you could use if you were to lead a discussion by this class on the subject, "A Sensible Plan for an International Police Force," or some other subject of your own choice.
2. Select a topic suitable for discussion by persons engaged in the vocation or profession you intend to enter and prepare an outline for a discussion of this topic by a study group of such persons.
3. Choose some current problem in which members of the class would be interested and prepare a plan for discussion of this problem.
4. Make a list of problems likely to arise at the next meeting of one of your classes (or other groups) and, assuming you are to act as chairman, *(a)* arrange these problems in the most effective sequence for discussion and *(b)* prepare an appropriately abridged discussion plan for each of them.
5. Analyze the discussion on page 308. Note the contribution to the discussion made in each speech. How well did the leader perform his duties?
6. Listen to a radio panel discussion (such as the University of Chicago Round Table). Evaluate the performance, considering the effectiveness of each member's delivery, his knowledge of the subject, and his contribution to the problem.
7. Assume you have been selected to arrange for a panel discussion to be held before the entire student body. Select a subject of importance to the students and select the speakers whom you would ask to participate as members of the panel. Then prepare a discussion plan suitable *(a)* for the series-of-speeches-plus-open-forum type of panel discussion and *(b)* for the give-and-take type of participation by the panel.
8. Outline a suitable order of business for the following:
    a. A special meeting of the senior class called to select an appropriate class gift.
    b. A regular business meeting of some specified club.
9. For a meeting of some organization to which you belong—
    a. Phrase five proposals as main motions.
    b. Phrase amendments to each of the five main motions prepared above. Be sure that your amendments are germane and that they embody a real change.

10. Taking one of the main motions stated for Problem 9, phrase correctly a motion (*a*) for the previous question, (*b*) to postpone, (*c*) to lay on the table, (*d*) to refer to committee.

11. Organize the class into a hypothetical meeting of one of the following (or similar) organizations and proceed to conduct business. Be careful to follow correct parliamentary procedure and not to allow others to violate it.

   a. The student council.
   b. The sophomore class.
   c. The dramatics board.
   d. The city council.
   e. The Y.M.C.A. or Y.W.C.A. cabinet.

Chapter 9 S P E E C H E S

F O R

S P E C I A L   O C C A S I O N S

Chapters 6 and 7 gave directions for preparing and presenting talks of the two kinds you will most often be called upon to make: those for instruction and for argument. Special occasions sometimes arise, however, which require slightly different treatment. As a presiding officer, you may have to introduce a visiting speaker or welcome a distinguished guest. You may be asked to announce awards or pay brief tribute to someone's achievements or devotion to duty. Or local groups may ask you to talk before them representing the business or profession to which you belong.

This chapter will not attempt to give full instructions on these many varying situations, but we shall consider here the basically different situations requiring special techniques and at least the essential requirements for making talks to suit them.

Special methods of beginning

Before taking up the different situations, consider two methods particularly useful in starting speeches for special occasions:

1. Reference to the occasion.

Speeches which are called forth by the nature of the occasion are often best begun by a reference to that occasion. For example, President Arthur Twining Hadley of Yale University began his address given at the centennial celebration of the Yale Medical School in the following way:

> We meet to celebrate the one hundredth anniversary of the founding of the Yale Medical School. A department of Medicine is and always has been regarded as an essential element in every well-equipped university. The importance of the public service rendered by its graduates and the careful theoretical training necessary to prepare them for such service make it at once a duty and a privilege for a great university to take part in medical training. And there are certain special circumstances in the history of Yale which give to its Medical School a more than ordinary significance as an integral part of the Yale life and organization. In the first place, ... [1]

This method is particularly useful at anniversaries, dedication ceremonies, and other such special events, where the occasion is the central motif for the whole program.

2. Personal greeting.

At times a personal word from the speaker serves as an excellent starting point. This is particularly true when the speaker is one of position or prestige. General Dwight D. Eisenhower began his talk before the New York Chamber of Commerce in this way:

> Mr. President, Mr. Grimm, Gentlemen: I am keenly sensible of the great honor this Chamber has done me. And it is doubly welcome because this award—the priceless token of your honorary membership—comes to me so quickly after my own transfer to this city. It is a distinction I shall always treasure.
>
> I could only have wished as I listened to the overgenerous remarks of Mr. Grimm that the people really responsible for the achievements for which

1 *Modern Short Speeches,* compiled by J. M. O'Neill (Century, N. Y., 1923), p. 67.

I am honored today—for which I have often been so honored—could be here to hear them: The GI's, the officers, the Brass Hats—indeed, every single citizen of the United States, that each in his own sphere attempted to do his job in the late war. . . .[2]

So long as such a beginning is modest in its attitude and sincere, it may serve to establish goodwill as well as to get the attention of the audience. Beware, however, of apologizing. Avoid saying, "I don't know why the chairman picked me out to talk on this subject when others could do it so much better," or "The man who was to speak to you couldn't come, and so at the last minute I agreed to speak, but I haven't had much time to get ready." Such apologetic beginnings defeat their own purpose by suggesting that your speech isn't worthy of attention. Be cordial, sincere, and modest, but don't apologize.

Of course, you will not always limit yourself to one of the two methods described above; the other methods of getting attention at the beginning of a talk (described in Chapter 6—reference to subject, illustration, question, etc.) are effective. But reference to the occasion and the personal greeting are particularly useful in beginning many talks for special occasions.

The rest of this chapter is devoted to the purpose and special requirements of four special types of talks you may be called on to make.

Introducing speakers The success of many a program, whether it is a lecture, a dinner meeting, or a celebration, is often determined by the effectiveness with which the chairman presides. A good presiding officer does not say much; he does not parade himself, yet his presence is felt. The audience feels his unobtrusive control in the smooth running of the program. Sincerity, energy, and decisiveness—these are the personal qualities which mark him as a good leader.

2 From *Vital Speeches of the Day*, Vol. XIV, May 15, 1948, p. 461.

The chairman's preparation must often be just as thorough as that of the speaker. Do not rely on the inspiration of the moment; prepare yourself as follows:

1. Determine the exact purpose of the meeting.
2. Acquaint yourself with the program. Know who is going to speak or sing or play; know each speaker's subject or the name of each artist's selection; understand the function of each part of the program in advancing the purpose of the meeting.
3. Make a time schedule. Determine how long the meeting should last; apportion the time among the various persons on the program and, before the meeting begins, tell each of them tactfully how much time is at his disposal.
4. Prepare your own remarks. Know what you are going to say in your opening speech and in your later remarks. You may modify these remarks according to the turn of affairs, but you must always be ready with something.
5. Start the meeting on time. Be on time yourself and see that the others on the program are, too; then keep things moving as nearly on schedule as possible.

If you prepare yourself in this way, the chances of success for your meeting will be greatly improved.

The person who presides over a meeting has the obligation of introducing speakers. Apparently an easy task, this duty is not so simple as it appears to be on the surface. Too often the introduction serves merely to "let the wind out of the sails," or to bore the listeners with a long recital. Although brief, the speech of introduction is extremely important.

There are times when someone else is better acquainted with the speaker than you are. When this is true, you may well request that person to introduce the speaker. But when you make such a request, be sure that the one who is to make the introduction understands that he is to introduce the speaker and not to tell a long series of anecdotes about their acquaintanceship.

PURPOSE: CREATING A DESIRE TO HEAR THE SPEAKER

Remember that your main object is to create a desire to hear the speaker; everything else must be subordinated to this aim. Your duty is to introduce, not to make a speech. Do not take this as an opportunity to air your own views on the subject. You are only the advance agent; your job is to "sell the other man" to your audience. This implies two things: (1) You must arouse curiosity about the speaker or his subject; by doing this, you will make it easier for him to get the attention of the audience. And (2) you must make the audience either like him or respect him—or both; in this way you will make his listeners more likely to believe what he says and to do what he asks.

MANNER: APPROPRIATE ENTHUSIASM

The dignity or informality of your manner will depend entirely upon the type of occasion, upon the closeness of your acquaintance with the speaker, and upon the prestige of the speaker himself. If you were introducing a justice of the Supreme Court, for instance, it would hardly be appropriate for you to poke fun at him. On the other hand, if you were to present an old friend to a group of your associates at an informal occasion, a manner of stilted dignity would be just as foolish.

Regardless of the dignity or informality of the occasion, one characteristic of presentation is absolutely essential: you must talk with sincere enthusiasm. You will never make an audience want to listen to a speaker unless you suggest by the way you talk about him that you yourself are enthusiastic about him.

SIX PRINCIPLES FOR CONTENT

As you are not the speaker of the day, but are merely introducing another, let the content of your speech follow these principles:

269

1. *Be brief.* To say too much is much worse than to say too little. What many consider to be the best introductory speech ever made was that of Shailer Mathews introducing President Woodrow Wilson; he said, "Ladies and Gentlemen: the President." The prestige of the man you introduce will not always be great enough for you to be so brief as this, but it is better to err in this direction than to speak too long.

2. *Don't talk about yourself.* There is a great temptation to tell your own views on the subject, or to tell anecdotes about your own experiences as a speaker. This should be strictly avoided, for it calls attention to you rather than the speaker.

3. *Tell about the speaker.* Who is he? What is his position in business or government? What experiences has he had that qualify him to speak on this subject? Caution: beware of emphasizing what a good *speaker* he is. Such comment may embarrass him. Let him demonstrate his own speaking ability; you tell who he is and what he knows. Never introduce a man as "a distinguished orator."

4. *Emphasize the importance of the speaker's subject unless the audience realizes the impo, tance already.* This does not mean to give a great deal of information about it. Don't make his speech for him. Merely point out to the audience the particular value of the information the speaker is about to offer. For example, "All of us drive automobiles in which we use the products made from petroleum. A knowledge of the way these products are manufactured and marketed is therefore certain to be valuable to our understanding and to our pocketbooks. . . ."

5. *Mention the appropriateness of the speaker or subject whenever possible.* If a golf club is considering the construction of a new course, a speech on types of grass is very timely, and this fact should be mentioned. Or if the occasion is the anniversary of the organization of a firm, it is appropriate that the founder should be one of the speakers. Statements of such facts are obviously in order and serve to connect the speaker more closely with the audience.

6. Use humor if it suits the occasion. Nothing serves better to put an audience at its ease and to create a friendly feeling than congenial laughter. Take care, however, that the humor is in good taste. Do not destroy the prestige of the speaker by making too much of a "goat" of him. If there is danger of offending the speaker, it is better to let him inject his own humor into the situation when he arises to speak.

Usually, the better known and more respected the speaker is, the more abbreviated should be your introduction; the more completely unknown he is, the more you will need to arouse interest in his subject and build up his prestige. But always remember that four primary virtues of the introductory speech are tact, brevity, sincerity, and enthusiasm.

Courtesy talks: welcoming visitors, accepting awards

Many times one is faced with the problem of performing public acts of courtesy, either as a personal obligation or on behalf of the organization which he represents. The ability to say the appropriate and effective thing on such an occasion is a valuable asset.

TYPICAL SITUATIONS

Courtesy talks are given most frequently to fulfill one of three obligations:

1. *Welcoming visitors.* For example, when a distinguished guest is present, someone, usually the presiding officer, is expected to extend to him a public greeting.

2. *Responding to a welcome or a greeting.* Whenever an individual is so welcomed, the obligation of course falls upon him to express his appreciation of that greeting.

3. *Accepting an award.* Occasionally an individual is presented with a medal or an award for some special accomplishment. In such

events, the recipient of the award may be expected to acknowledge and express his appreciation of the honor. Sometimes, of course, the award is made to an organization as a whole rather than to an individual, in which case someone is selected to act as spokesman in acknowledging it.

Purpose: expressing genuine sentiment

The speech for courtesy has a double purpose. So far as the speaker is concerned, its purpose is *to express a genuine sentiment:* the speaker gives audible evidence of his feeling of gratitude or hospitality. Often the success of a speech for courtesy depends upon the degree to which it makes the audience feel that the appropriate thing has been said. When guests are present or acknowledgments are due, the audience expects the proper courtesies to be extended. Courtesies of private life put people at ease; public acts of courtesy create good feeling in an audience.

Manner: sincerity

Emerson once said, "What you are speaks so loudly I can't hear what you say." This criticism might well be leveled at many persons who have made speeches of courtesy. In no other type of speech is the temptation so great to repeat with oratorical flourish a series of flowery platitudes without any genuine feeling. Above all else, let your manner of speaking be sincere. Do not try to overdo yourself in graciousness. Speak straightforwardly and honestly. Let your manner, moreover, fit the spirit of the situation. Whether the mood in which you speak is to be serious or jovial, brisk or tranquil, will be determined largely by the occasion. Usually, however, a note of optimism is appropriate; imply by your remarks that the presence of this guest is an honor.

Three requirements of content

Remember that your duty is to perform tactfully an act of courtesy. With respect to the content of your speech keep in mind the following points characteristic of the better speeches of this type:

1. *Indicate for whom you are speaking.* In many instances you will be acting as spokesman for a group. Be sure to make clear that the greeting or acknowledgment comes from all and not from you alone. Note the following excerpt from a speech by Theodore Roosevelt: "It is a pleasure to be here this afternoon to accept in the name of the nation the monument put up by your society to the memory of those who fell in the war with Spain. . . . " References to yourself or the group you represent should, of course, always be modest.

2. *Present complimentary facts about the person or group to which you are extending the courtesy.* The emphasis in a speech of this sort should be upon the accomplishment or good qualities of the person or group you are greeting or whose gift or welcome you are acknowledging, rather than upon yourself or the group you represent.

3. *Illustrate; don't argue.* Let the incidents and facts which you present serve to illuminate and develop the importance of the occasion or the group you are addressing, but do not be contentious. Avoid so far as possible points of disagreement. Do not use the courtesy talk as a chance to air your own views on controversial subjects. Let the content of your speech serve to make concrete and vivid the thoughts which are already in the minds of your listeners.

Paying tribute: memorials, farewells, awards

Many times one wishes to pay tribute in public to another's personal qualities or achievements. Such occasions range all the way from the award of a trophy after a contest to the eulogy given for one who has died. Sometimes tribute is paid to groups—such as pioneers, soldiers, and mothers—rather than to an individual.

TYPICAL SITUATIONS

1. *The memorial.* Services to pay public honor to one who is dead are sometimes held, and there is a speech of tribute. Occasionally a

speech of this kind is given years after—witness the many speeches on Lincoln. More often the speech concerns someone personally known to the audience.

2. *Dedication.* Memorials, in the form of buildings, monuments, etc., are sometimes set up to commemorate the life of some outstanding personality. At the dedication it is appropriate that something be said in honor of him to whom the memorial is dedicated.

3. *Farewell.* When an executive with whom a group of men have long been associated leaves to enter another field or when anyone generally admired is about to leave the community or the office which he has held, the opportunity is frequently taken to express public appreciation of his fellowship and work.

4. *Presentation of award.* In the situation just mentioned, the one who is leaving is sometimes presented with some tangible token of remembrance. When someone has performed his duties with unusual skill or devotion, a suitable award may be given him and a tribute paid to his merit or achievement.

Purpose: securing appreciation

The basic purpose of a speech of tribute is to secure appreciation of the commendable traits or accomplishments of the person to whom tribute is paid. If you can get your audience to feel deeply the essential worth or importance of the man, you have succeeded. But you may go further than this. You may, by honoring him, arouse deeper devotion to the cause he represents. Did he give all he had for his company? Then strive to impart depth to the audience's feeling of loyalty toward the company for which he worked. Was he noted as a friend of boys? Then arouse a feeling that boys' work deserves your audience's support. Create a desire in your listeners to emulate him. Make them want to follow in his footsteps, to develop the same virtues, to demonstrate the same devotion.

Manner: simplicity and honesty

A farewell banquet usually mingles an atmosphere of merriment with a spirit of sincere regret. Memorial services, the unveiling of monuments, and the like are on the whole dignified and formal, while the awarding of prizes usually takes place at a time when enthusiasm is the keynote. Regardless of the general tone of the occasion, however, avoid high-sounding phrases, bombastic oratory, obvious "oiliness"; these things will mar the effect of a speech of tribute more quickly than anything else. A simple, honest feeling of admiration expressed without the attempt to be flowery is most likely to be appreciated.

Focusing the content

Too often speeches of tribute are mere enumerations. Many speakers do nothing but name the items concerning a man's life and accomplishments. Such a speech is little better than an obituary. Remember the impossibility of telling everything about a man in the brief time during which you are to speak. Pick out a few of the most outstanding things and emphasize them. Focus the content of your speech on one of three things:

1. *Dominant personal traits.* Select the aspects of the man's personality which are outstandingly worth admiring and then relate incidents from his life or work which will bring these before your audience. Show how they influenced his decisions, impressed others, or enabled him to overcome obstacles.

2. *Outstanding achievements.* Pick out a few of his most notable accomplishments. Tell about them in detail to show how important they were to others and how influential he was in securing results. Let your speech say, "Here is what this man has done; see how important it is."

3. *Influence upon his associates.* Show the effect he had on those with whom he worked. This point is not much different from the other two except in the point of view taken. In showing what the man's influence

has been, you will quite naturally mention his personal traits and achievements. The difference is in the emphasis. The importance of many men lies not so much in any one or two traits or any material personal accomplishment as in the influence they have had on others.

Keep in mind that the three methods outlined above are not mutually exclusive. Every speech of tribute will contain all three characteristics to some extent. But in the interest of unity and effect upon the audience you can well emphasize only one of the three.

In developing the points you have chosen to emphasize, beware of complicated statistics and of long enumerations. Do not name organization after organization to which the man belongs. What few things you do tell about, relate in an interesting human way. Let each event you talk about become a story, living and personal. Only in this way will you get your audience to admire the *man.*

Goodwill talks

Every speech, of course, seeks the goodwill of the audience, but the type of speech here considered has this object as its direct and primary aim. In a sense, the goodwill speech is informative in character, telling as it does about the organization for which public support is sought; in another sense, its purpose is to convince, yet it must not be argumentative— the appeal for support must be subordinated or at times even hidden. In short, the goodwill speech is an informative speech the object of which is to convince—a sort of hybrid, combining the characteristics of two basic types of speech considered in Chapters 6 and 7. Goodwill speeches of this sort have within recent years begun to play an important part in the public relations of many business firms. More than eighteen hundred speeches of this type were made in one year by the representatives of a single large Chicago corporation. But business firms are not alone in this practice; many such talks are now being made by spokesmen of public institutions to build up and maintain public support.

276

Typical situations

1. *Luncheon club meetings.* Luncheon club meetings present an excellent opportunity for such talks. Clubs of this sort offer an audience composed of leading men or women from all types of business and professional life. Meetings are semi-social in nature and good feeling is practically guaranteed. Such groups are interested in civic affairs and in the workings of other men's professions. To gain the support and goodwill of groups like this is relatively easy and extremely valuable.

2. *Educational programs.* Educational programs are often arranged by school authorities, clubs, and religious organizations. Speakers are asked to talk about their business or profession and to explain to the young people in the audience what opportunities exist and what training is required. By tactful reference, goodwill may be secured for the particular organization you represent.

3. *Special demonstration programs.* Special programs are frequently presented by corporations and by university extension departments. For example, the county farm agent, referring to experiments which have been conducted at the state university, may show better methods of grading butter or of feeding poultry. Although the speech is primarily informative in character, the speaker indirectly points out that the experimental work was done by the university to aid farmers such as those who make up the audience.

There are, naturally, many other situations in which goodwill speeches are in order—indeed, there are few situations in which they are not—but these three are typical.

Purpose: securing goodwill unobtrusively

It is obvious from what has already been said that the primary aim so far as the speaker is concerned is to secure goodwill. But this is somewhat too simple a statement of the case. Although the *real* purpose of the speech, this object must not be the *apparent* purpose. So far as the audience is concerned, the purpose must appear to be primarily informative

277

(or sometimes persuasive: urging joint action toward a common goal). Moreover, in order to secure goodwill, the speaker must necessarily present information about his organization; he must get his audience to understand and appreciate it in order to secure goodwill for it. Thus, the purpose of the speech will be to present information about the speaker's profession or the organization he represents in order to secure support for it *unobtrusively*.

Manner: modesty, tolerance, humor

Three terms—modesty, tolerance, and good humor—characterize the manner of speaking required on such occasions. The speaker quite naturally will be talking about his own vocation and he must make that vocation seem important to his audience, but he should beware of bragging. Let the facts speak for themselves. Moreover, show a tolerant attitude toward others, especially toward competitors. Finally, exercise good humor. The goodwill speech is not for the crusader. Take the task more genially.

Four essentials of content

Essentially four things are characteristic of what you should say:

1. *Novel, interesting facts about your organization.* In one sense, a speech of this kind implies indulgence in a little gossip. Make your listeners feel that you are "letting them in on the inside." Avoid talking about what they already know, but give them first-hand information about things that are not generally known.

2. *Indication of definite relation between your profession and the lives of the members of your audience.* Make them see the importance of your activities to their safety and happiness.

3. *Avoidance of any definite request for their approval (assume that you have it already).* Don't make the mistake of telling your listeners that they don't know anything about your organization and that you are trying to get their goodwill. Instead, suggest that they already know a

good deal about it (if they don't, they will probably think they ought to) and then proceed with points 1 and 2.

4. *Offer of some definite service.* This may be in the form of an invitation to visit your office or shop, or even the simple offer to answer questions. Leave the impression that you are at your listeners' service.

The suggestions outlined above will need to be modified to suit the needs of the occasion at which you speak. But never lose sight of one fact: indirectly, *you must demonstrate to your listeners that your work is of value to them.*

problems

1. Prepare a plan for a meeting at which you might be expected to preside.
2. Preside for one day during the next series of class speeches. See that the program runs on schedule; maintain a lively atmosphere; and introduce each speaker in an appropriate manner.
3. Prepare a speech suitable for an occasion such as
   a. Welcoming a distinguished visitor.
   b. Accepting a citation or award for some achievement.
   c. Responding to a welcoming speech.
   d. Accepting an office to which you have been elected.
4. Prepare a speech paying tribute to a man whom you admire.
5. Prepare a speech to secure goodwill for your intended business or profession suitable for presentation before—
   a. A county farmers' institute.
   b. One of the local luncheon clubs.
   c. A parent-teacher association.
   d. A convocation of students in high school.
   e. A convention of dentists, doctors, or some other professional group.
6. Assuming that you are to introduce one of the speakers whose remarks are printed in the Supplement, prepare an appropriate introduction.

President Roosevelt was the acknowledged master of the art of speaking by radio. From the expression on his face in the picture below it is clear that Mr. Roosevelt was *thinking* of his audience while talking to them through the microphone just as much as when talking to them directly. Thus his whole personality came across to his listeners.

Chapter 10 BROADCASTING

A TALK

Every speaker should have at least a general knowledge of the technique of speaking over the air, because he is likely to be called on at times to broadcast his remarks. You will observe as this analysis proceeds that important differences from ordinary speaking do exist. Still, the fundamental principles laid down earlier continue for the most part to apply, and more often than not what is good speech before a visible audience is good speech for broadcast purposes.

The radio and television audience

To understand the basis for the modifications which are necessary for broadcast speaking, an appreciation of the nature of radio and television audiences is required. First of all, any such audience is universal: that is, anyone who has a receiving set within the power range of the broadcasting station can "listen in," so that your listeners are likely to be of both sexes and of all ages, creeds, occupations, interests, and degrees of intelligence. There is no such thing as a radio or television audience

281

composed entirely of young men, or of Democrats, or of Baptists, or of labor-union delegates. This puts an additional premium on tactfulness and on the ability to give a subject universal interest.

The influence of the hour and of the location of the broadcasting station serves to limit the universal nature of broadcast audiences somewhat. Surveys have shown that women listeners predominate during the morning hours when husbands are away at work and children are at school; this is also true early in the afternoon. At mealtimes anyone is likely to listen, but most people prefer musical programs or brief announcements (markets, weather, news, etc.) at this time. More children are apt to be listening in the late afternoon and early evening than at any other time; late evening audiences contain few children. Men are likely to have more leisurely interest during the evening and on Sundays and holidays. The location of the station, of course, modifies the nature of the audience in that the power of the station is weaker at a distance; as a result the audience probably consists of more people from the immediate neighborhood than from a distance. This is less true of large, powerful stations than of small ones, of course; and network broadcasts will cover every kind of community.

A third and very important characteristic of radio and television audiences is that the listening is done by individuals or by small intimate groups. In spite of the large and universal character of your audience in general, the individuals in that audience will not be gathered in a large mass but will be scattered about in living-rooms, offices, hotel rooms, automobiles, and the like. While no doubt aware that others are also listening to the same program, the radio or television listener is primarily influenced by his own environment and expects the speaker to talk to him in an informal, conversational manner suited to that environment. Such listeners do not like to have speeches made at them; they prefer to be talked with.

Two further characteristics need to be remembered: listeners can easily tune off at any time, and they are likely to be more subject to distraction. People hesitate to make themselves conspicuous by getting up and leaving an audience which a speaker is addressing personally, but the radio or television listener feels no hesitation at all about tuning you out. In addition, he is likely to be surrounded by household noises—the baby's crying, the clatter of dishes, a conversation at the other end of the room—which compete with the broadcast for his attention. Both of these facts require of the broadcast speech a high degree of interest value.

Two types of broadcast Apart from the more specialized forms such as play-by-play sports broadcasts, dramatized dialogs, and the like, there are two principal types of speech broadcast: those which are broadcast directly from the studio without an audience, and those which are presented before actual audiences in the studio or broadcast from the speaker's stand in an auditorium.

BROADCASTS FROM THE STUDIO WITHOUT AN AUDIENCE

When you speak directly from the studio for the broadcast audience alone, the style of speaking should be very informal and conversational. The novice is likely to think of the "millions" of listeners in his audience and to make an oration to them, forgetting that actually he is talking directly to one, two, or three persons in each place. A good plan is to imagine that you are talking with someone over a very clear-toned telephone, or that you are sitting across the room from someone and conversing with him personally. Indeed, some speakers bring a friend into the studio with them and direct their remarks to that person, or if the announcer is in the same room, they talk as if conversing with the announcer. Do not strain for overdramatic effects. You needn't shout; the transmitter will add all the power needed to carry your voice miles away. An audition before the broadcast will help determine how loud to talk and how close to the microphone you must be.

Sometimes a speech made before an audience present in person is of sufficient general interest to justify broadcasting it, or public interest in an occasion (such as an anniversary or a dedication) is great enough to warrant broadcasting an entire program of which a speech is a part. On nearly all such occasions the speaker's primary duty is to the audience before him; radio and television listeners are allowed, as it were, to listen in through the window. They seem to accept this fact. When they know that an actual audience is before you, they do not mind your talking in the manner of public speech rather than of intimate conversation. They use their imaginations to project themselves into your presence and in a sense become a part of the crowd in the auditorium. The situation is quite different from that of studio broadcasts, where the listeners somehow expect you to come to them. When the broadcast is by radio alone without television, you can help the imaginations of your radio listeners, however, by occasional remarks referring pointedly to the specific audience before you or to the occasion which has brought them together. Laughter drawn from the audience or applause or any audience participation which can be heard will help remind the radio listener of the audience before you.

The manner of speaking for radio

The main thing to remember in broadcasting a radio talk is variety of voice. Remember that without television your radio audience can't see you and must get its impression of you from your voice. Change the rate of speed at which you talk and vary the pitch of your voice. Do not, however, make sharp changes in its loudness or shift away from the microphone. Remember that the microphone is sensitive and that you must adapt yourself to it. Go back to page 83 and review the discussion of microphone technique given there.

Groping for words is a major sin in broadcasting. Since the audience cannot see the speaker anyway, most people solve the problem by writing out radio speeches word for word and reading them from manuscript. This procedure has the further advantage of insuring the completion of the remarks within the allotted time. There is one disadvantage: some persons cannot write with the informality of oral style, and, even when they can, they have difficulty in reading aloud in a natural, easy, conversational manner. This disadvantage can be overcome with a little practice, however; whereas even the best speakers find keeping a swift extemporaneous flow of words on the air a bit difficult. The advice of experts is to use manuscript for radio speech and to learn how to read from it naturally, avoiding both monotony and artificial emphasis.

Avoid monotony, then, by varying the pitch and rate of speaking; learn to read from manuscript in an easy, natural fashion, avoiding long pauses; and keep in mind the listeners around the receiving sets at home—talk *at* the microphone but *to* the listeners.

The manner of speaking for television

Unlike the "blind" radio broadcast, television permits your audience to see you while you talk. Thus your physical behavior—your appearance, facial expression, and movement—may help to convey your thought just as when you are speaking face to face. Likewise, irritating mannerisms will annoy your listeners, and a monotonous "dead-pan" expression or slavish reading from manuscript will cause them to lose interest. Indeed, the intimacy with which your audience views your image on the receiving set makes your appearance and movement even more important than when your audience sees you face to face.

Neither can you merely forget you are broadcasting and talk as you would if only facing an immediate audience. Your voice and action must still conform to the limitations imposed by the microphone and the television camera. In addition, you must adapt yourself to the distractions of the dazzling lights, to the movement of cameras on their booms or dollies, and to the restriction of your movement within the area upon which the lights and cameras are focused. And yet this adaptation must seem natural, avoiding equally a stunned or disconcerted appearance and the tendency to overact, to "play the gallery."

The technical aspects of television are changing rapidly and the facilities available at different stations vary considerably. Hence you will need special advice from the technicians in charge each time you broadcast in order to adapt your presentation to the special conditions which prevail. For this reason, detailed instructions would be inappropriate here.

Factors deserving special emphasis

Although the principles of speech development laid down in previous chapters apply to broadcast speech as well, some deserve special emphasis. In particular, bear the following suggestions in mind:

1. *Remember that the time limit is exact.* Most broadcasting stations operate on a schedule that is adhered to within thirty seconds; you cannot run over time or you will be cut off. Moreover, programs start on time too; allow yourself time to get to the studio and catch your breath before you have to begin speaking. If you are to speak on a fifteen-minute program, you will not have a full fifteen minutes to speak; allowance must be made for announcements and introduction. Ask just how much time to allow for these things so that you will know exactly how much time is actually yours, and find out what sort of signal you will be given to indicate how the time is going. Many people find that they talk much faster in a studio than elsewhere without realizing it. Allow for this possibility by having an additional illustration or story prepared, which can be inserted near the end conveniently if you see that you are getting through too early. Be prepared also to cut if the time grows short in order to finish promptly.

2. *Make your appeal as universal as possible.* Remembering that all sorts of people may be listening, reach out to interest them by the varied nature of your illustrations, comments, and applications.

3. *Use animated, lively, concrete material.* Avoid abstract theorizing; listeners will tune you off. Use a wealth of stories, illustrations, comparisons, and the like, especially those which are "believe it or not" in type, those which contain plenty of action, and those which relate to the everyday experiences of your listeners.

4. *Apply as many of the factors of interest as possible.* Go back to pages 179-184 and study again the principles of attention there discussed. Give special emphasis to (a) the *Vital*—relate your material to the important needs and desires of as many types of people as you can; (b) *Activity* and *Reality*—keep your speech free from abstraction and full of movement in the manner indicated in the preceding paragraph; (c) *Suspense*—early in your speech arouse curiosity or give promise of valuable information which is to be presented later, always indicating that there is something more of value to come.

5. *Use simple (but not childish) wording and sentence structure.* Avoid the use of technical terms where common terms will do; if you must use such terms, explain them. But do not talk down to the audience; even children like to be talked to as if they were grown up. Use relatively simple sentences.

6. *Use a simple type of speech organization.* Avoid complex reasoning; rarely will you have time to make such reasoning clear, and without being able to watch your listener you can't tell whether he is understanding it or not. A few main ideas, clearly related and moving definitely in a straightforward direction, should serve as the main structure of your speech.

7. *Mark your transitions clearly.* When you move from one idea to another, be sure to indicate this fact by a word or two or by a distinct change of rate or pitch. On the platform or on television you can indicate such transitions by movement or gesture, but over the radio your

287

voice must do this work. Such transitions should not become stereotyped, however; vary them and keep them informal. Such phrases as "In the first place" and "Secondly" sound a bit stilted for the conversational type of speaking called for in the studio. It is much better to say, "Now I want to tell you—" or "But let's look at something else for a minute."

8. *Give a sense of continuous movement and development.* Don't let your speech run down or ramble. Keep your listeners aware that you are getting somewhere, that you have an objective and are moving toward it steadily.

9. *Avoid profanity and remarks offensive to special groups.* Extreme care must be taken to avoid remarks that could be interpreted as slurs upon any religious, racial, or occupational group. Remember that the air is public property and that all types of people may be listening. Profanity or risqué stories are never necessary to a good speaker; on the air they are absolutely taboo—the station will shut you off in order to save its license if you use them.

These are a few of the considerations that should be kept in mind in preparing the material for speaking on the air. You can observe their application by listening to speakers broadcasting from the better stations every day.

problems

1. Acting as an announcer, introduce some famous person to the "radio audience" as if he were about to speak.[1]
2. Give a five-minute survey of the day's news (or cover the week's news in ten minutes). Write out the opening and closing statements verbatim and outline the intervening material. Set a clock on the table before you and adjust your remarks so that you close exactly on time.

1 If a loud-speaker system is available with the microphone in an adjoining room, its use will make these exercises more realistic and valuable. A workable substitute consists of having the speaker talk from behind a screen or from the rear of the room so that he will be heard but not seen.

3. Prepare for radio or television presentation talks of the types described in Chapters 4, 5, and 7 as assigned by your instructor, fitting them to definite time limits.
4. Listen to some skilled radio speaker broadcast and report to the class what you think are the factors of his effectiveness. Comment both on his manner of speaking and on the organization and content of his speech.
5. Suppose you are to broadcast a five-minute speech to a general evening audience. Cut one of the speeches printed in the Supplement, adapting it for the audience.
6. Adapt the speech you have prepared in Problem 5 for television broadcast. Indicate with marginal notes what visual aids you would use and what special adaptations of movement and gesture would be appropriate.
7. Prepare for television broadcast a speech similar in purpose to the one prepared for Problem 3. Include marginal notes as suggested in Problem 6.

SUPPLEMENT

Principles of Speech has set up specific formulas about the characteristics, structure, and supporting material of each of the types of speech—to provide an ideal and to give the student at least one good way of preparing a given type. It is important to remember, however, that not all good speeches will conform precisely with the outlines presented in this text. Although the following speeches have been classified according to types, the student perhaps will not find all the characteristics exemplified in every case. He may find a speech that embodies elements of several different types, or he may find a very good speech that is effective because of its excellence in a single characteristic. It is hoped that the student will study the speeches carefully, analyzing the structure and method used and deciding how effectively the speaker achieved his purpose.

290

291

The Revolution in
Our Political Parties

by WILLIAM G. CARLETON

GREAT changes are taking place in our political parties, changes which amount to a slow revolution. These changes will influence our lives deeply, for it is through our parties that we make our important government decisions; it is through our parties that the democratic process operates. The changing nature of our parties, therefore, will have consequences for all of us.

Through the years, particularly in the last several decades, our two major parties have reversed their fundamental arguments, their principles, their philosophies. The Jeffersonians—that is, the Democrats—who once stood for less government now stand for more. The Hamiltonians—that is, the Republicans—who once stood for more government now stand for less. And curiously enough, both parties have been consistent in this apparent inconsistency. These reversals are logical. They make sense.

Prior to this twentieth century, it was the business men—the manufacturers, the bankers, the railroad investors—who wanted to extend government. Business men wanted tariffs, subsidies, bank charters, railway grants. In general, business men were committed to the old mercantilistic philoso-phy that prosperity slides down from the top, that in order to make the nation strong, government should intervene positively to stimulate business and encourage the capitalists. By so doing, it was argued, all classes in the nation were benefited. So long as these views prevailed among business men, the Republican party, to which most business men belonged, favored an extension of government, particularly an extension of the federal government. On the other hand, the Democratic party, which contained relatively few business men but many laborers and farmers, stood out against the extension of government and proclaimed the doctrines of little government, of individualism, of laissez-faire, of states rights. The groups composing the Democratic party contended that few benefits from the government went directly to them but that instead they bore the burdens of government aids to business, that they were forced to pay higher taxes and higher prices as the result of government intervention in behalf of the business interests.

By the twentieth century conditions and circumstances had changed, and the parties responded to these changes. America was now a land of big business,

292

and twentieth century big business had less reason than the smaller and developing business of the nineteenth century to ask aid from the government. Big business, while not averse to direct favors from government, primarily wanted to be left alone. The old mercantilistic philosophy of government stimulation to business gave way to the new social-democratic philosophy of government regulation of business, which business men resented and resisted. The new philosophy that prosperity bubbles up from the bottom (and does not percolate down from the top), that the chief need is for wide and continuous purchasing power to buy the avalanche of goods that can now pour from the machines, steadily gained ground. Increasingly government stepped in to regulate business and to insure to the mass of consumers, to labor, and to farmers a greater share of the national income. Laboring men and farmers, many of them in the Democratic party, favored this trend, and the Democratic party increasingly became the champion of more government, particularly more federal government. Business men, most of them in the Republican party, felt they were being curbed and restricted and then taxed to pay for the restrictions, and consequently the Republican party increasingly opposed the trend toward more government.

And thus it has come about that the Democratic party, which once resisted the trend toward more government, now spearheads the trend; that the Republican party, which once spearheaded the trend toward more government, now resists it. To be sure, even the conservative Republicans like Senator Robert A. Taft know full well that we cannot go back to the simple government of the nineteenth century, and even Taft is a "welfare-stater" of a sort. Nevertheless, the historic roles are now reversed, and reversed with good reason. The Democrats now invoke the name of Jefferson to give us more government and to hasten centralization of government; the Republicans now invoke the name of Hamilton to slow the trend toward more government and to discourage centralization.

In another sense, our political parties are now undergoing a revolution. An important realignment of groups is taking place between the parties. True, business still remains the chief pillar of the Republican party, and labor still remains the chief pillar of the Democratic party. But some other important groups are shifting allegiances.

The Republican party tends to lose Midwestern and Western progressives and to pick up Southern conservatives. The Democratic party tends to pick up Midwestern and Western progressives and to lose Southern conservatives. The Republican party is becoming more consistently conservative. The Democratic party is becoming more consistently leftist. The differences between our two major parties are becoming more logical, more ideological, more clear-cut. We are getting a fundamental realignment of our parties, and we are getting that realignment not by way of the growth of a third party, as many had predicted. We are getting that realignment within the pattern of our traditional two-party system.

The old Republican one-party states of the corn and wheat belt are now visibly becoming two-party states. The old Democratic one-party states of the South are now gradually becoming two-party states.

During and following the Civil War, the corn and wheat states of the agricultural Northwest became Republican one-party states. At the close of Reconstruction, Southern states became Democratic one-party states. Both areas thus became political abnormalities, and the one-party system of both sections represented, in part, a carry-over of the emotional and sectional issues of the Civil War. Before the Civil War all sections of the country had been two-party sections. After the Civil War only the area East of the Mississippi River and North of the Mason-Dixon Line enjoyed a genuine two-party system, and even in this area there were some one-party states. The country at large enjoyed a two-party system only because the two one-party sections represented *opposite* parties—the Northwest was a *Republican* one-party section and the south was a *Democratic* one-party section.

Today, however, the one-party sections are becoming two-party sections again, and this is resulting in a more logical party division nationally.

Until Franklin D. Roosevelt's campaign of 1932, the corn and wheat states of the Northwest—Kansas, Nebraska, the Dakotas, Iowa, Minnesota, and Wisconsin—were usually overwhelmingly Republican. Democratic organization did not exist at all in many of the counties of these states. For the most part, Democratic state organization was formal and perfunctory. True, enough Democratic organization existed to allow Democratic presidential nominees, upon occasion, to carry some of these states—for instance, Bryan in 1896 and Wilson in 1916. But such occasions were extremely rare. And at all times Democratic organization remained weak in the localities and Republicans pretty well monopolized the local jobs.

What explains the tremendous hold of the Republican party on this area? There are a number of explanations: the issues and memories of Civil War and Reconstruction times; slavery; the great part played by the Northwest on the side of the Union; the strength of Grand Army of the Republic veterans; the Homestead Act passed by the Republican party; the trans-continental railroads sponsored by Republican policies. The "Cleveland" panic confirmed the Republicanism of the farm belt. The "Wilson" panic of 1920, particularly devastating in the farm belt, reaffirmed that Republicanism.

However, since 1932, since the "Hoover" panic and the Roosevelt New Deal, the Democrats have been growing stronger in this area, and the Truman victory of 1948 gave additional impetus to the Democrats. A new and vigorous Democratic party is developing in the farm belt. Democratic organization is extending to the grass roots. Full Democratic tickets are appearing in more and more of the towns and counties. "Respectable" leaders more and more are willing to accept Democratic nominations. The "rotten borough" type of leadership is disappearing in the Democratic party, and a new, a young, an able, an enthusiastic, an aggressive leadership is appearing—a leadership not satisfied with dispensing Washington patronage but bent on winning mass elections in all the subdivisions of these states. The one-party system is disappearing. A vital two-party system is in the making.

And why this phenomenal growth of Democratic strength in the corn and wheat states? There are a number of reasons: memories of the "Hoover" depression; the repeated national victories of the Democratic party; the large amount of federal patronage; the popularity of Democratic measures with respect to farm relief and public electric power; the fact that Democratic policies seem to fit in with post-depression and post-war thinking better than do Republican policies; the tendencies of progressives and young people to go into the Democratic party.

The paramount issue in the farm belt is parity price, and Democratic farm subsidies and price supports are popular in the farm belt. There is a suspicion in the farm belt that the Republicans are not as firm friends of crop supports as are the Democrats. Even the Administration's Brannan Plan has considerable support in the farm belt, but with the Brannan Plan defeated the Democrats are in an even stronger position. To the cities, consumers, wage-earners, and Farmers' Union, supporting the Brannan Plan, the Democrats can claim that they would have enacted the Plan into law but for Republican opposition. To the advocates of high and fixed price supports, strong in the farm belt, the Democrats can point out that the current Democratic Congress enacted a law extending price supports at the high and fixed level of ninety per cent of parity. And to all farmers, the Democrats can boast that the present Democratic Congress was more generous to the farmer than the Republican Eightieth Congress, which enacted the Aiken Act, an act which under some conditions allowed crop supports to fall as low as sixty per cent of parity.

Another issue benefiting the Democrats is public electric power. In the public mind, the Democrats have managed to get themselves on the side of the proposed Missouri Valley Authority and the proposed Columbia Valley Authority. Also, they have managed to get themselves on the side of public power districts which enable consumers to get cheap electric power from federal dams. These are popular measures in the farm belt and in the West.

In terms of organized group support the Democrats are gaining. The AAA committeemen, grass-root farmers elected by fellow grass-root farmers to administer federal farm legislation in the localities, tend to be Democrats and to influence others strongly in favor of the Democratic party. The Farmers' Union is a rapidly growing organization in many of the farm states and tends to support the Democrats. Republican progressives and progressives of Republican origin tend to go into the Democratic party; Farmer-Laborites in Minnesota; LaFollette Progressives in Wisconsin; the Norris following in Nebraska. Perhaps most significant of all, young people and first voters tend to register as Democrats.

The Republicans, of course, are still very strong in the farm belt. The tradition there is overwhelmingly Republican. Many progressives—both leaders and the rank and file—still cling to the Republican party. But in the farm belt and in the West there is an unmistakable and a significant tendency for liberals and progressives to quit the Republican party and go over to the Democratic party.

Over the years, then, the Democrats of the farm belt have been gaining and the Republicans weakening. At the same time, over the same years, the Democrats of the South have been weakening, and the Republicans, at least in presidential elections, have been gaining. What has caused this weakening of the Solid South? In order to answer this question we must go back a bit into history.

At the close of Reconstruction, only one party remained in the South—the Democratic party. All white men, of whatever faction or shade of opinion, joined together in the Democratic party to preserve "white supremacy" and to prevent effective Negro participation in politics. Men who would have been Republicans had they lived in the North, men who actually had been Whigs in the days before the Civil War, not only became Democrats but frequently assumed the leadership of the Democratic party. The Democratic party had always been the strongest party in the South, even in the days before the Civil War when the South had a two-party system, for the ideals and policies of Jefferson and Jackson made a powerful appeal to the majority of small farmers of this agrarian section. But during and after the Civil War, almost all white voters, whatever their economic interests, joined the Democratic party in opposition to "Northern interference" and because of their opposition to Negro influence in politics. The Democratic Solid South, then, can be explained almost exclusively in terms of the determination of nearly all groups of white men to exclude the Negro from politics. And as long as the national Democratic party was relatively conservative on economic questions and was led by conservatives like Seymour and Tilden and Cleveland, the conservatives of the South felt fairly comfortable within the Democratic party on all counts.

But since the turn of the century, Southern conservatives have been increasingly perturbed over the new direction of the national Democratic party. They resented the Bryan leadership, and many rebelled against it. They were restless under Wilson and feared the strong labor influence in that administration. And under the Roosevelt and Truman leadership, conservative fears have grown and intensified.

So long as the Democratic party was still the vehicle of "white supremacy," at least in the South, conservatives felt compelled to stick to the party, in spite of their dislike of the party's economic policies. But by now it has become clear that the New-Deal and the Fair-Deal Democratic party, even more than the Republican party, has become the spearhead of policies which widen the economic, political, and legal rights of the Negro. Even in the South the Democratic party is becoming a weaker and weaker vehicle for preserving "white supremacy." The white primaries have been outlawed by federal judges appointed by Democratic administrations. Since 1944, every Southern primary and election has seen a significant increase in Negro voters. About nine-tenths of Southern Negroes participating in politics now register and vote as Democrats. The one-party system was a device to prevent Negro participation in Southern politics, but Negro participation in Southern politics can no longer be prevented. The reason for the one-party system is gradually disappearing. And as the reason disappears, so will the one-party system. The one-party system is on the way out—"gone with the white primary." Why, then, should Southern conservatives remain in a party which no longer serves either their economic or their avowed racial interests?

The Republican party is growing stronger in the South, particularly in presidential elections. In 1948, Dewey carried about thirty-six per cent of the popular vote of the South. In other words, Southern conservatives increasingly vote Republican in presidential elections. So far as presidential elections go, the Republican party is adult in Kentucky; it is near adult in Tennessee; it is a lusty youth in Virginia, North Carolina, Texas, and Florida; it is a growing adolescent in Georgia, Alabama, Louisiana, and Arkansas; and only in South Carolina and Mississippi is it still an infant.

Where Southern conservatives are still reluctant to vote Republican, they tend to go into the Dixiecrat movement. On the main economic issues of the day, Dixiecrats see about eye to eye with Republicans. Dixiecrats are those Southern conservatives who, for one reason or another, still want to cling to some kind of Democratic label, who still cannot bring themselves to register or to vote as Republicans. But where Dixiecrats fail to hold or win their state organizations, where they are defeated by national Democrats, by New-Deal Democrats, they will more and more incline to the Republican party. The Dixiecrats have no long-time or permanent place in Southern politics; sooner or later they must merge with those who feel as they do, who are numerically stronger than they are even in the South—the Republicans.

In the farm belt, then, a genuine two-party system is reviving, and the Democrats are steadily growing stronger. In the South, a genuine two-party system is reviving, but more slowly than in the farm belt, and the Republicans are gradually growing stronger. Expressed in national terms, this means that the Democrats are losing Southern conservatives and winning farm belt progressives, that the Republicans are losing farm belt progressives and winning Southern conservatives. *But the Democrats are winning Western progressives more rapidly than the Republicans are winning Southern conservatives.* And if all the conservatives of the South were suddenly to find themselves in the Republican party—which is still a long way from the fact—and a vigorous two-party system in actual operation in the South, even then the Democrats probably would win more of the South more frequently than the Republicans. The Democratic tradition is strong in the South. A majority of Southerners were Democrats long before the Civil War and Reconstruction, long before the Negro issue entered Southern politics. Even when the South was a two-party section, even in Federalist and Whig days, the South went Democratic much more frequently than it went Federalist or Whig. Today the majority of Southern people—white and black—are poor folks. They regard the Democratic party as the party of poor folks. As poor folks they stand to benefit enormously from the expanding social services of the federal government.

What significance has this for our practical politics of today? Simply this. The Republicans should be extremely cautious about making a frontal attack on the welfare state, on the basic trend of our time, for they need to check their losses in the farm belt and in the West. They will not do this by making a general attack on the welfare state, for the welfare state includes farm price supports and public electric power, popular in the West. To keep their progressives and liberals, the Republicans need not go as far toward a controlled economy as the Democrats, but they cannot keep their progressives and liberals by preaching old-fashioned and straight-out free enterprise. They can attack specific extravagances and specific pressure-group evils, but they cannot attack the whole trend toward a welfare state. Even if all the conservatives in the country were in the Republican party, it is doubtful if there would be enough of them to win on the issue of "statism." But all the conservatives are not in the Republican party. Many Southern conservatives are still in the Democratic party. These Southern conservatives are on the way to Republicanism, but they have not yet gone all the way over. In short, the Republicans have not yet arrived at the position where they can exploit to their political advantage a majority of Southern conservatives, where they can count on some Southern states in the Republican column at election time. Until they have arrived at such a position, they will be well advised to be resilient, to see to it that they do not lose any more of their farm belt and Western liberals than they have already lost.

We are, then, confronted with a paradox. A two-party system is reviving in the farm belt. A two-party system is reviving, more slowly, in the South. But a revived two-party system in the farm belt and the transitional situation in the South might actually lead in practice to a Democratic one-party system nationally, at least for a time.

Have the Republicans of today enough political sense, enough flexibility, to prevent this? A few decades ago, conservative Republican leaders like William McKinley and even Mark Hanna would have had the political wisdom to deal with this situation effectively. But today? Will the Republicans follow realists like Ives, Driscoll, Dewey, Lodge, Aiken, Flanders, Youngdahl, Thye, Beardsley, Morse and Warren? Or will they follow the doctrinaire free-enterprisers like Hoover, Bricker, Wherry, McCarthy, Gabrielson, and Fulton Lewis, Jr.—and go down the certain road to disaster? We shall see.

CONVINCING

National Crime Syndicates

by DELESSEPS S. MORRISON

MY name is deLesseps S. Morrison. I am the mayor of the City of New Orleans and the immediate past president of the American Municipal Association, whose viewpoint and recommendations I have been asked to present here today. The AMA speaks directly and indirectly for 10,152 towns and cities of America.

On September 20, 1949, our Association addressed to Attorney General McGrath a letter expressing concern over the growing menace of organized nationwide gambling syndicates. We proposed federal government coordination and cooperation with local agencies in coping with this problem.

This conference is an unprecedented and significant milestone in the history of crime-fighting in the United States. Certainly it marks the first coordinated step to be taken by the federal government in recognition of the growing power of organized crime syndicates in our country.

On behalf of the American Municipal Association, I should like to express our genuine appreciation to Attorney General McGrath for his interest and initiative in calling this meeting. And to President Truman, certainly, for his presence and expression of interest and cooperation. Both the conference and the stature of the participants offer the greatest encouragement to public officials and civic-minded citizens who are sincerely concerned with the problem and who believe that an immediate, strong and effective plan of coordinated action is necessary.

Before going further I would like to make plain and clear two important points. We of the AMA recognize fully the responsibilities and duties of local officials for local law enforcement. We do not ask the federal government to take over this task—nor do we condone the failure of indifferent or inefficient local officials to work for enforcement in their communities.

But we do say, however, that when local officials wage war on nationally organized underworld elements whose supply lines, communications, and general operations cut across municipal, county, state and even national lines— then this problem is no longer a local

one to be handled solely by local officials whose jurisdiction and information is so limited.

Secondly, I would like to say that we do not pretend to be experts on this subject. There are many gaps in the information available to us and to the other municipal officials present—gaps which we hope will be corrected to some extent by this conference.

For instance, the federal government agencies have an extensive data on nationwide operations of racing wire services, the slot machine syndicates, and allied activities. Yet much of this is not available to municipal officials, and some not even available to other U. S. departments.

A few days ago we learned of an extensive report on racing wire services compiled several years ago by the FBI. Yet, when our police superintendent asked for a copy he was told that none was available in New Orleans. And, even if there were, the FBI said, it could not permit us to see such a confidential document.

There is an urgent need now of central coordination for such information among federal departments, making same available to law enforcement agencies of the cities and states.

We do not have the whole picture— but each of us present—and hundreds of other mayors, public officials and crime commissions in various states— have seen small segments of this national scene of organized interstate crime. These pieces fit together in a pattern of mounting evidence concerning several highly organized gambling and racketeering syndicates whose wealth, power, scope of operations and influence has recently grown to gigantic and alarming proportions. It is an ugly, vicious, un-American picture of systematic law violation, huge profits, corruption of public officials who can be bought—and operations outside the jurisdiction of those who cannot be purchased.

According to our information, there are two major criminal syndicates operating in America today. One controls the large slot machine industry and engages in allied gambling rackets; the other dominates the racing wire service. On the basis of checkable information, these activities are the largest steady sources of income in the underworld.

Their shrewd and efficient overlords have adopted the techniques and methods of business. They operate in a loose confederation of mutual respect, cooperation, allocated territories and huge profits.

Here are the most conservative figures on these operations.

The annual slot machine take in the United States is estimated by the best authorities from $1 billion to $2 billion a year. This figure is based on the fact that 105,000 gaming machines, mostly one-armed bandits, were registered in 1949 with the Bureau of Internal Revenue. The total number operating is considered double or triple that figure. The average net take of each machine is $10 to $15 a day.

The principal racing wire service in the country is Continental Press Service which is the key to the multi-billion dollar betting business. Its 16 thousand miles of leased wire service cover 300 key handbook areas. It is difficult to pin down the annual take of this industry but the best estimates put it at double or treble the volume of pari mutuel betting at legalized race tracks—or from $3 to $8 billion per year.

There is an abundant fund of facts which point to control of this wire service by the old Capone gang. Although the wire service has been domiciled in Cleveland since its late operator James M. Ragan was killed, the Chicago Crime Commission and other sources believe that Continental is dominated by the Chicago underworld interests.

We have good reasons to believe that the slot machine syndicate is controlled by Frank Costello. The shy and retiring czar of the slot machine racket always understates his interest in rackets and government in his public denials of the facts about his potency and influence.

The numerous case records of his interstate operations could take our entire day. For the record I will briefly sketch a well documented case and the one with which I am most familiar— the Costello syndicate operations in Louisiana.

According to his own federal grand jury testimony some years ago, Costello moved his New York slot machine operations to New Orleans in 1936. He said that he sent down Dandy Phil Kastel, ex-convict and one time associate of Arnold Rothstein, to incorporate and run the business. Today he lives and operates in Jefferson parish above New Orleans beyond our jurisdiction.

Kastel first formed the Bayou Novelty Company which later became the Pelican Novelty Company, and which today is the Louisiana Mint Company, to handle the distribution of slot machines and other coin devices.

From 1936 until 1946 the Costello-Kastel interests operated in New Orleans under an exclusive monopoly.

Some idea of their profits may be seen in the figures revealed during the income tax evasion trial of Costello, Kastel and five associates in the New Orleans federal court in 1939. The government charged that they had conspired to evade payment of about $500 thousand taxes on income approaching $3 million from their New Orleans slot machine business in 1936-37. That was before they installed their maximum amount of 5,500 slot machines in New Orleans. We have no figures on their take between 1937 and 1946, but at $10 to $15 a day per machine it must have been enormous.

With the election of the present city administration in 1946 the syndicate retreated across the parish line. No slot machines have operated in New Orleans since that time.

One day in 1947 our police superintendent learned of a cache of new slot machines stored in New Orleans for shipment to nearby distribution points. Police raided the place and destroyed 390. Kastel, as an owner of Louisiana Mint Company, promptly filed a suit against us for $117 thousand. Listed in the suit as Company Manager was Dudley Geigerman, brother-in-law of Frank Costello.

Their suit was dismissed, but the Louisiana Mint Company continues to thrive and prosper outside of New Orleans. They own most of the 8 thousand gambling devices for which the Bureau of Internal Revenue issued $100 tax stamps in Louisiana last year.

Meanwhile, Kastel was following another of the syndicate's recognized techniques—that of entering into allied businesses. This syndicate built the Beverly Club in Jefferson Parish, Louisiana, a luxury gambling house. Its charter, copy of which is attached, shows its registered agents to be Phil Kastel and Carlos Marcello. The latter is a local ex-convict and syndicate man. In addition to operating the Beverly Club, this group finances bar and tavern proprietors at lower interest rates than the banks charge—with the understanding, of course, that these places must install their machines.

The Continental Wire Service, as already noted, does not come into New Orleans. Its leased Western Union wires do service their Louisiana distributor at several points just above and below our city. Through batteries of telephone relays they service handbooks below and above our city limits. Despite the continuing enforcement efforts of our police there are still sporadic bookie operations in our city. But the lack of direct wire service and our insistence that the telephone company pull out telephone lines of all raided establishments has held these operations down to a minimum.

To our knowledge, the Costello Syndicate and the wire service heads today are not personally violating any municipal or state law in New Orleans. But they are doing it all around us. And they are causing the law to be violated in our city.

Major Bowron of Los Angeles and the California Crime Commission headed by Admiral Standley have called attention to similar situations in the Far West. The Citizens Crime Commissions of Chicago and Greater Miami have compiled almost identical facts. So has the Massachusetts Crime Commission. Others present, including Mayor Darst of St. Louis and Mayor Cobo, of Detroit have similar corroboration.

Mayor Dorothy Lee of Portland, Oregon has publicly stated:

"Seven weeks after my election, slot

machine operators sought to organize in Portland and at the same time get me out of office."

Municipal officials everywhere will tell you that in investigations of local criminals we continually run into frustrating blind alleys and dead ends—and the trail often winds out of the local jurisdiction over a city, county or state line.

Does all this not point up the very vital fact that the great need is not to get at the small fry, but the absentee syndicate bosses who direct the financing, supplying, strategy and rapid movement of law breakers back and forth across the country? All states and cities are not yet infected, but no state or community is immune from invasion.

It should also be made a part of this record that for several years the U. S. Immigration and Naturalization Department has had complaints in its files that Costello committed perjury in swearing to his final citizenship papers in 1926. When he swore that he was not in violation of any U. S. laws, it is our understanding that he was at that time the nation's top-ranking rum runner.

The American Municipal Association proposes to attack the problem on three levels: at home, within the states, and through joint efforts of city, state and federal governments. In presenting our recommendations, I wish to make three preliminary comments.

The first goal of the AMA is to assure the basic honesty and integrity of municipal officials, so they will deserve the respect of the people. One of our major efforts will be to strengthen the backs of those municipal officials who have the courage to uphold the law.

Here questions of state laws arise—laws designated to protect individuals and free enterprise from undue governmental interference—but laws whose loopholes have been exploited for years by high priced legal talent defending illegal operators. The Attorney Generals are the most competent authorities to go into this point. Then there are federal-city problems.

I should like here to express the admiration and implicit confidence of municipal officials in the law enforcement agencies of the federal government. We believe that they are doing the best possible job under conditions laid down by Congress and within the limits of their budgets.

Insofar as permissible, there exists today excellent teamwork between local and federal enforcement agencies. Many of the best city police are graduates of the FBI academy, or have served actively with the bureau—and this suggests a further expansion of this type of training.

Wise legislation in the recent past has extended the jurisdiction of the Federal authorities so that they may assist local police in combatting crime. For example, kidnapping, bank holdups, interstate transportation of stolen cars. No responsible persons would consider this a usurpation of local power.

If the federal government can invoke its powers against those who use its mails to defraud, does it not follow logically that similar powers should be invoked against those who use interstate shipments and communications against the public interests.

Today it is a federal offense to traffic in prostitution across state lines, but responsibility for suppressing prostitution remains local. Similarly, unauthorized possession of narcotics is a Federal offense, but the local war against the dope traffic goes on strong as ever.

This all adds up to the fact that the last major area of big profits from illegal enterprise in which the jurisdiction of the federal government has not been extended is that of interstate gambling operations that violate the laws of 46 states.

Here is where federal action truly seems to be indicated—not to centralize police power—but to move into a field that needs its help.

We must conclude that for the world's best investigators to materially help us in this problem there must be new legislation to extend their jurisdiction and fill in the gap that now exists.

We know, too, the political power of the underworld lies primarily in its financial strength. And its financial strength stems largely from the syndicate operation of slot machines and the control of racing and sports pool news.

The key objective before us is an attack on the supply lines and income of organized gambling as a nation-wide industry.

Today the records of any Collector of Internal Revenue will tell you who has bought gaming tax stamps and where the business is situated. We believe that it would be equally valuable to know who owns the machines as well as those in whose place of business they are installed.

Finally, if we can deport those who have fraudulently obtained their priceless American citizenship, we will rid the country of undesirable elements who are a menace to American democracy and our way of life.

Consequently, the American Municipal Association proposes and will actively support these concrete recommendations:

1. Development of a coordinated master plan of action on the whole system of nation-wide rackets by Federal, state, local governments and citizens' groups. The Attorney General for the United States should be coordinator for the entire effort.

In that connection, it would be of tremendous help if we could receive a confidential quarterly or semi-annual report from the Attorney General, correlating all available data—giving municipal officials a continuing, complete picture which cities do not have the facilities or jurisdiction to obtain themselves.

2. Support of the Kefauver bill to investigate the entire problem of interstate gambling rackets and allied operations. A Senate investigation that can call witnesses and make them tell the truth under threat of perjury indictments is the only way some of these "dead ends" can be routed out.

3. Legislation to outlaw dissemination of race results across state lines by telegraph, telephone or radio for illegal gambling purposes. Such a law would not be designed to prohibit dissemination of sports information through the generally accepted press associations and newspapers.

4. Legislation to prohibit the interstate shipment of slot machines, other gambling devices, and their parts; requiring Federal registration of all such machines sold within states, and prohibiting foreign export of such devices. The Preston bill to prohibit shipment of gambling devices in interstate or foreign commerce and which has been endorsed

in principle by FBI Director Hoover, deserves our fullest study.

5. Amending the Bureau of Internal Revenue tax regulations on gaming devices to require registration of owners of devices on which tax stamps are purchased, as well as the user of such gaming devices. Penalties for failure to register gaming devices should be stiffened.

6. Legislation to extend the jurisdiction of the FBI to permit that agency to lend needed assistance and information to state and local officials.

7. Amending the immigration and naturalization laws providing that aliens obtaining citizenship by fraud or perjury may have that citizenship revoked at any time after discovery of said fraud or perjury.

8. Complete and continuing tax investigations of the head bosses of the rackets syndicates.

9. Amending Bureau of Internal Revenue regulations to provide that the now closed income tax records of known police characters and ex-convicts may be inspected by law enforcement agencies of the Federal, state and local governments.

10. Inter-city cooperation, exchange of information and action. This was begun some months ago through the AMA by Mayor Bowron, myself and the Chicago Crime Commission, Mayor Lee of Portland and several others. We will work to strengthen and improve the facilities of exchange of information among local police departments, through AMA as a coordinating agency.

11. While all the recommendations above are important, if we are to accomplish all of our joint objectives, there needs to be a thoroughly coordinated Federal effort or agency through which the cities and states can work.

To sum up—I wish to acknowledge the interest and assistance of numerous Mayors and the Crime Commissions of Chicago, California, Greater Miami and of Massachusetts.

The American Municipal Association believes that the flourishing existence of these nationally operated gambling-racketeering syndicates presents one of the greatest threats to society and to good government. At the very least, the alliances between the wealthy organized criminal element and local gamblers make more complex and difficult the problem of law enforcement at the local level. At the very worst, these underworld czars, through entrenched special privileges in a community, can wield tremendous influence over its government. From profits and power in one locality they go on to another. That is a danger and threat to our democratic way of life hardly less real than the Communist menace. Indeed, nothing could please the Russians more than the crumbling corruption of democracy by large segments of the American people.

I do not believe that the combined resources of the organized underworld rackets are greater than those of the Federal, state and municipal governments of the United States.

It is our firm conviction that if everyone in this room determines to do something about the problem it can and will be conquered. Our cooperative action must not end when this meeting adjourns.

In this objective we pledge you the full and active cooperation of the American Municipal Association.

The Qualifications of a College President

by EDWARD C. ELLIOTT

Your Honor, Mr. Toastmaster; Mr. baby president, and Mr. brother president; presidents, deans, directors, professors; and most important of all, you fathers and sons of Wabash:

This has been an auspicious day for Wabash College. If I have heard aright today and tonight, the greatest man in Christendom has been secured as the President of this Institution we here celebrate.

This is a great day for education in Indiana. A new captain has come to aid us in our campaign to gain new knowledge and to lose old ignorance. Indiana has a right to be proud today in that another distinguished citizen has been added to the rolls of service for the Hoosier State.

You will, I am sure, indulge me some expression of the pleasurable satisfaction which we of Purdue University have in welcoming this new leader of yours. We know that our tasks are to be made the easier, and we feel that the new successes in prospect for Wabash College will be shared by us. We of Purdue wish for you of Wabash new strength, new power, new victories all the while—save when you come to the Ross-Ade Stadium!

I have heard, Your Honor, that you are a stern judge. Therefore, I hesitate to take any liberties with you on this occasion. Nevertheless, I am constrained to observe that, in your court tonight, your witnesses or your jurymen, whatever they may be called, have paid absolutely no attention to your early admonitions for brevity. Presumably watches are for the purpose of recording the passage of time, or at least of providing insurance against that procrastination born of verbosity. Apparently, however, those displayed along this board are intended to be decorations for the banquet table and not for the guidance and limitations of their owners. Mine, I trust, is a timely and not a temporizing instrument.

Mr. President, you have received much wise counsel and even more sound advice during this inauguration day. The mere fact that you still retain some semblance of human expression after the inaugural ordeal is convincing and persuasive testimony of your ability to carry the hidden responsibilities of your new office.

As I sat through the dignified and appropriate ceremony of this afternoon and listened to the wise philosophy and high instructions of your distinguished brother, I well knew that, being what you are, when you get into your job you will not pay the slightest attention to him or to his ranking experience. I also have two brothers. I am the eldest and, therefore, I speak with that foreknowledge gained only from fraternal humiliation.

It seems to me that, from their wealth of wisdom and from their oceans of experience, your wellwishers and your counsellors have neglected to contribute some of the little things that you will very greatly need. You have been told how essential to the success of Wabash were your capacity for leadership and your broad scholarship. The learned and indulgent President of Northwestern University has just painted an artistic word portrait that invests you with the halo of supernatural power.

Now, Gentlemen, in my humble capacity as the maker of the last, as well as the best, speech of the evening, I regard it as my solemn duty to exhibit in this presence certain small though precious bits of garden variety philosophy which this neophytish President is going to need. In a sense I am betraying professional secrets. Yet as I look about me and note the high intelligence and the fine professional interest in everything that is going on, I feel certain that what I am about to say will be received with profit, if not with confidence.

The first requisite for success in the Presidential office, I submit, is not learning, is not scholarship, is not sacrificial devotion to service for youth—is not any one of the things to which high tribute has been paid today. Mr. President, I beg of you to know that the most necessary thing for your success at Wabash is that you have *a sound stomach*. Speaking from personal experience, I am certain that your first, if not your greatest, responsibility is not that of establishing higher ideals for the College, is not that of selecting the right youth for your student body, is not that of providing effective leadership for your faculty— the hardest task you will have, Sir, especially during these first years in this hospitable Hoosier State, will be to eat all of the meals placed before you in public. If you succeed during your first year in running the gastronomic gauntlet, no one will thereafter have any major reservations as to your presidential potentialities. I am tempted to say that a good executive digestion contributes as much to the external peace, to the internal harmony, and to the all-round success of a college as do those other things customarily mentioned.

Next, in the category of essentials for presidential success, I would call your attention to the invaluableness of *a good thick skin*. Unless you are naturally pachydermous, or acquire by artificial means a rhinoceros-like hide, not only your days but also your nights will contain unnumbered hours of torture. The capacity for resisting, without seeming effort, your foes and particularly your friends, you will find to be the great first aid to physical peace and mental comfort in the high office to which you have been elevated.

Even the combined value of these two so often forgotten prerequisites is scarcely equal to the value of the third one. If you possess, as you are said to, that profound human organ known as the *conscience,* I advise that at the earliest possible moment you have a psychological operation performed completely extirpating that part of your physical and professional system. With normal human beings this organ is at the best a daily nuisance. For a president it is a discouraging handicap.

My good friend, President Bryan, during his address this afternoon, read to you certain mortality statistics of presidents. Personally, I did not think that this was in timely taste. However, statistical science is more often testy than it is tasty. The thought was registered in my own mind that the high professional death rate among college presidents is due more to faint stomachs, to thin skins, and to super-sensitive consciences than to any of the ordinary causes referred to in the post mortem reports. President Bryan wondered what happened to presidents between the fifty-eighth and sixty-eighth birthdays. I believe I know. During their days of repentant retirement, each of these ex- and emeriti presidents tries to regain his digestion, to rebuild a normal human exterior, and covets that one thing without which the day of resurrection is postponed unto eternity—his conscience.

I suppose, indeed I know, Sir, that you are proud tonight. Any one of us in your place would be even prouder. But please do not be too proud. This ceremony and this gala occasion have a unique significance if I know the history of Wabash College.

My friend, Bishop Overs, lately returned from the Episcopalian Diocese of far-off Liberia, recently related this incident to me; or rather related it to my Rockne-interested son to whom President Walsh referred a little while ago. I have a suspicion that the Bishop spoke to the boy trusting that the moral would not be wasted upon me. It appears that an emigrant son of the Emerald Isle had spent his long life in this land of the free and equal as a humble street sweeper in one of our great American cities. In the due course of time and according to the inevitable law of nature, Michael was translated to the Great Beyond. There, to his great surprise, he found his spiritual self outside of the well-known pearly gates. His spiritual heart sank within him. He feared insuperable difficulties. To his overwhelming surprise, the gates immediately swung open and he was welcomed by the Keeper in a very matter-of-fact manner. "Good morning, Mike," said the Keeper handing him his tickets. "This red ticket is for your harp and the white one is for your place in the choir. Now step along lively because there are others coming this morning."

Our hero took his place in the golden grandstand and performed his tasks with harp and Celtic voice industriously and effectively through several aeons. Eternity appeared to him to be a dullish long time as it did to his neighbors. One day from his high place in the celestial choir, he became aware of great excitement all through heaven. The bands were playing and there was much marching and counter-marching. Apparently much ado was being made over someone. From his distant seat among the heavenly musical host, Mike could not see all that he desired. That night after the day's work was done, he began to feel a resentment in the democratic heart which he had brought with him from earth. Having been on earth a Democrat, he retained a heavenly belief in the doctrine of equality.

The morning following the unexplained and disturbing celebration, Mike left his place in the grandstand

and went down to the heavenly head-quarters. There he made bold to inquire of the Great Keeper why it was that after all these years heaven began to show personal discrimination. He referred feelingly to the simplicity of the exercises by which he had been admitted, and compared these to the hullabaloo and fanfare of yesterday when some unknown occupant of a new space in heaven had been welcomed. Saint Peter listened patiently to his protest and then said, "Now Mike, please do not get excited; to be sure there was an extraordinary celebration yesterday. Even while I tell you that this was held on account of the sudden and wholly unexpected arrival of Bishop X, you may not understand. You will understand though when I tell you that only about once in every one hundred thousand years does a Bishop ever get up here."

Therefore, President Hopkins, I beseech you to be humble. This inaugural celebration is in reality a testimony of honor to your office. Wabash College has done its utmost to be gracious,

hospitable, and enthusiastic today; only once in every generation is there an opportunity to receive a new President to this Institution.

This afternoon, as you ended your notable address, Sir, there was loud and enthusiastic applause. For a moment I wondered why. First I thought it was because you had finished. Then I thought that it was because of the things you had said. But these were not good reasons. Then I realized what I and many others now know to be the real explanation of that spontaneous outburst, expressive of your enthusiasm and the enduring loyalty of your Wabash community. Your new supporters were not applauding time; they were not applauding logic or sentiment; they were applauding Hopkins, the man newly come among them. He is far greater than any speech, and he transcends the limits of time.

President Hopkins, may you ever have wisdom in your head. Better still, throughout all the many Wabash years ahead, may you have a song in your heart.

GROUP DISCUSSION

The Census Shows Us Up

by THE UNIVERSITY OF CHICAGO ROUND TABLE

Mr. Wirth: What will the census show us? How will it change our notions about America? What surprises are in store for us?

Mr. Hauser: Without question the most important single surprise will be the great increase in total population of the United States during the last ten years, much greater than was expected.

Mr. Ogburn: The most unexpected conclusion, I think, which will come from the census is the fact that the family is not a dying institution, as some people have said. We will have really had more marriages in the United States than we have ever had before.

Mr. Wirth: To me the most important finding of the census will be the tremendous number of babies that have been born during the last decade—thirty-two million of them.

Mr. Hauser: Right. And also the tremendous increase in our labor force—the number of people in the United States working or seeking work.

Mr. Ogburn: These may be unexpected, but I would submit that the most significant change which we expect to find in the census is the great growth in the standard of living, which puts us very high indeed among the nations of the world. We will also have shown a very great advance in education.

Mr. Wirth: These, and other important facts, for the America of today and the America of tomorrow, we will get from the seventeenth census of the United States which is to begin to be taken this week.

You have had a great deal to do with the planning of that census, Hauser. Tell us about it.

Mr. Hauser: This will be the seventeenth census of population taken since 1790. It also will include a census of housing and a census of agriculture. It is a major administrative and technical undertaking. It will cost over ninety-two million dollars. It will require a field staff of over one hundred and fifty thousand people. It takes a lot of organization to count over one hundred and fifty-one million people, forty-five million dwelling units, and six million farms. As a matter of fact, there will be several million punch cards into which fifteen billion facts will be punched; and the results of the census will be published in literally tens of thousands of pages.

Mr. Wirth: This undertaking, we think, is significant because it is going to reveal where we stand in 1950 and might furnish us with a guide of where we are going to go in the future.

Let us go into the question of what we expect to find from the 1950 census and compare it with our older notions about what we would find.

Mr. Hauser: It is expected that the 1950 census will reveal that the United States is today a nation of one hundred and fifty-one and a half million people. This will represent an increase of almost twenty million people since the 1940 census—about nine million more than expected.

Mr. Wirth: This nine-million figure, nine million more than we expected, shows that apparently there was something wrong with our predictions, was there not?

ABOUT THE MEMBERS OF THIS DISCUSSION: PHILIP M. HAUSER, Professor of Sociology and Associate Dean of the Division of Social Sciences at the University of Chicago, is acting director of the United States Bureau of the Census. WILLIAM F. OGBURN is the Sewell L. Avery Distinguished Service Professor of Sociology at the University of Chicago and served as chairman of the Census Advisory Committee from 1920 to 1926. LOUIS WIRTH, Associate Editor of the *American Journal of Sociology* since 1926, is Professor of Sociology at the University of Chicago.

Mr. Ogburn: I would like to comment on that and to say that we did miss in the projection of our population estimates but that this miss was due largely to the war, which was not foreseen.

If I could take just a couple of minutes, I would like to explain how I think that that takes place. What we do when we project population estimates is to project the trend lines and not the fluctuations about a trend line. If one takes any annual series, like foreign trade, or pig-iron production, or immigration, and draws this series on a piece of paper, it turns out to be a zigzag line going either up or down. But if one draws a smooth line right through the middle of these zigzags, we get what is known as a trend. The population projections are of the trends and not of the zigzags. This population of 1950 is a zigzag upward, so to speak, owing to the influence of the war. And I think that the question which is very interesting is whether the long-time trend is going to be affected very much by this temporary zigzag due to the war.

Mr. Wirth: But that zigzag is quite a zig in the zag, because it means nine million people whom we underestimated. And today we are in trouble in this country because we went on the predictions of the population experts, and we did not plan for the schools, we did not plan for the housing, and we did not plan for a lot of other things for which we should have planned to accommodate this population.

Mr. Hauser: I quite agree. We have to revise our notions to the extent that they have been based on projections of population. On the other hand, it is awfully important to recognize the significance of what Ogburn has just said about the long-time trend. It takes more than one swallow to make a summer, and the fact that we have had this startling increase during the past decade does not mean that we should forget about the trend of one hundred and fifty years of declining rate of population growth, not only in the United States but in Western civilization in general.

Mr. Wirth: But there are some who believe that this trend might very well be reversed. I am of the opinion, right now at any rate, that the 1950 census will be as wholesome a corrective for the population experts as the 1948 election results were for the pollsters.

Mr. Hauser: In some respects, I should agree, although I am not sure that those two illustrations are exactly parallel.

On the other hand, I should like to warn that the burden of proof of reversing a long-time trend like that of one hundred and fifty years, in terms of the experience of any one decade, lies with the people who are impressed with the decade results.

Mr. Wirth: Yes, but I am not so much interested in what is going to happen a thousand or two thousand years from now as I am in what is happening today and what is going to happen in the decade which lies ahead of us. On that, I think, we have to revise our figures upward.

Mr. Hauser: On that we quite agree.

Mr. Wirth: Ogburn, what do you see in this population increase which is startling as you seem to feel it is?

Mr. Ogburn: The point which you made a few minutes ago—that we have had thirty-two million babies born in a decade and that we probably have had, last year, three million babies born.

That, by the way, amounts to, if it carries on at that rate, about one hundred and eighty babies born while we are presenting this ROUND TABLE.

Mr. Wirth: But those babies who were born during the past decade are going to go to school in the next decade, and they are going perhaps to get married and have babies of their own in the decades to come, are they not?

Mr. Hauser: Right.

Mr. Wirth: And that is going to change our picture, too, of America's future.

Mr. Hauser: Right. And it is important to realize that this large crop of babies is primarily what is responsible for the net increase in our population of about two million a year which we have experienced throughout the decade.

Mr. Wirth: Births and deaths are not the only ways in which a population increases or decreases. After all, there is such a thing as migration—people coming in and going out. And there must be a surplus of births over deaths in order to make up a population increment.

Mr. Hauser: That is right, although we should recognize that immigration has become a negligible factor in the population growth of the United States. One of the amazing things about the increase in the last ten years is that it is almost entirely due to natural increase—an excess of births over deaths.

Mr. Ogburn: Of course, we do not know what the future may be about immigration, some ten or fifteen years from now, though we could change the policy on that, of course.

Mr. Wirth: And our planning for the future, therefore, depends upon the possibility of predicting other things, such as prosperity, wars, depressions, and a lot of other phenomena in the world which we cannot just say we have definitely before us as facts.

Mr. Hauser: Right. A student of population really cannot predict population accurately in the long run until after we learn to predict depression and war and so forth.

Mr. Wirth: Suppose then that we look at the question of who composes this population. Is there any important change in the age grouping of this population? Are there more old or more young, or more middle-aged? How does the picture look from that standpoint?

Mr. Ogburn: We will have both an increase of the old and an increase of the babies. This, of course, will have lots of effects upon our economic and social order. The number of youth and the number of babies will present aspects of buoyancy and optimism; and it, of course, affects the nature of businesses. We will have to have, for instance, more sales and manufacturers of toys to take care of the children, more children's clothing. This changing population will cause a considerable revision in the preparation of goods for the markets.

Mr. Wirth: Housing is one instance in point, is it not? There are nine million more people to be housed, and that means more shelter for them for which we have not made provision.

Mr. Hauser: And, of course, in connection with housing, the census is also going to reveal the change in the number of families during the last ten years. It is going to be a startling thing, I believe, to realize that since 1940 we shall have increased by about six million families, three million more than expected.

Mr. Ogburn: That is rather an odd thing, too, because, while the population during the last ten years has increased 15 per cent, the number of married couples has increased 22 per cent.

Mr. Hauser: Right.

Mr. Ogburn: And the mere increase in population does not tell us how much the increase in housing is needed. I would like to say in relation to housing that the expected number of new needs for households runs, during the next two or three years in my guess, at something over a million a year.

Mr. Wirth: In any case the family, as you see it, and as the 1950 census will show, is not a dying institution in America?

Mr. Ogburn: No. The family has shown certain tendencies to break up every now and then. We have quite a high divorce rate, and we will show, I think, increasing number of divorced persons, but not as much as the divorce rate. What we will have, really, is a very muchly married population. And while I am on that point I would like to say that I have looked over the statistics of the world, and we have, at the present time, a marriage rate which is higher than has ever been shown in the history of marriage statistics of any nation in the world. We are much the most married people, much the most married country. That also carries the correlative that we have a smaller proportion of unmarried people over fourteen years of age. There is only about one in every five over fourteen years of age who is single.

Mr. Hauser: We have got to realize another point in relation to housing. As Ogburn pointed out, the great increase in our marriage rate and the great increase in the number of families is going to create a problem in terms of number of housing units. But, in addition, the census is going to tell us about a lot of what has happened to the quality of housing during the last ten years and what has happened to rents. For example, despite the fact that we have had rent control, the census will tell us just how much rent has increased during the last ten years. In Chicago, for instance, where we have taken a preliminary survey, it has gone up some 38 per cent.

Mr. Ogburn: While the number of families is producing a distress and a dilemma with regard to housing, as has just been said, there are also certain positive advantages about this large number of families.

Mr. Wirth: They represent mouths to be fed and people to have clothing provided for them; and they are going to constitute the market of today and tomorrow. Is that what you have in mind?

Mr. Ogburn: Yes. That is the best news for the business world which we have had in a long time.

But I would also like to say that, as a sort of social significance and appraisal of our country, the married people are favored over the single. For instance, the death rate is lower among married couples than it is among the single. The sickness rate is less among the married than it is among the single. And the insanity rate is very much less among the married than the single. There is also less crime among the married than the single. So, this increase in marriage is a desirable thing for our population.

Mr. Hauser: That is certainly true. And, looking at it from the standpoint of the future, it is important to emphasize that many types of businesses, in many parts of our country, are affected by the number of families and the number of consumer units as families, rather than total population. There is reason to believe that for some time the increase in number of families will actually continue to be greater than the increase in the number of people.

Mr. Wirth: You have already spoken of some of the evidence that the census will give us about our economic future, but I should like to raise, particularly, the point about the incomes of the American people. The census will show, I assume, that they have gone up substantially.

Mr. Ogburn: We are going to have a question on incomes in the census, and it will be interesting to see how that question turns out. It will be particularly interesting to the business people. You have no doubt that that income question will be on the census, I take it, Mr. Director? Some people have been objecting to its inclusion.

Mr. Hauser: "Ex-director," Ogburn! But I think that the question will remain on the schedule, and certainly it is to be hoped that it will remain on the schedule.

It is worth observing that the inclusion of income questions in the 1950 population census schedule simply represents a continuation of experience with census schedules exactly one hundred years old this time.

Mr. Wirth: How much will our income have gone up, as consumer units, in the 1950 census since 1940?

Mr. Hauser: The 1950 census results will probably confirm what we are able to guess at the moment—that real purchasing power has increased by perhaps 40 per cent during that period.

Mr. Wirth: That is, despite the fact that the cost of living has gone up, the wages and other incomes have gone up more. I do not find that that is true in my case, but I am glad to hear you say it about the rest of the people.

Mr. Hauser: Each according to his merits, perhaps, Wirth.

Mr. Ogburn: I would like to say a little more on that income question you asked, Wirth. I would like to make the guess that the average family income in the United States will be shown by the census to be as high as or over three thousand dollars a year per family.

Mr. Wirth: Does that mean in 1950 dollars, or some other kind of dollars?

Mr. Ogburn: That means in 1950 dollars. But I would also compare that with the average family income about 1910, when you express it in 1950 dollars. In those days it was about fifteen hundred dollars. In other words, the standard of living has doubled within about thirty or thirty-five years for the American people. That is one of the most significant things which is to come out of this census.

Mr. Hauser: I should like to point out, however, that, although we have the highest standard of living probably ever achieved by any people in the history of man, the census results will probably also confirm the facts recently announced by a Senate committee that there are still about one-third of our families having an income of less than two thousand dollars per year.

Mr. Wirth: That indicates that we have not abolished poverty in the United States as yet.

Mr. Hauser: Oh, by no means!

Mr. Ogburn: That is because of this peculiar thing called the "average"— some below and some above the average. If we were looking ahead, though, and if we should double the standard of living during the next (I am not forecasting now; I am simply projecting this forward)—what if we should double that during the next thirty-five years? That would mean that the average family income in 1950 dollars would be six thousand dollars, and we might very well have abolished poverty. So, I think that we can look forward, as an interpretation, to hope that some day we may abolish poverty in this country.

Mr. Wirth: One sign of the better way of life is, of course, education. We have already spoken of the fact that we have missed, by a very large margin, the number of school children whom we would have in the next few years in the elementary schools. What about the educational level of the American people? That, too, has gone up, has it not?

Mr. Hauser: Yes, appreciably, as a result of prosperity during the war and after the war, the G.I. Bill of Rights, the number of people going to school has tremendously increased. The 1950 census results will probably show that the average number of years of schooling among the people of this country will have increased by more than a year since 1940.

Mr. Ogburn: You interpret that in terms of high-school education. My guess is that we shall show that between 65 and 70 per cent of the young people of this country of high-school age are in high school. That large number of persons in high school is going to have the effect of raising the level of education, which will mean a great deal for those who make radio programs, for those who sell books, for those who write for the newspapers. It is going to affect our cultural level immeasurably and for the better, very much so.

Mr. Wirth: That is, if these agencies like the radio, the press, the magazines, and the books want to meet the needs and expectations of young America, they will have to raise their sights.

Mr. Ogburn: And let us warn them not to put the sights too low because of this education.

Mr. Hauser: Without question I think that the census results, for the first time in the history of this country, will show that the average person in this country has entered high school and has had some high-school training.

Mr. Wirth: And that means a proportionate amount of them have gone to college and beyond?

Mr. Hauser: Right.

Mr. Wirth: What does the census mean to us in America with reference to jobs and opportunities to make a living? What about this question of the people who are working? Do we have more or less? You may recall that, a few years ago, Henry Wallace talked about sixty million jobs. Where are those sixty million jobs? Was that a good guess, or a bad guess?

Mr. Hauser: It turns out, despite what a lot of people thought at the time, that Henry Wallace was too conservative in his estimates. There are now over sixty-two million people either working or seeking work. There has been a tremendous increase in the number of people in the labor force. At the beginning of the century, only 37 per cent of our people were workers.

Mr. Ogburn: What percentage of those were women?

Mr. Hauser: In the beginning of the century, only 18 per cent were women. But in the 1950 census, it will be shown that about 43 per cent of our population will be workers; and, of the workers, about 28 per cent will be women.

Mr. Wirth: And do you expect, too, that the census will show that the unskilled labor has been declining in number and importance, that we are getting more semiskilled people working with automatic tools in modern factories, and that we will have more clerical and white-collar occupations?

Mr. Hauser: Without question. The 1950 census results will, I think, reveal an acceleration of that trend toward more white-collar and service trades and fewer unskilled.

Mr. Ogburn: That drop in the unskilled will be quite appreciable in my guess. We do not know exactly what it will be, but the number of clerical and professional have increased very greatly. That will change, of course, the complexion of occupational life. I would like to mention one other thing there. The census will show quite a marked decline in the number of farmers. That is a big occupation and has stood for much of value in our life. But they have been declining for some time.

Mr. Wirth: What about employment and unemployment?

Mr. Hauser: That is a very interesting thing. Largely as a result of the rate of total population growth and the aging of the population, we are now experiencing currently, based on the Census Bureau's month-to-month reports, the unusual phenomenon of seeing both number of people working and number of unemployed increasing. In other words, the problem before our economy is whether we can grow fast enough on the economic side to maintain jobs for our new workers.

Mr. Wirth: On that, too, then we have to raise our sights as to what is needed to keep America prosperous?

Mr. Hauser: Without question.

Mr. Wirth: Now may I turn, then, to a question which is of great interest to all of us. Where are these new Americans? Are they going to be in the same places where they were before, or has there been a shift? We have undergone two great decades of upheaval—one great decade of depression and another great decade of war. What is happening? Are they shifting around from place to place?

Mr. Ogburn: There has never been as much migration, moving back and forth in the United States, as there has been during the past decade, as the railroad people will tell you. But these shifts have been of two kinds: one has been the shift as between the city and the country and the suburbs and the other has been a regional shift. And in both cases they have been very marked changes.

Mr. Hauser: For example, this census will show a greater increase in the population in the West than any other census. At the beginning of the century, the West had only about four million people.

Mr. Ogburn: What do you mean by "the West"?

Mr. Hauser: All the Rocky Mountain States and the Pacific Coast combined. The West, this time, will have close to nineteen million people and make up about 12 per cent of the total population growth, incidentally largely at the expense of the North.

Mr. Wirth: I note in some of the preliminary figures, for instance, that Mississippi had actually declined in population. Illinois has been moved from the third state in the Union to the fourth state in the Union, giving place to California. The New England States, too, have been experiencing a slowing-down of their growth and development.

Mr. Ogburn: My guess is, though, that the states in the former dustbowl area will be the ones which will show the greatest loss in population.

Mr. Hauser: They will also show a loss, but the amazing thing is that, while these changes which you have just indicated have taken place, the West Coast states increased, each of them, by 50 per cent or more during the last ten years. And this has, of course, very important implications from the standpoint of shifts of the balance of political power and apportionment in the Congress.

Mr. Wirth: That is, of course, one of the reasons the census is taken—to determine the number of representatives. What will result? Mississippi will probably lose. . . . New England will lose. The Middle West will lose. And who will gain?

Mr. Hauser: More specifically, it is likely that the West Coast will increase its number of representatives by around ten or more congressmen at the expense of a loss of one or so in New York, in Pennsylvania, and in Illinois, and a loss of three or four representatives throughout the South.

Mr. Ogburn: On this question of the shift of political power, I am wondering whether this decline in the number of farmers is going to cut down the farmers' influence. We have heard a lot about the farmers' influence lately. Do you think that that is going to be cut down by the changes in the rural population?

Mr. Wirth: It may mean that perhaps the farm-support programs are not going to be as popular as they were.

Mr. Hauser: It is rather interesting that, despite the farm-support programs, the population on farms in the 1950 census will probably be about twenty-eight million—a net loss of about two million during the last ten years.

Mr. Wirth: And in the light of the mechanization and modernization of farming, probably the loss ought to be even greater, should it not?

Mr. Hauser: That is quite possible.

Mr. Wirth: Finally, let us talk about the cities. What is going to happen to them? We have been taught to believe that the cities were declining in growth, that they were losing their population at the center, and that the great suburbs were springing up and emptying the cities.

Mr. Ogburn: We are due for a little surprise there—not so much, but a little one. It is of this nature: You know, during the census from 1930 to 1940, a lot of cities did not gain in population, and some lost. And I think, however, that there will be a gain in the cities, but the gain will be, of course, very much greater in the suburbs, as it was during the previous decade. But the center of the city, which has been losing population to the periphery for perhaps thirty, forty, or fifty years, will, I think, continue, except in a few cities. There are about a half-dozen cities where even the center of the city will probably gain in population.

Mr. Wirth: And that will be very significant for city planning . . .

Mr. Ogburn: Oh, very much so.

316

Mr. Wirth: . . . and redevelopment and slum eradication to make these centers of the cities habitable.

Mr. Hauser: And if Ogburn is right, that, of course, will be a startling change from what we have experienced in many of our cities in the preceding decade.

Mr. Ogburn: Of course, you might raise the question of whether you want to make the center of these cities habitable, or not. It is adding to the congestion and makes a target for the bombs.

Mr. Wirth: Now, then, we are agreed here, are we not, and particularly you, Hauser, since you have had so much to do with it, that the census is going to show us some very important things and that it is vital for us.

Mr. Hauser: Without question. This census, quite apart from being taken because the Constitution requires it for apportionment purposes, is designed to meet the needs of various segments of the American people.

Mr. Wirth: In 1950, America, contrary to expectations, is fearfully growing. Far from being a dying nation, we are a still increasing nation. We are not merely growing in numbers, but we are continuing to develop economically. We are more productive. Our standard of living is rising. The 1950 census makes it urgent to revise our ideas about our opportunities and our needs. We must raise our sights to meet the requirements for food, for housing, for schools, for hospitals, for recreational facilities, for job opportunities, for investment, and to meet the higher educational and cultural level of the American people.

Our focus of attention in the past has been very much upon the old. The 1950 census reminds us that we must redirect our attention to the young, the future America.

INTRODUCTORY

Introducing Ricardo J. Alfaro

by CORDELL HULL

The Chairman has the very special pleasure of presenting to you an old associate and colleague in the diplomatic service. He is a former President of the Republic of Panama, where he made a distinguished and outstanding record of public service. He was long in the foreign service and, as you know, was Minister to this country for some years. I am delighted to join with you in listening to him this evening. We are most fortunate to have him with us, and I am pleased now to present to you Dr. Ricardo J. Alfaro, of the Republic of Panama.

317

Introducing Francis A. Callery

by MERRILL C. MEIGS

Mr. Chairman, Gentlemen: I have here the notice which went out to you that Harry B. Woodhead would be here to address us today. There has been a change in this schedule. I am sure that, when Mr. Woodhead made this commitment back in October, none of us, including Mr. Woodhead, knew what was going to hit us between that time and now. As it is, he must be in Washington for some very important meetings. I was there all of this week myself, and I assure you what is going on in the capitol is much more important than any speaking engagement. I told Mr. Woodhead I would assure you of his regret and explain that his boss, Uncle Sam, just said, "You have to stay here on this job."

But we are very fortunate in having as a substitute one of his associates and Vice President of the Consolidated Vultee Aircraft Corporation, Mr. Francis A. Callery.

Now, Mr. Callery has had a rather checkered past, in that he was a banker. (Laughter) As a banker, he had a con-siderable responsibility in effecting the largest aviation merger since we got into this war—the merger of Vultee and Consolidated into one corporation. And, as a banker, he has a lot to do with their finances. It is no secret that the volume of those companies this year will approach one billion dollars—so he has to know about money. However, he is a flier. He was a flier in the last war. He was a former director of American Air Lines, and, when somebody had to go to Washington to appear as spokesman for the Aircraft Association on the Coast, they chose Mr. Callery to go and take the rap, and he was very successful in that effort. He knows the subject of aviation and aircraft fully as well, I think, as Mr. Woodhead. He isn't quite as old or quite as heavy physically, but he is taller. (Laughter) So I am very glad indeed, gentlemen, to introduce to you Mr. Francis A. Callery, Vice President of Consolidated Vultee Aircraft Corporation, who will speak on the subject "Air Power." Mr. Callery. (Much Applause)

Introducing Bishop G. Bromley Oxnam

by GEORGE V. DENNY, JR.

Our next speaker is one of the best-known clerical leaders in America. Bishop G. Bromley Oxnam, who's a native of California, has received his education in California, Boston, and three countries of the Far East. In 1936,

318

he was made Bishop of the Methodist Church, and served as head of the Federal Council of Churches from 1942-46. He's the author of several books, was one of the organizers and is one of the six presidents of the World Council of Churches that met last year in Amsterdam.

COURTESY

California Welcomes the United Nations

by EARL WARREN

M R. President, Ladies and Gentlemen: The people of California are highly honored by your presence. We are profoundly grateful to the United Nations for the unity which has pushed the war to a stage that makes timely such a Conference as is now being opened. We share with you the full realization of the importance and the solemnity of the occasion.

You are meeting in a State where the people have unshakeable faith in the great purposes which have inspired your gathering. We look upon your presence as a great and necessary step toward world peace. It is our daily prayer that the bonds of understanding forged here will serve to benefit all humanity for generations to come.

We here on the Pacific Coast of the United States of America are fully aware of the special recognition you have given us. Ours is a young civilization, a civilization that has made its greatest development during the lifetimes of men now living. Many of you represent nations which are not only ages old, but which have for centuries been making the struggle for a better world, the struggle in which we are now all joined. It is a double compliment to us, therefore, to have our young and hopeful segment of the world chosen as the drafting room for a new era in international good will.

We recognize that our future is linked with a world future in which the term "Good Neighbor" has become a global consideration. We have learned that understanding of one another's problems is the greatest assurance of peace and that true understanding comes only as a product of free consultation.

This Conference is proof in itself of the new conception of neighborliness and unity which must be recognized in world affairs. The plan to hold this Conference was announced at Yalta—half way around the world—only two and a half months ago. Yet, in spite of all the tragic events of the war, including the sad and untimely death of our own President, it opens today here in

319

San Francisco on schedule and without the slightest interference with the greatest military undertakings in all history.

Unity has created the strength to win the war. It is bringing us ever closer to the end of world conflict. This same strength of unity, continued and cultivated here, can be made to develop a sound pattern of world affairs with a new measure of security for all nations.

It is in the spirit of neighborliness that we join you in advancing tolerance and understanding, the tools with which we are confident a better and happier world can be built.

It is in expression of this spirit that I, as Governor of California, welcome you.

Response to Welcome

by ANTHONY EDEN

Mr. Chairman, Fellow Delegates, Ladies and Gentlemen: No more suitable setting could have been found anywhere for this assembly than the splendid city of San Francisco, one of the main centers of the United Nations war effort—San Francisco, whose confidence in the future is only equalled by its sense of comradeship today. Our deep gratitude, Sir, is due to the city itself and to the whole State of California, which with traditional hospitality has opened its gates to us, and also to the Government and the people of the United States who in a wider sense are our hosts at this momentous function. We thank you, Sir, and through you all those who have helped to organize this Conference, for the labor which they have given so generously in the common cause.

TRIBUTE

Address at the Grave of Franklin D. Roosevelt

by WILLIAM O. DOUGLAS

The hemlock hedge that surrounds his grave sets it apart as a quiet place of meditation, consecrated to earth and sky. It is a shrine for ordinary people the world around. Here they will come to make their pilgrimage and to bow

320

their heads in thanks that the mind and heart of Franklin Roosevelt were dedicated to humanity.

The men and women who come here will recapture for a moment the precious sense of belonging that Roosevelt gave them. The sense of belonging is important to man. The feeling that he is accepted and a part of the community or the nation is as important as the feeling that he is a member of a family. He does not belong if he has a second-class citizenship. When he feels he does not belong, he is not eager to assume responsibilities of citizenship. Being unanchored, he is easy prey to divisive influences that are designed to tear a nation apart or to woo it to a foreign ideology.

Franklin Roosevelt, like no other public figure in our history, was alive to this fact. And he knew how to fashion from it a positive and cohesive force in American life. He was in a very special sense the people's President, because he made them feel that with him in the White House they shared the Presidency. The sense of sharing the Presidency gave even the most humble citizen a lively sense of belonging, a keen feeling that he was an important part of a vital and vibrant system.

Roosevelt was acutely aware of the sorrows, perplexities, burdens, and fears of the common man. By his conquest of suffering and despair he removed forever from the American vocabulary the words "handicapped person." Moreover, he had a great appetite for ideas—and none was too startling or explosive to be unwelcome. He was a magnet for new ideas. Hence they flowed in from all sections of the country. His quick perception and sixth sense also drew from the minds of people ideas which the authors themselves had not yet matured. Thus did Franklin Roosevelt draw upon the energies and enthusiasms of the common people. Thus did they in fact as well as in feeling share the experience of leadership. As a result, no enterprise in history had more partners than his great crusade to make crusading practical.

So it was that men and women from every walk of life felt they were members of a great family. So it was that they wept when he died. And so it is that they will come to his shrine as long as America lives and there in the solitude of his grave pray for strength. For they know from the life and works of him who sleeps there that faith and love can work miracles—that faith and love can make even the lowliest of men noble.

Those Names Are Words in Stone

by V. O. KEY, JR.

We are not gathered to mourn the dead. Their passing has been marked by the tears of mothers and fathers.

We can only see, not share that anguish. Nor do we gather to honor the dead. In death they achieved an honor which

321

the living cannot embellish by word or by ceremony or by sign.

Peoples and institutions, above all colleges, live by their memories, their hopes, their faith. We are gathered to refresh our memories, to renew our hopes, to reaffirm our faith.

Names have been cut into marble and cast in bronze. Names, they are, one may say, which for a short moment are meaningful to classmates and to friends who soon depart, names which become quickly only anonymous lists at which the curious stare.

Yet architects and workmen wrote more than they knew. Between the lines in the lists, unwittingly, they etched our memories, our hopes, and our faith.

Adams, Bancroft, Bronson. Morrison, Otis, Porter. Such names, and there are many more, evoke memories of our country's long and honorable past, of old crises and tribulations, always surmounted. They remind us that we are the beneficiaries of a heritage bought not only by blood, but by the sweat and toil and devotion of generations, a heritage not to be accepted lightly but only with the hope that, by the fulfillment of our duty, it can be maintained unimpaired.

Adelman, Danowski, Levin. Andrews, Gallagher, O'Keefe. These cannot be read as but names. They symbolize the magic amalgam that is America. They remind us that we have drawn our strength from the corners of the earth; that the venturesome and unafraid have come to us and become of us; that oppressed men have sought here liberty and opportunity and that they have not been disappointed.

Biddle, Carey, Chickering. Rabin-ovitz, Scholtz, Siegel. Are these mere names? Not at all. They are words in stone which recall that we have lived, and now live, by a faith in liberty and equality. They remind us that our hopes, ever approached, never attained, are goals that give us courage and guidance. And they destroy the pretensions of those of little faith who would call the American dream only a mad fantasy.

Crawford, Hungerford, MacDougal. Frankenthal, McMullen, Randolph. What titles did they carry? Colonel and second lieutenant. Cadet and lieutenant-commander. Captain and machinist's mate. Apprentice seaman and private. We are reminded that we gain strength in the achievement of our great purposes by each contributing according to his ability; indeed, that it is the genius of a free people to clear the way for each to give his best to the common cause. And we recall that once the anger of debate is dissolved by decision we are accustomed to act together, united by the firm will of democratic discipline, be it a matter of war or peace.

Irwin, Morton, Schumann. Dugan, Newcomb, Waldman. Where did they fall? Aachen and the Argonne. Bremen and Subic Bay. Cambrai and New Caledonia. Chateau-Thierry and Corregidor. Tunisia and the Coral Sea. Verdun and Mindanao. Thus is written in stone our fearful power, a power pyramiding up from the mines of Minnesota, the arsenals of Connecticut, the fields of Nebraska, the refineries of Oklahoma, the furnaces of Pittsburgh, and the men and women of America. We recall that we command our destiny.

Architects and workmen wrote more than they knew. Little reveries etched imperceptibly into stone between the lines fade and form, gradually grow and transform themselves into a mighty epic.

Adams, Adelman, Biddle. Carey, Crawford, Danowski. Dugan, Gallagher, Hungerford. MacDougal, Morrison, O'Keefe. Porter, Randolph, Schumann—our memories, our hopes, our faith.

GOODWILL

A Century of Great Awakenings

by LIAQUAT ALI KHAN

Mr. President, honorable Members of the Senate, in welcoming me within these walls and giving me an opportunity of addressing this august assembly, you have bestowed upon me high prerogative, and honor for which I am deeply grateful to you.

This is my first visit to your great land, but I have long been an admirer of the vigor of your enterprise, your indefatigable spirit of inquiry, your optimism, your high respect for individual effort, your belief in equal opportunities for all, your reverence for the sanctity of the home, the frankness of your speech and manner and the liveliness of your language. Above all I have admired your jealous and uncompromising regard for the supremacy of the people's will, your firm belief that civil liberty gives man the greatest scope for his faculties and your faith that "morality is the best security of law and the surest pledge of freedom." In seeing America, I hope to see

more than America. I hope to see the men and women whose enterprise and vitality have made your country great and the faith that sustains them in their efforts.

I thank you for your welcome, and value it the more because the people whom I have the honor and privilege to represent, although the inheritors of ancient faiths and cultures, are, as a nation among sovereign nations, young; and on the threshold of new experiences, both exciting and grave.

In the geography of the world, Pakistan's name is not yet 3 years old. What led to the emergence of this new state on the map of Asia, is perhaps not universally known. Nor do I expect it yet to be common knowledge what urges stir and inspire us in the task that we know lies ahead of us.

Pakistan was founded by the indomitable will of a hundred million Muslims who felt that they were a nation too numerous and too distinct

323

to be relegated forever to the unalterable position of a political minority, especially when, in the vast subcontinent which was their homeland, there was enough room for two great nations—the Hindus and the Muslims—to enjoy peace and full sovereignty in their respective dominions. They believed that thus alone would the vast multitude of the followers of Islam be uninhibited in the development of their culture and free to follow their own way of life. Pakistan was founded so that millions of Muslims should be enabled to live according to their opinions and to worship God in freedom. That self-same freedom which they sought for themselves, they conceded to others, with the determination to live as peaceful neighbors when to live as more than neighbors seemed to be more than hazardous. Like some of the earlier founders of your great country, these Muslims, though not Pilgrims, nevertheless embarked upon an undertaking, which, in aim and achievement, represented the triumph of an idea. That idea was the idea of liberty which has had its ardent followers in all climates and all countries. When our time came, its call summoned us, too, and we could not hold back. The partition of our subcontinent into two independent sovereign states did not, nor was it expected to, eliminate or efface minorities. But it brought magnitudes within focusable limits and saved the political architecture of the new Asia from a strain which might well have proved excessive and dangerous.

But this, we realize, is only the beginning of a new life. The achievement of freedom is not an instantaneous event; it is a process. The seed is planted, but before the tree can take root and grow and spread it has to be nurtured untiringly by innumerable hands. Our constitution is yet on the anvil and elected representatives of the people are engaged in making it a true mirror of our live beliefs and our sincere aspirations. To frame a genuine constitution, a people need to scrutinize their own mind and soul very closely. Time-honored maxims and hallowed principles embodied in a constitution are of little validity, unless a nation feels that it possesses the spiritual strength to live up to them, unless they echo the voice that is heard unfalteringly in the innermost recesses of its soul. We have earnestly searched our hearts; and though much yet remains to be done, the main features of our constitution to which we can put our seal with a conscience free of all restraints, doubts, or qualms, are to us unequivocally clear.

We have pledged ourselves a federation with autonomous units, wherein shall be guaranteed fundamental human rights, equality of status and opportunity and before law, social, economic, and political justice, freedom of thought, expression, belief, faith, worship, and association.

We have pledged that the Muslims in our state shall be enabled to order their lives in accordance with their faith; but not forgetful of that perpetual fear of the majority from which Pakistan has delivered millions of Muslims and in humble thanksgiving to God for this deliverance, we have solemnly pledged that our minorities shall enjoy full rights of citizenship and shall freely profess and practice their religions and develop their cultures and that their legitimate interests and the interests of the backward and

324

depressed classes shall be adequately safeguarded.

We have pledged that the state shall exercise its powers and authority through the chosen representatives of the people. In this we have kept steadily before us the principles of democracy, freedom, equality, tolerance, and social justice as enunciated by Islam. There is no room here for theocracy, for Islam stands for freedom of conscience, condemns coercion, has no priesthood and abhors the caste system. It believes in the equality of all men and in the right of each individual to enjoy the fruit of his or her effort, enterprise, capacity and skill—provided these be honestly employed. It firmly believes in the right of private ownership, although it frowns on large accumulations of unearned wealth and is greatly concerned over menacing inequalities.

These are articles of faith with us and by them we are irrevocably bound. They are our way of life; and no threat or persuasion, no material peril or ideological allurement can deflect us from the path we have chosen. In proclaiming the objectives of our Constitution, we have called on almighty God, to Whom alone sovereignty over the entire universe belongs, to bear witness to our resolve and to guide our footsteps so that the people of Pakistan may prosper and attain their rightful and honored place among the nations of the world and make their full contribution toward international peace and progress and happiness of mankind.

In our short life as a free nation, we have learned not a little about the world and the times we live in and about ourselves. We have learned that freedom, whether of the individual or of countries, is not everywhere and at all times safe and that the integrity of our own homeland which is dearer to us than our lives will demand of us unceasing vigilance. Our people are deeply distressed at the thought that world-wide destruction might overtake not only the fuller life to which they aspire but the entire human civilization with all its magnificent achievements and illimitable opportunities for good. For youthful countries like ours, which are experiencing but the first pulsations of a free existence, this prospect is profoundly disturbing and not without a touch of irony. We sincerely hope that leaders of world opinion will pursue the path of understanding and will use their wisdom and power to dispel and not to enhance the fears of an apprehensive world. Though freedom has had many births, greed, aggression, and intolerance continue, alas, to rear their ugly heads. This is the century of great awakenings in all parts of the globe; and it depends entirely on the leaders of the world whether mankind will awaken to the horrors of darkness or to a glorious dawn.

We have learned much about ourselves too. Our State began under a number of handicaps, both natural and man-made, and almost before we had time to unfurl the flag to which we now bear allegiance, millions of refugees—the largest number in world history—crossed our borders and sought shelter within our territories. This put us to a test which might have proved disastrous; instead of which our calamities strengthened the determination of our Nation, and the hard work demanded of us fortified our faith. If the test was to come, we are glad that it came early and when we least expected it. For it gave us the measure of our moral and spiritual resources and even in our immature years filled us with courage for the future that has yet to unfold itself. The task that lies before us is truly immense and we are fully aware of it. We are aware that liberty does not descend upon a people, a people must raise themselves to it. We are aware that recent centuries of progress and advancement in the world have bypassed us leaving our resources untapped, our capacities unused and our genius inactive. In all humility but with great faith in our destiny, we the people of Pakistan are resolved to make up for lost centuries within the shortest possible time so that we shall never be a source of disquiet to our friends or a temptation to our adversaries. Peace is essential for progress, but progress is no less essential for peace. As peace and war today are indivisible, so is progress, and in its name we offer our good will to all nations great and small and earnestly ask for theirs.

INAUGURAL

Second Inaugural Address

by ABRAHAM LINCOLN

Fellow Countrymen: At this second appearing to take the oath of the presidential office, there is less occasion for an extended address than there was at the first. Then a statement, somewhat in detail, of a course to be pursued, seemed fitting and proper. Now, at the expiration of four years, during which public declarations have been constantly called forth on every point and phase of the great contest which still absorbs the attention and engrosses the energies of the nation, little that is new could be presented. The progress of our arms, upon which all else chiefly depends, is as well known to the public as to myself; and it is, I trust, reasonably satisfactory and encouraging to all. With high hope for the future, no prediction in regard to it is ventured.

On the occasion corresponding to this four years ago, all thoughts were anxiously directed to an impending civil war. All dreaded it—all sought to avert it. While the inaugural address was being delivered from this place, devoted altogether to saving the Union without war, insurgent agents were in the city seeking to destroy it without war—seeking to dissolve the Union, and divide effects, by negotiation. Both parties deprecated war; but one of them would make war rather than let the nation survive; and the other would accept war rather than let it perish. And the war came.

One-eighth of the whole population were colored slaves, not distributed generally over the Union, but localized in the Southern part of it. These slaves constituted a peculiar and powerful interest. All knew that this interest was, somehow, the cause of the war. To strengthen, perpetuate, and extend this interest was the object for which the insurgents would rend the Union, even by war; while the government claimed no right to do more than to restrict the territorial enlargement of it.

Neither party expected for the war the magnitude or the duration which it has already attained. Neither anticipated that the cause of the conflict might cease with, or even before, the conflict itself should cease. Each looked for an easier triumph, and a result less fundamental and astounding. Both read the same Bible, and pray to the same God; and each invokes his aid against the other. It may seem strange that any men should dare to ask a just God's assistance in wringing their bread from the sweat of other men's faces; but let us judge not, that we be not judged. The prayers of both could not be answered—that of neither has been answered fully.

The Almighty has his own purposes. "Woe unto the world because of offences! for it must needs be that offences come; but woe to that man by whom the offence cometh." If we shall suppose that American slavery is one of those offences which, in the providence of God, must needs come, but which, having continued through his appointed time, he now wills to remove, and that he gives to both North and South this terrible war, as the woe due to those by whom the offence came, shall we discern therein any departure from those divine attributes which the believers in a living God always ascribe to him? Fondly do we hope—fervently do we pray—that this mighty scourge of war may speedily pass away. Yet, if God wills that it continue until all the wealth piled by the bondmen's two hundred and fifty years of unrequited toil shall be sunk, and until every drop of blood drawn with the lash shall be paid by another drawn with the sword, as was said three thousand years ago, so still it must be said, "The judgments of the Lord are true and righteous altogether."

With malice toward none; with charity for all; with firmness in the right, as God gives us to see the right, let us strive on to finish the work we are in; to bind up the nation's wounds; to care for him who shall have borne the battle, and for his widow, and his orphan—to do all which may achieve and cherish a just and lasting peace among ourselves, and with all nations.

BROADCAST

Report to the Nation

by GENERAL DWIGHT D. EISENHOWER

Fellow Americans:

As a soldier, I have been given an Allied assignment that directly concerns the security of the free world, with special reference to the countries bordering upon the North Atlantic Ocean. I have approached the task, aiming at the good of the United States of America, conscious that a strong, solvent America is the indispensable foundation for a free world.

While I have reached definite conclusions, the subject of the free world's security is so vast and complex that no man could hope to master its elements to the last critical item or, in a quarter hour, to answer all questions in his fellow-citizens' minds. Consequently, though I speak to you out of deep conviction, I do so in all humility, trusting to your sympathetic consideration.

Our hope remains the achievement of peace based on understanding and forbearance, the only sure foundation for peace.

We must never lose faith that such a peace can be ultimately established. We seek only peace. No one can honestly interpret our modest preparations otherwise.

But we should examine the current situation, fearlessly and clearly, neither shutting our eyes to obvious dangers nor permitting fear to warp our judgment. America's record and America's strength certainly should prevent hysterical apprehension of the future. Today we are faced by an aggressive imperialism that has more than once announced its implacable hostility to free government. Therefore, we strive to erect a wall of security for the free world behind which free institutions can live. That wall must be maintained until Communist imperialism dies of its own inherent evils.

One of the great questions before us is the will and capacity of Europe to cooperate effectively in this aim. Unless there exists in Europe a will to defend itself, no amount of outside help can possibly make it secure. A nation's defense must spring from its own soul; and the soul cannot be imported.

For years we have heard that Western Europe is plagued, confused, and divided far more seriously than we are; we have heard that in their homes, in factories, on the street millions of honest workmen are daily subjected to Communist bullying; that their days and nights are haunted by the specter of invading hordes whom they cannot hope to equal in numbers or physical strength.

Furthermore, the discouragement, destruction and confusion visited upon the peoples of Europe by two world wars sapped their productive capacity and, in some instances, reduced them to levels of near-starvation. More than this—their spirit was smothered in war-weariness.

That is a story often told. If it were the whole story, then all I could honestly do would be to recommend that we abandon the NATO [North Atlantic Treaty Organization] treaty and—by ourselves—attempt, however futilely, to build a separate fortress against threatening aggression. Two striking facts make such a recommendation, for me, impossible.

The first fact is that the utter hopelessness of the alternative requires our participation in European defense. We can all understand that America must be strong in air and sea power. These elements are vitally essential to the defense of the free world and it is through them that we protect the approaches to our homeland and the routes of commerce necessary to our existence.

But this alone is not enough. Our ships will not long sail the seas, nor our planes fly the world airways, if we stand aside in fancied security while an aggressive imperialism sweeps over areas of the earth with which our own future is inseparably linked.

Western Europe is the cradle of our civilization; from her originally we drew our strength, genius, and culture. But our concern in Europe is far more than sentimental. Our own security is directly involved. Europe is a highly developed industrial complex with the largest and most varied pool of skilled labor on earth. This huge potential would be a rich prize for a totalitarian invasion. Its direct importance to us is the stark fact that its possession by communistic forces would give them opportunity to develop a preponderance of power. Even this disaster would not tell the whole story.

If Western Europe should be overrun by communism, many economically dependent areas in Africa and the Middle East would be affected by the debacle. Southeastern Asia would probably soon be lost. Thus, we would be cut off from the raw materials of all these regions— materials that we need for existence. World destiny would then be dictated by imperialistic powers whose avowed purpose is the destruction of freedom.

The second fact bearing upon our participation in European defense is that the people of Europe are not spiritually bankrupt, despite the validity of many pessimistic reports. Great sections of its population have for years labored on and fought the creeping paralysis of communism. Now, the North Atlantic Treaty has brought new fuel to the flames of hope in Europe. It has noticeably lifted morale, the fundamental element in this whole situation—the force which powers all human progress.

In every capital, there is growing a desire to cooperate in this mutual security effort. All the Governments that I have recently visited agreed that their defense programs must be stepped up despite economic and other difficulties— in spite of preoccupations that constitute abnormal drains upon particular nations. For example, France now wages a relentless and costly war against communism in Indo-China. Britain, still existing on an austerity level, shoulders heavy burdens in Malaya. However much those nations may differ from us in their diplomatic thinking with respect to Asiatic states, there is no question concerning their solidarity in opposing communistic aggression.

They and others on the Continent are taking measures to effect substantial increases in their defense establishments. Within the past few days, Britain has stepped up drastically its rate of preparation. The new military service program in France bars all exemptions, of every kind whatsoever. The Norwegians impressed me with their unshakable determination that never again will they be victims of occupation. To them, a fighting resistance, even to their own destruction, is preferable. And in Italy, there are unmistakable signs of a stiffening courage and determination. The same is true of Belgium, Holland, Denmark, Luxembourg and Iceland.

On every side, I saw heartening evidence of a regeneration in Europe's spirit. Its morale, its will to fight, will grow with every accretion to physical strength. The arrival in Europe of new American land and air units, though modest in protective influence by themselves, will certainly produce added confidence and accelerate the production of military force throughout the member nations. The European nations must, of course, produce and maintain the great bulk of the land forces necessary to their defense.

For this purpose the most immediate need of Europe is munitions and equipment. Every one of the continental nations I visited can rapidly and markedly increase its resistance power if it can be promptly furnished additional supplies of this kind. To fill this need, our loyal neighbor, Canada, with Britain and others, is shouldering part of the load.

In military potential, the free nations have everything they need—natural resources, industrial genius, productive capacity, and great reservoirs of leadership ability. Given the ingredient of morale—the determination to combine for mutual protection—the military strength necessary will be produced at a speedy pace. With every increase in strength, there will be an upward thrust in morale, an ever-mounting spiral of confidence and security.

With respect to time, our hour of attack, no man can know at what hour, if ever, our defensive organization may be put to the ultimate test. Because our purpose is entirely defensive, we must be ready at the earliest possible moment. Only an aggressor could name the day and hour of attack. We have no time to waste. Our current mobilization, properly adjusted to our peaceful security needs, should be as rapid as any required by the emergency of war.

To you, the people of America, I repeat—as I have to the Congress and to the President—I believe that:

First, the preservation of free America requires our participation in the defense of Western Europe.

Second, success is attainable. Given unity in spirit and action, the job can be done.

Third, while the transfer to Europe of American military units is essential, our major and special contribution should be in the field of munitions and equipment.

By no means do I believe that we Americans can support the world militarily or economically. In our own interest, we must insist upon a working partnership with every nation making the common security its task of first priority. Every one of the member nations must realize that the success of this combined effort to preserve the peace rests as directly upon America's productive, economic, and political strength as it does on any amount of military force we can develop. Only cooperative effort by all of us can preserve for the free world a position of security, relative peace, and economic stability.

Attainment of this result is largely a matter of morale and the human spirit. The free world now must prove itself worthy of its own past.

If Frenchmen can rise to the heights their fathers achieved at Verdun in 1916; if Italians can recapture the fervor of Vittorio Veneto; if the British can re-live the days of 1940 when they stood alone against Hitler; if our other Allies can react to today's threat in the mode of their own revered patriots; if we here in America can match the courage and self-sacrifice of the ragged, freezing members of Washington's Army at Valley Forge; indeed, if each of us now proves himself worthy of his countrymen fighting and dying in Korea, then success is sure—a glorious success that will bring us security, confidence, tranquility.

Each of us must do his part. We cannot delay, nationally or individually, while we suspiciously scrutinize the

330

sacrifices made by our neighbor, and through a weasling logic seek some way to avoid our own duties.

If we Americans seize the lead, we will preserve and be worthy of our own past. Our children will dwell in peace. They will dwell in freedom. They will read the history of this decade with tingling pride and, from their kinship with this generation, they will inherit more than can be expressed in millions, in acres, or in world acclaim.

It is not my place as a soldier to dwell upon the politics, the diplomacy, the particular treaty arrangements that must accompany and go forward with such an effort. But I do conceive it my duty to report from time to time, both to this Government and to all others in the coalition, as to progress achieved. Thus our own and all other peoples may constantly review their decisions and plans—and if necessary, revise them. This evening I come back to you only as an individual with some experience in war and peace, of some acquaintance-ship with our friends of Western Europe, to bring you what is in my heart and mind. I shall go about my own task in this undertaking with the unshakable confidence that America will respond fully when the basic issues are understood.

We know that 150,000,000 united Americans constitute the greatest temporal force that has ever existed on God's earth. If we join in a common understanding of our country's role today and wholeheartedly devote our-selves to its discharge, the year 1951 may be recorded in our history in letters as bright as is written the year 1776.

INDEX

In page references, *d.* refers to a diagram.

333

334

4 5 6 7 8 9 10 11 12 13 14 15 16 17 18 19 20 21 22 23 24 25   58 57 56

This chart is useful for indicating criticisms of outlines, manuscripts, or speeches as delivered. The numbers (21, 34, 315, 43, etc.), when placed at the *top* of the sheet, indicate that the fault is general; when these numbers are placed in the *margin,* they refer to the section of the outline or manuscript immediately opposite. The instructor can also record the numbers in a similar fashion on a card when listening to a speech.

The page references direct attention to the discussion in the text.

1. *Errors in outlining*

11. Indentation improper. (pp. 150-151)
12. Subordination lacking or illogical. (p. 150)
13. Symbols improperly used. (pp. 151-152)
14. Too many items per unit. (p. 149)
15. Sentence incomplete. (p. 152)
16. Not neatly written.
17. Vague or clumsy wording of main points. (pp. 143-145)

2. *Faults in analysis*

21. Audience not specified.
22. Audience diagnosis incomplete. (pp. 44-51)
23. Primary interests of audience not indicated, or incorrectly stated. (pp. 46-51)
24. Audience attitude not correctly analyzed. (pp. 51-56)

25. Occasion not well analyzed. (pp. 17, 42)
26. Subject too broad. (p. 16)
27. Wrong general end. (pp. 37-41)
28. Purpose not specific, or impossible of attainment. (pp. 41-43)

3. *Faults in content*

31. INADEQUATE SUPPORT FOR PROOF OR ILLUMINATION OF IDEAS
311. Needs explanation. (pp. 113-114)
312. Needs analogy. (pp. 114-115)
313. Needs illustration. (pp. 116-118)
314. Needs instances. (pp. 118-119)
315. Needs statistics. (pp. 119-120)
316. Needs testimony. (pp. 120-122)
317. Needs restatement. (p. 122)
318. Use charts or models. (pp. 122-128)
32. WEAK REASONING (pp. 218-221)
33. INADEQUATE MOTIVE APPEAL
331. Wrong motive for audience. (pp. 46-51)
332. Weak appeal. (p. 50)
333. Tactless appeal. (p. 51)
34. INTEREST FACTORS WEAK OR LACKING (pp. 178-184)
35. POOR WORDING (pp. 18-19, 287)

4. *Faults in organization*

41. Stringy: too many main points. (pp. 146-149)
42. Hazy: sequence of ideas not progressive. (pp. 139-143, 167-168, 200-20)
43. Wrong development for general end indicated. (p. 38)